Judicial organisation in Europe

Council of Europe Publishing

French edition:

L'Europe judiciaire

ISBN 92-871-4244-0

Cover design: Graphic Design Workshop of the Council of Europe
Layout: DTP Unit of the Council of Europe
Edited and published by: Council of Europe Publishing
F-67075 Strasbourg Cedex

ISBN 92-871-4245-9

Printed and bound in Germany by Koelblin-Fortuna-Druck

The Council of Europe

THE Council of Europe was founded in 1949, in the wake of the second world war, in order to promote European construction, firmly rooting it on a common set of values, contempt for which had thrown Europe into a time of strife and inhumanity.

The Organisation currently comprises 41 member states representing some 800 million Europeans – in other words almost all the countries of the European continent. Since 1989, the Council has contributed to bringing together the different countries of Europe. It works towards creating a common democratic and legal area structured around the European Convention on Human Rights. The Council of Europe develops many forms of co-operation on a wide range of issues to be addressed by our societies today, including education, social cohesion, protection of national minorities, the fight against all forms of intolerance, the prevention of crime and corruption, the consolidation of local democracy and the enhancement of Europe's cultural heritage.

Council of Europe Publishing is the official publisher of the Council of Europe, and reflects the many different aspects of the Council's work, addressing the main challenges facing European society and the world today. Our catalogue of over 1 200 titles in French and English includes topics ranging from international law to human rights, ethical and moral issues, society, environment, health, education and culture.

Contents

Contents

INTRODUCTION

ACCEPTANCE of the principles of the rule of law and of the enjoyment by all persons within their jurisdiction of human rights and fundamental freedoms is one of the basic conditions which states accept when they accede to the Council of Europe.

When the previous edition of this work was published in 1975, eighteen states contributed to it. Promoting the rule of law has always been central to the activities of the Council of Europe and it says a great deal for the success of those endeavours that the present edition has contributions from thirty-three of the present forty-one member states.

This book will have considerable practical value. Increased freedom to travel within Europe inevitably leads to increased use of the courts in civil and criminal cases. Basic information about the structure and operation of judicial systems in such a large number of countries collected in one place represents an invaluable resource.

The information gathered in this volume will also be of considerable academic interest to scholars of the different systems of law in Europe; some enjoy the benefit of centuries of tradition, whereas others have had relatively little time to develop the conditions necessary for ensuring that their democratic society is soundly based.

The contribution of the Council of Europe to the acceptance of the rule of law throughout Europe cannot be overvalued. This is not, however, a time for complacency and there is no time to rest. Serious problems still exist in some parts of Europe. A freely elected parliament and countries' declared acceptance of the rule of law are only the first steps towards making the avowed intentions a reality. Institutions and cultures need to be put into place if this is truly to be the case. In countries which maintain democracy and the rule of law, attachment to these fundamental values must find expression in the whole constitutional framework which regulates the relationship between the individual and the state.

Adherence to the rule of law can only be a reality if government itself is subject to the rule of law. The right must exist – in practice as well as in theory – for citizens to challenge unlawful acts by governments and emanations of government including, for example, the police.

Such a possibility can only exist if there is an independent judiciary. Central to the rule of law is the basic conception that judges must be independent of government, with absolute power over the decisions taken within their own courts, which can only be overturned by equally absolute decisions of senior judges in higher courts.

In return, the trust we place in the judiciary is that they will carry out their duties fairly. Judicial impartiality, the absolute recognition and application by judges of their obligation of fidelity to the law, is the counterpart, the quid pro quo, from the judiciary for the guarantee of their judicial independence provided by the state.

The media too have a crucial role to play as the contact between the judiciary and the general public. Just as judicial impartiality is the fair exchange for judicial independence, so open justice as witnessed and reported by an attentive media is a strong encouragement to judicial impartiality in practice. This was recognised by the authors of the European Convention on Human Rights, which guarantees, in Article 6, a hearing which is not only fair but also public. The obligation always rests with the courts, should they wish to exclude any part of proceedings from public scrutiny, to demonstrate that justice in a particular case cannot otherwise be done.

Another crucial ingredient in developing the rule of law through judicial transparency and fairness is education for democratic citizenship. People should have the confidence to claim their rights and challenge the *status quo* while, at the same time, understanding that rights carry with them responsibilities, respect particularly for the rights of others. Education in democracy should foster respect for law, justice and democracy; it should encourage concern for the common good as well as independence of thought, and it should generate in each individual a sense of society based on shared, fundamental values.

I am confident that these principles, implemented throughout Europe, will one day enable us to say with confidence that we have made a reality of (to use the words of the Strasbourg Declaration) an area of common legal standards throughout Europe.

LORD IRVINE OF LAIRG
The Lord Chancellor

ALBANIA

A SHORT description of the three-level court system which follows will provide useful and efficient recommendations for court standards, infrastructure and systems.

I. The district courts

Albania is divided into 29 judicial districts. Page 13 shows a map with the different districts. These are courts of first instance and the starting point for all civil and penal cases. Several courts also have military courts attached to them with 11 military judges. Albania is in the process of separating the Military Courts from the District Courts. The main type of case handled by the Military Court has to do with violations of the Military Code.

Albania's district courts employ the majority of judges and administrative staff. The number of judges have doubled since 1992 without planning for any additional facilities.

The courts are headed by a Chief Judge and many larger courts have a Deputy Chief Judge. Judges work in three-judge panels which, in civil cases and misdemeanour penal cases, consist of one judge and two assistant judges. On felony penal cases the new code requires three judges. The other court staff consist of:

– A secretary whose duties are to take notes by hand during a trial and type up decisions;

– A chief secretary who is responsible for registering the case, tracking its progress and communicating with the other levels of courts and preparing the statistical reports for the Ministry;

– An archivist (or it may be the chief secretary) who is responsible for archiving the closed files;

– A bailiff who is responsible for giving notice of the filing of the case as well as the date of trial;

– A finance clerk who is responsible for carrying out the budget and preparing the next budget.

The courts are divided into Penal and Civil panels. Civil panels are further divided into specialities of family, administrative and commercial, where the district is large enough to provide such divisions.

On average, from 1994 through 1997 only 8% of the cases brought before the court were penal cases and 92% civil matters.

II. The Court of Appeal

The Court of Appeal has recently changed from a single court in Tirana to six courts of appeal based in the cities of Tirana, Durres, Vlore, Shköder, Gjirokaster, and Korcha. Somewhat less than 10% of all the cases filed in Albania are appealed. The judges are arranged in three-judge panels. Each judge has his or her own secretary whose responsibility it is to handle the trial work when the judge is the one in charge of a case. That work includes calling the parties for trial, taking notes, and typing the decision. The process of registration of cases is similar to the process in the District Courts.

III. The High Court

About 25% of all the cases appealed are then brought to the High Court. The High Court consists of judges, the Chief Justice and two Deputy Chief Judges. Judges do not have assigned clerks and many clerks work independently of the judge giving a preliminary opinion as to the validity of the case.

There are a number of secretaries who are not assigned to judges, but are responsible for administrative work and typing up decisions.

Cases are heard in three-judge panels in a similar manner as the other courts, however, no record of the proceedings are taken and decisions may not be presented to the parties in person. The sentence will be handed out when the file comes back to the Court of First Instance. There is also a provision for an appealing party to have its case heard in joint college when they are dissatisfied with the decision by the three-judge panel.

In order to bring a case from a lower court to either the Court of Appeal or High Court, a request is made by the citizen's attorney for examination under the provision that the lower court has violated the law. That request comes to the Chief Secretary who registers it. The file must be requested from the District Court.

The High Court is in the process of reconstruction. This will provide for more courtrooms and a better arrangement of offices with the filing window having its own entrance for the public. This should eliminate some security problems as well as frustrations for the attorneys.

Organisation of the court system into 29 judicial districts

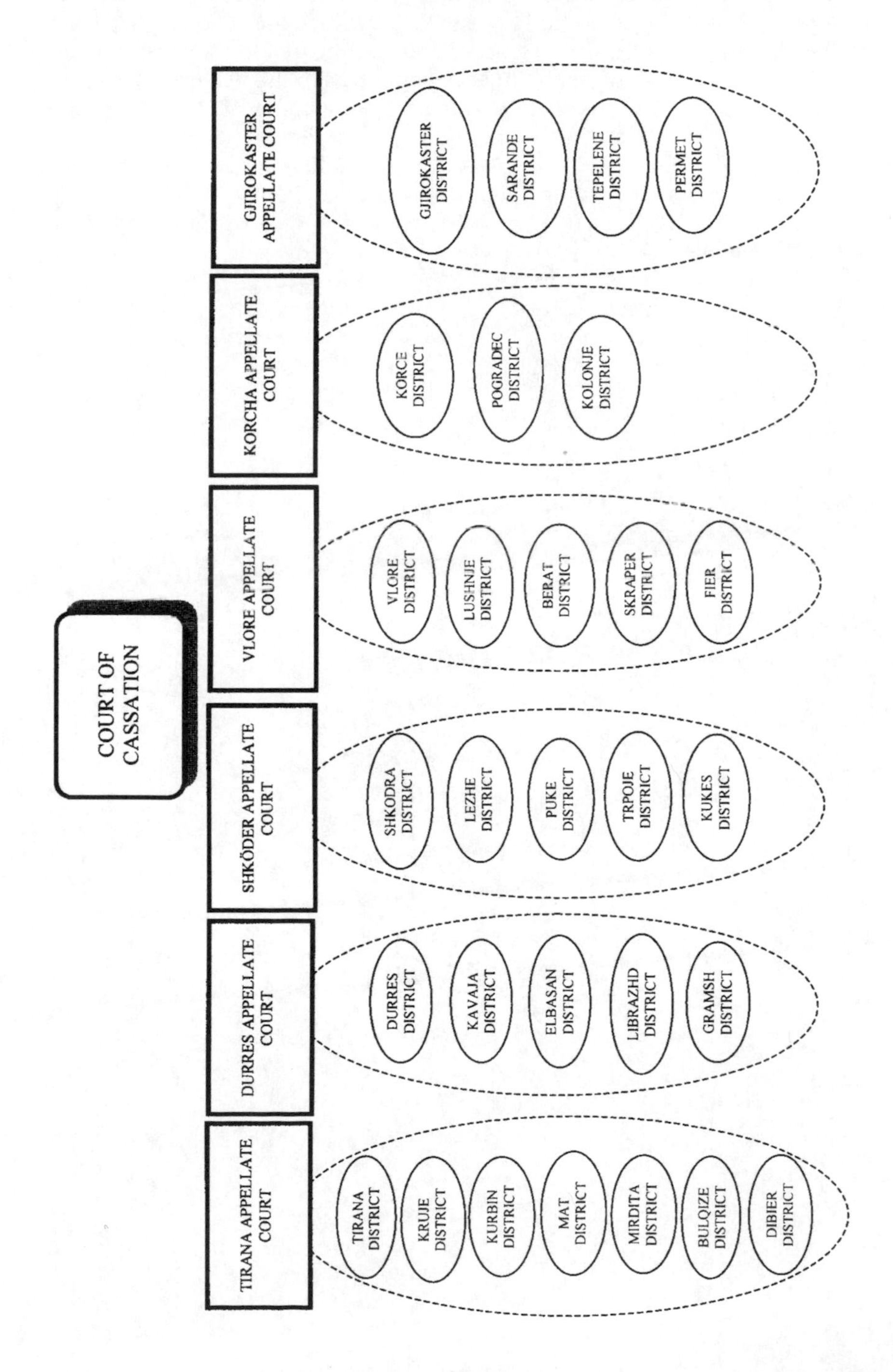

ANDORRA

I. Introduction and general principles

After the *Pareatges* of 1278 and 1288, which settled the disputes arising from the exercise of feudal power over the valleys of Andorra between the bishops of Urgel and the counts of Foix (the latter being succeeded by the kings and, subsequently, the Presidents of France), the judicial system in Andorra remained one of the main features of the joint sovereignty that was exercised by the co-princes in accordance with a complex and decentralised system and underwent only minor changes as a result of the privileges they granted and the decrees they issued, on the one hand, and of the evolution of legal custom, on the other.

This system was completely transformed when the Constitution, which was approved in a referendum, entered into force on 1 January 1994. It proclaims the independence of the Principality of Andorra and the sovereignty of the Andorran people and institutes a parliamentary system in which the co-principality is based on the separation of powers and the independence of the judiciary.

The present system has resulted from the implementation of the principles enshrined in the Constitution by the Special Law (*Llei Qualificada* = law requiring adoption by a special majority) on the Administration of Justice, the Special Law on the Constitutional Court, the provisional Law on Judicial Procedure and the Special Law relating to the Public Prosecutor's Department, pending the adoption of definitive laws relating to judicial procedure currently being drafted.

The judicial system is unitary. Its structure, its composition, the way it functions and the legal status of its personnel are laid down by a Special Law. Special, exceptional or customary courts or courts dealing with sectional or professional interests are prohibited. The powers of the courts and the rules of procedure are based on the law.

Justice is dispensed exclusively in the name of the Andorran people by judges who are independent, cannot be removed from office and are solely responsible in the exercise of their judicial powers to the Constitution and the laws.

Judicial authority is exercised, in conformity with the law, by the Magistrates (*batlles*), the Magistrates' Court (*Tribunal de Batlles*), the Criminal Court (*Tribunal de Corts*) and the High Court of Justice (*Tribunal Superior de Justicia*), as well as by the Presidents of these courts. There is no jury system.

Each court is a single court, sits at Andorra la Vella and has jurisdiction for the entire country.

Andorran judges are called *batlles* in the Courts of First Instance and *magistrats* in the Criminal Court and the High Court.

II. The Legal Service Commission *(Consell superior de la justicia)*

The Constitution entrusts the task of safeguarding the independence and proper functioning of the judicial system to a separate, independent constitutional organ, the Legal Service Commission. It is defined as an organ of representation, control and the administration of justice.

The Legal Service Commission consists of five members, one appointed by each of the co-princes, one by the Speaker of Parliament (*Sindic General*), one by the Head of Government (*Cap de Govern*) and one by judges and magistrates from outside their own ranks. Their term of office is six years and may be renewed only for one consecutive period. The Commission is presided over by the Speaker, who holds an election among its members to appoint a Vice-President and a Secretary.

The duties of the members of the Legal Service Commission are incompatible with any other public office or function and with the exercise of the function of a lower court judge or the profession of a lawyer. A member may not be removed from office by the authorities or the body that appointed him or her except for gross misconduct and unless the other members of the court unanimously endorse the dismissal.

The functions and responsibilities of the Legal Service Commission are defined by the Constitution and governed by the qualified law on the administration of justice.

In general terms, it mainly has to ensure that the means are available for the proper functioning of the administration of justice. For this purpose, it produces a draft annual budget based on the proposals submitted to it by the Presidents of the courts and the Chief Public Prosecutor. The draft is then sent to the government for inclusion in the general state budget and adoption by Parliament.

At the request of the government or Parliament, or on its own initiative, the Legal Service Commission may draw up reports concerning the application of the laws relating to the administration of justice. At the beginning of the judicial year, its President makes a public statement on the state of the administration of justice and its functioning.

The Legal Service Commission also has special and exclusive responsibility for arranging for the recruitment and appointment of all magistrates and judges, members of the Public Prosecutor's Department and registrars.

It also exercises disciplinary powers over the judges and members of the Public Prosecutor's Department in accordance with the procedures and conditions laid down in the Special Law on the Administration of Justice. Depending on the seriousness of the misconduct, it can issue a written warning, impose a fine of up to one hundred thousand pesetas, suspend the person concerned for from one to six months or remove him or her from office. Its decisions are not subject to appeal. The only remedy possible is an *empara* appeal to the Constitutional Court in the cases provided for by the Special Law on the Constitutional Court.

III. Judicial authority

All judicial authority is vested in the magistrates, the Magistrates' Court, the Criminal Court and the High Court of Justice. Their jurisdiction is divided into three branches: civil, criminal and administrative.

Criminal jurisdiction covers all criminal offences and, in the absence of an international treaty, includes decisions to request, allow or refuse extradition in accordance with the conditions and rules of procedure laid down by domestic legislation in this particular area of the law.

Administrative jurisdiction covers the government's compliance with the law when exercising its power to make regulations, the adoption and implementation of legal provisions by the public administrative authorities and compliance with the purposes that legitimise the action taken. It embraces:

– social security disputes;

– appeals in cases involving officials in the service of all public institutions in the Principality;

– electoral disputes arising from party lists and candidatures;

– disputes concerning the pecuniary liability of public administrative authorities and their officials;

– disputes arising from contracts entered into by the public administrative authorities for the supply of goods and services or for the management of public services; and

– appeals against decisions of the competent authority to fix the level of compensation for the expropriation of property in the public interest.

Civil jurisdiction covers all private legal disputes. Generally speaking, it includes all cases not expressly placed under some other jurisdictions.

A. The Magistrates' Court *(Tribunal de Batlles* or *Batllia)*

The magistrates normally constitute the jurisdiction of first instance and the investigating authority for all types of case. Sitting either alone or as benches of three, they are responsible for giving judgment on all contentious issues in accordance with the rules laid down in the procedural laws, with the exception of the serious criminal offences specified in the Criminal Code, which are the responsibility of the Criminal Court.

The Magistrates' Court is divided into four sections: civil, criminal, administrative and investigative. The magistrates, who must number at least eight in addition to the President, are distributed among them.

B. The Criminal Court *(Tribunal de Corts)*

The *Tribunal de Corts,* the traditional Criminal Court, consists of a President, a Vice-President and one judge. Its members may be replaced on a rotation basis by magistrates appointed as substitutes for a fixed period by the President of the Magistrates' Court with the agreement of the Legal Service Commission. At the request of the Criminal Court, the Commission can also appoint assistant judges for a specified period, when this is necessary to reinforce the court or to permit its proper constitution when one of its members is disqualified, challenged or excused.

The Criminal Court is responsible for dealing with serious offences at first instance and with appeals against judgments of the Magistrates' Court in respect of minor offences and against the decisions of single magistrates in cases involving summary offences. It also hears appeals against restrictions of freedom ordered by the magistrates or against provisional measures ordered when a case is being investigated. The President's functions also include the supervision of prisons and the enforcement of sentences.

The Criminal Court is also the only body competent to order, in response to a complaint by the prosecuting authorities or the victim, the institution of criminal proceedings against magistrates, judges, members of Parliament or of the government for offences committed in the exercise of their functions. In this case, the inquiry is entrusted to a judge of the Criminal Court.

The Criminal Court also deals with conflicts of criminal jurisdiction between the Magistrates' Court and its own investigation department, and between these authorities and itself.

C. The High Court of Justice *(Tribunal Superior de la Justicia)*

The High Court of Justice is the Principality's highest judicial authority. It consists of a President and eight judges assigned to three chambers: civil, criminal and administrative. Its jurisdiction covers all appeals against judgments delivered at first instance by the Magistrates' Court in civil and administrative cases and by the Criminal Court in proceedings involving serious criminal offences.

Only the civil chamber is competent to order the enforcement in Andorra of civil judgments delivered by foreign courts.

The criminal chamber has sole jurisdiction to try, at first instance, a magistrate or judge, a member of Parliament or of the government for an offence committed in the exercise of their functions.

In addition, the High Court, when sitting as a full court, is competent to hear:

– applications for ordinary or extraordinary review of its own decisions;

– actions seeking a finding of judicial error, miscarriage of justice, and an assessment of any damage caused;

– cases to decide on its own competence and conflicts of jurisdiction between the various sections of the Magistrates' Court;

– challenges and withdrawals of magistrates and of judges of the Criminal Court; and

– appeals against judgments of the criminal chamber in cases concerning the criminal liability of magistrates, judges, members of Parliament or of the government for offences committed in the exercise of their functions. These appeals may not be heard by the members of the criminal chamber.

D. Legal remedies

There is extensive provision for private individuals to appeal to a court or judge and bring an action to protect their interests.

The right to institute proceedings to defend the interests of the general public is provided for in all the cases specified in the procedural laws. In criminal cases, Andorran citizens can exercise this right in respect of all offences against the interests of the general public. They can also bring a suit against private individuals when the law does not make prosecution subject to a complaint lodged by the victim or, if this proviso does not exist, when the victim has not brought an action.

The right of appeal, which the Constitution provides for in criminal proceedings, also exists in civil cases within the limits laid down by the procedural laws.

The Appellate Courts have full jurisdiction both in civil disputes and in appeals to the Criminal Court. There is no court of cassation for these cases.

However, an appeal against decisions delivered by the Criminal Court at first instance may be lodged only by way of a petition to the criminal chamber of the High Court, whose jurisdiction resembles that of a court of cassation and which can give judgment on the facts only in the following cases:

– lack or abuse of jurisdiction or competence;

– error in assessing the evidence or violation of the right to be presumed innocent;

– breach of the accusatorial principle by imposing on the accused, without prior consultation of the prosecution and the defence, a harsher sentence than that requested or for a different offence from that being tried;

– infringement of an important rule of criminal law by directly breaching it, by interpreting it incorrectly or by applying it improperly; or

– a breach of any other rule necessary for the application of the criminal law.

E. Judicial protection of fundamental rights

Judicial supervision of respect for the fundamental rights enshrined in the Constitution consists in two types of action involving two separate procedures.

The first concerns the right not to be deprived of liberty and involves the application in Andorra of the principle of *habeas corpus*. The procedure regulates and facilitates access to a judicial body for anyone claiming to have been unlawfully deprived of their liberty – for whatever reason and whomever by – so that a ruling can be given on the lawfulness of the detention. The application is made either in writing or by the simple appearance of authorised persons or bodies before the President of the Magistrates' Court or, failing this, a magistrate appointed by him. An appeal may be lodged against the decision with the President of the Criminal Court or a judge delegated by him. If an enforceable decision is given acknowledging the unlawfulness of the detention, the prisoner is immediately released, without prejudice to the criminal proceedings.

In the wider framework of all the rights and freedoms enshrined in the Constitution, there is provision for an urgent procedure that takes precedence over other cases and is aimed at protecting fundamental rights or putting an end to an unlawful situation. The application is made either orally or in writing to the duty magistrate, who summons the parties concerned and reaches a decision. An appeal may be lodged with the High Court, the President of which designates the chamber competent to deal with it. The decisions taken in such a case may on no account be regarded as *res judicata* in respect of the ordinary proceedings, on which they have no suspensive effect.

F. Execution of judgments

The execution of judgments, whether in civil, criminal or administrative cases, is effected or supervised by the courts themselves – either of their own motion or upon application by the parties – subject to the conditions laid down in the procedural laws.

In civil cases, the execution of judicial decisions is the responsibility of the reporting magistrate of the civil section of the Magistrates' Court or the magistrate who heard the case at first instance. A judgment is enforced by attaching the assets of the person against whom it is given. Damages are payable if it is impossible to enforce an obligation to act. Issues that arise are dealt with by the magistrate responsible for enforcing the judgment; his decision, reached after hearing both parties, is subject to appeal.

In criminal cases, the enforcement of judgments is the responsibility of the magistrate for summary offences, the President of the Magistrates' Court for minor offences and the President of the Criminal Court for serious crimes. These courts deal with issues relating to the enforcement of judgments. Appeals against the decisions of the magistrate lie to the Magistrates' Court and against the decisions of the President of the latter to the Criminal Court.

In administrative cases, the enforcement of judgments and administrative decisions given against both citizens and the administrative authorities is the responsibility of the administrative section of the Magistrates' Court. The administrative chamber of the High Court deals with issues arising from such enforcement. Both central government bodies and local authorities must include an appropriation in their annual budget to cover any payments they may have to make. A delay by an administrative authority in executing a final judgment or decision will incur financial liability. An order to stay the execution of an administrative court judgment may be made only if there is a risk of a serious breach of public order or irreparable harm to public finances.

The administrative authorities can be held liable under the criminal law for negligently failing to execute a judgment of the Administrative Court. This involves the latter referring the case to the competent Criminal Court.

IV. Judicial personnel

A. Judges

Judges are recruited by advertising vacant posts and appointed by the Legal Service Commission for a renewable term of six years. Magistrates must, and judges should preferably, be of Andorran nationality. If there are insufficient candidates from within the Andorran career structure, posts may be filled, on an equitable basis, by Spanish and French lawyers.

All candidates must have either a bachelor's degree in Spanish law or a French master's degree, possess the requisite technical ability and personal qualities, as determined by the Legal Service Commission, necessary for the performance of judicial functions, and take part in an open competition, the procedures and organisation of which are determined by the *Consell.*

Appointments to higher posts are determined exclusively by the Legal Service Commission. The selection of candidates is made on merit by open competition and follows the order for the career structure laid down by the Special Law.

No one may be appointed to a more senior post within this structure without having held a less senior position for at least one full term, unless the Legal Service Commission considers that this is warranted by special circumstances. The *Consell* may also, without prejudice to the possibility of following the order laid down by the Special Law, decide to open the competition to persons who do not hold a post within the judicial career structure but meet the other general recruitment conditions.

During the period of their appointment, magistrates and judges cannot be removed from office. They may not be censured, suspended or dismissed except as a consequence of a sanction imposed by the Legal Service Commission for a criminal or disciplinary offence.

The procedural laws and the Special Law on the Judiciary specify the cases in which a function is incompatible with the position of judge. They list grounds on which a judge may be challenged or excused and lay down the procedure in cases in which it is to be feared that a judge lacks impartiality. They prohibit a trial court judge from sitting in judgment on appeal and, in criminal cases, an investigating judge from being a member of the trial court dealing with the same case. They also bar judges from participating in political elections apart from exercising their right to vote.

Magistrates and judges are liable under the civil law for any damage or injury caused in the exercise of their functions. However, they enjoy judicial privilege in respect of criminal liability for offences committed whilst carrying out these functions. Accordingly, they may be detained only if caught in the act of committing a crime. They may be prosecuted only by order of the Criminal Court on receipt of a complaint by the Public Prosecutor's Department or the victim. The investigation and committal proceedings are conducted by a judge of the Criminal Court. Judgment is given at first instance by the criminal chamber of the High Court, while an appeal is decided by the latter sitting in plenary session, but excluding the members of the criminal chamber.

When a judge is charged, he or she is automatically suspended from duty by the Legal Service Commission.

B. Court staff

Court administrative staff is made up of registrars, assistant registrars, ancillary staff and other employees.

The registrars record the acts and decisions of judges and the courts and assist them in the exercise of their functions. They issue instructions to all the registry staff, under the overall authority of the judges, and are responsible for the storage and safe-keeping of all documents made out or handed in, for the archives and the preservation of evidence and for the immediate transfer to the National Institute of Finances of deposits in the form of cash and securities, payments into court and sureties. They also supply duplicates of legal documents and arrange for the service of writs, summonses, etc.

Given the importance of their work, the registrars are subject to the same legal impediments and disqualifications as judges.

Registrars, who must be Andorran nationals with a degree in law, are recruited and selected by open competition and appointed as general administration-grade civil servants for an indefinite period by the Legal Service Commission. The latter demands the same formal qualifications from candidates as from judges and determines the programme and organisation of the tests making up the competition.

Other court staff are selected by open competition and appointed by the government.

Disciplinary authority over registrars, assistant registrars, ancillary staff and other employees is exercised by the President of each court, in accordance with the administrative regulations applying to all civil servants and other employees of the general administration.

V. The prosecuting authorities

The Public Prosecutor's Department consists of the Chief Public Prosecutor and a number of assistant public prosecutors.

The role, status and responsibilities of the public prosecutors and their relations with the judges and other organs of the state are defined and regulated by the Constitution, the Special Law relating to the Administration of Justice, the law relating to the Public Prosecutor's Department and the Code of Criminal Procedure.

Although judges and prosecutors are in certain respects very close to one another given the nature of their work and their status, they each have their own functional autonomy and are not subordinate to or dependent upon one another in any way.

The Chief Public Prosecutor and the assistant public prosecutors are selected by open competition and appointed by the Legal Service Commission for a renewable term of six years. They are chosen from a list of persons proposed by the government who meet the conditions for being appointed magistrates or judges.

Without prejudice to their independence from the hierarchy of the courts, they are included in the judicial career structure as far as appointments, promotions and pay are concerned. The budget of the Public Prosecutor's Department is drawn up according to the same rules as the budget of the courts. The Legal Service Commission includes it in a section of the draft general budget for the administration of justice.

The Chief Public Prosecutor is responsible for the organisation of the prosecution service and acts as its statutory representative.

The number of assistant public prosecutors is determined by government decree after consulting the Chief Public Prosecutor. They act on the latter's instructions and are subject to his authority with regard to the organisation of their work and the substance of their opinions and as far as legal classifications and conclusions are concerned.

In the event of disagreement among members of the Public Prosecutor's Department, the Chief Public Prosecutor confirms his instructions in writing. However, the assistant prosecutors are free to voice their own opinions in the oral observations they make in the course of a trial.

Members of the Public Prosecutor's Department may be dismissed for committing a criminal or disciplinary offence. Disciplinary authority is exercised by the Legal Service Commission in the same way as for judges.

The general task of the Public Prosecutor's Department is to uphold the law, the legal system and the independence of the courts and, through them, to promote the application of the law in order to protect citizens' rights and preserve the public interest.

In accordance with the constitutional principle of mandatory prosecution, the Public Prosecutor's Department institutes criminal proceedings on its own initiative or at the request of any institution, public or private legal entity or individual, without prejudice to the right of the magistrates to take action on their own initiative. It also brings civil actions in conjunction with criminal proceedings, except when the injured party intends to do so later, renounces its right to do so or withdraws from the action.

It takes part directly in criminal proceedings, attends and participates in hearings, lodges appeals as appropriate and sees that decisions are executed; it takes part in civil actions concerning missing persons, minors and persons without legal capacity, as well as in proceedings relating to civil status; it acts in disciplinary proceedings held before the Legal Service Commission against magistrates and judges; and it may institute *habeas corpus* proceedings before the President of the Magistrates' Court or the magistrate appointed for the purpose.

In addition, in cases brought before the Constitutional Court the Public Prosecutor's Department must: be a party to, and file submissions in, proceedings concerning the unconstitutionality of laws and legislative decrees; give its prior opinion, if it is involved in a case in which the Ordinary Court makes an interlocutory application for a ruling on unconstitutionality; and it is a party to proceedings before the Constitutional Court if the latter allows such an application. It must also file submissions in *empara* proceedings concerning a violation of fundamental personal rights and public freedoms, as well as the political rights of Andorran citizens. Furthermore, in cases where it has given leave, which is necessary for lodging this type of appeal with the Constitutional Court, it is an applicant in *empara* proceedings concerning a violation of the rights of the defence during or in relation to judicial proceedings.

The government may make general recommendations to the Public Prosecutor's Department concerning the prosecution of offences and protection of the public interest. These recommendations are always made in writing. Whatever these recommendations, members of the Public Prosecutor's Department must always act according to the principle of mandatory prosecution, and they remain free to make such observations as they consider relevant with regard to the offence and its classification, even if these observations are contrary to the government's recommendations.

The Chief Public Prosecutor must provide the government with information on request, unless there is a legal impediment, on any matter in which it is involved and on the general functioning of the administration of justice. It sends the government a copy of the annual progress report it presents at the beginning of the judicial year.

As far as its relations with the police are concerned, when an investigating magistrate is not involved in a case the Public Prosecutor's Department directs police work with regard to the establishment of any facts that may constitute a breach of the law, orders all investigations necessary to obtain evidence and examines whether the length of detention on remand is appropriate and within the limits laid down by law. To this end, it transmits its instructions to the Chief of Police.

The Public Prosecutor's Department may also be asked to work with the legislative authorities when the Speaker of Parliament decides to bring to its notice the conclusions of a committee of inquiry or parliamentary commission on any question of public interest.

VI. Other personnel of the law

A. The criminal investigation police

All Andorran police officers are required to undertake criminal investigation duties whenever necessary. The police force, which is entirely under the control of the executive authorities, can, however, set up and organise specialised criminal investigation units within its internal structure.

The police act under the supervision of, and take orders from, the magistrates, the Public Prosecutor's Department and the courts, which they assist with regard to all aspects of their work and the enforcement of all court decisions. They carry out the tasks and inquiries assigned to them in the context of investigating offences and obtaining evidence.

The Police Chief's Office is required to send a daily report to the Magistrates' Court and the Chief Public Prosecutor.

B. Barristers

It is usual for a barrister to be present at all court proceedings, but this is not mandatory in minor civil cases, in social security disputes or in criminal proceedings for summary offences.

In order to practise, a barrister is required to have Andorran nationality or to be a legal resident of good character, to possess a bachelor's degree in law, to have obtained the necessary administrative authorisation, to have no other occupation that is incompatible with the dignity of the legal profession and not to have been declared unfit to practise law or hold public office. A limited number of registrations are accepted by the Governing Council of the Andorran Bar Association after checking the applicant's credentials. Admission to the bar becomes effective only when the registration file is sent to the High Court and the latter raises no objections after receiving a report from the Public Prosecutor's Department.

By way of exception, the interests of the Andorran state may be defended by lawyers registered only with the government's legal department, but the government is not prevented from asking other lawyers to act for it in specific cases.

Lawyers are free and independent in the exercise of their profession before the judges and the courts. They enjoy the rights inherent in the dignity of their position, enjoy freedom of expression and freedom in the defence of their clients. They are required to observe professional secrecy.

The right to counsel and to the technical assistance of a barrister are guaranteed by the Constitution, as is the right to justice free of cost in order to ensure equality of access to the courts. In general terms, these rights are guaranteed by laws that provide that judicial acts are free of charge and provide for the appointment of official defence counsel for people who, after supplying evidence to this effect, have been declared poor or insolvent by a magistrate.

The remuneration allocated to legal-aid lawyers is not regulated. At the request of the Bar Association, the overall annual sum, based on the number of lawyers appointed by the courts, is entered by the Legal Service Commission in the budget for the administration of justice, and included in the general state budget.

C. Solicitors

Solicitors in Andorra are persons who offer their services as legal representatives to act in conjunction with barristers on behalf of the parties when they do not want to appear before a court in person, unless the rules of procedure provide otherwise. They are obliged to observe secrecy with regard to all facts and information that become known to them in the course of their professional work.

Until such time as specific requirements to be fulfilled by Andorran solicitors may be laid down by law, it rests with the Legal Service Commission, after receiving a report from the Public Prosecutor's Office, to draw up an annual list of persons authorised to represent parties in proceedings before the Andorran courts.

VII. Functions of the Judicial Court

The Constitutional Court checks the constitutionality of laws, international treaties, legislative decrees and the rules of Parliament and settles disputes between the constitutional organs.

It also hears *empara* appeals for the protection of constitutional rights. Its responsibilities are exercised through three types of proceedings provided for by the Constitution and regulated by the Special Laws on the Administration of Justice and the Constitutional Court and the Transitional Law on Judicial Procedure, which relate to the Ordinary Courts and those subject to their jurisdiction:

The first occurs when, in the course of a trial, a court has reasonable and justified doubts about the constitutionality of a law, a legislative decree or a rule with the force of a law the application of which is indispensable in order to give judgment in the case or determine a subordinate issue.

In this case, the court, either of its own motion or at the request of a party, can ask the Constitutional Court to rule on the constitutionality of the legal rule concerned before it delivers its judgment. The Constitutional Court can declare the application inadmissible. Otherwise, it must give its ruling within two months.

The second is the *empara* appeal to the Constitutional Court against the final dismissal of an action by the Ordinary Courts under the urgent, priority procedure for securing immediate protection of rights and freedoms (see III.E above).

The appellants or associated parties to this latter procedure may exercise the *empara* appeal direct. If it is admitted by the Constitutional Court, the defendants and the Public Prosecutor's Department participate in the proceedings, state their claims and make submissions. Within two months of admitting the appeal, the Constitutional Court gives its decision on whether to allow it in full or in part or to dismiss it.

The third type of proceedings is an *empara* appeal in the specific case of a violation, during or in relation to a trial or pre-trial proceedings, of one of the general rights of the defence guaranteed by the Constitution. In this case, the person concerned must make a claim in defence of his her right before the competent judicial organ by employing the means and remedies provided for by law. If the appeal is unsuccessful in the Ordinary Courts, he or she may, within six days of the final decision to dismiss it, make application in writing to the Public Prosecutor's Department, requesting it to lodge an *empara* appeal with the Constitutional Court. The decision of the Public Prosecutor's Department is final. If the application is granted, both the appellant and the Public Prosecutor's Department are applicants in the *empara* proceedings, which are held according to the same rules as the previous type of *empara* appeal.

AUSTRIA

I. INTRODUCTION

Austria is a federal state formed of nine independent *Bundesländer*.

Pursuant to Austria's Federal Constitution, jurisdiction is exclusively the responsibility of the federal state. Consequently, there exist only federal courts but no judicial authorities of the *Bundesländer*. In 1988, however, independent tribunals (Independent Administrative Boards) were established in each *Bundesland* that have – amongst others – the task to review decisions of administrative authorities that impose administrative penalties (fines and sentences of imprisonment). These tribunals took up work in 1991.

According to Article 83, paragraph 1, of the Federal Constitutional Act as amended in 1929, the court system is laid down by federal legislation. The Constitutional Court and the Administrative Court have been created as guardians of the Constitution and the administration under the Federal Constitutional Act itself, which also provides detailed rules for these judicial authorities. These two courts are also called courts of public law. Since 1991 the Independent Administrative Boards provide legal protection against administrative decisions. Applicants have to address their appeals first to an Independent Administrative Board, in cases that are within its competence. An appeal against the ruling of the board can be launched with the courts of public law.

According to the rules concerning the organisation of Austrian courts, the latter are classified:

– as to their field of activity: courts of public law, civil courts and criminal courts; and

– as to the delimitation of their competences: ordinary courts and other (extraordinary) courts.

II. CIVIL AND CRIMINAL COURTS

A. Ordinary courts

1. Definition

Ordinary courts are the courts competent under Article 1 of the Judicature Act (*Jurisdiktionsnorm*) to exercise civil jurisdiction and the courts competent under Article 8 of the Code of Criminal Procedure of 1975 to exercise criminal jurisdiction. They include:

– District courts (*Bezirksgerichte*);

– Regional courts (*Landesgerichte*) (courts of first instance);

– Criminal courts of assize (*Geschworenengerichte*);

– Courts of appeal (*Oberlandesgerichte*) (courts of second instance): they have been established in Vienna, Graz, Linz and Innsbruck;

The Supreme Court (*Oberster Gerichtshof*) which has its seat in Vienna.

2. Circuits of district courts

Circuits of district courts are, as a rule, formed of coherent areas of one or several communes. The circuits of all district courts taken together extend over the whole of the Austrian territory.

Each of the circuits of the Courts of First Instance covers the areas of several district courts and the circuits of the various courts of appeal comprise the circuits of two or more courts of first instance.

The Supreme Court is competent for the whole of the national territory.

3. District courts and courts of first instance

District courts and courts of first instance, as a rule, exercise jurisdiction both in civil matters and in criminal matters. Exceptions to this rule are the following:

For jurisdiction in commercial matters a special district court for business matters (*Bezirksgericht für Handelssachen*) and a commercial court serving as a court of first instance (*Handelsgericht*) have been established in Vienna; outside the circuits of these two courts, jurisdiction in commercial matters is within the competence of district courts and regional courts;

Special district courts and special courts of first instance have been set up in Vienna and in Graz for both civil jurisdiction and criminal jurisdiction;

A special juvenile court (*Jugendgerichtshof Wien*) has been established in Vienna which, acting as a court of first instance and as a district court, is responsible for handling matters in certain sections of civil and criminal jurisdiction;

A separate juvenile court (*Jugendgericht Graz*) has been established in Graz; it is charged with responsibilities of a district court in civil and criminal matters;

A special labour and social court (*Arbeits- und Sozialgericht*) acts in Vienna as a court of first instance in disputes arising from employment relations and certain branches of the social insurance system.

Jurisdiction in civil matters (civil jurisdiction) includes contentious jurisdiction and jurisdiction in non-contentious matters.

4. System of legal recourse, sphere of activity in civil matters

Ordinary civil jurisdiction is, as a rule, exercised in three instances, viz:

– in the first instance, by district courts or courts of first instance;

– in the second instance, by courts of first instance or by courts of appeal; and

– in the third instance, by the Supreme Court.

The material jurisdiction of district courts, in principle, covers financial disputes involving a value not exceeding 130 000 Austrian Schillings as well as certain disputes irrespective of the value in litigation such as disputes concerning paternity, the recognition or contestation of legitimate descent, maintenance payments due under the law, divorce actions and dissolution or nullification of marriage as well as all other disputes arising from the relations between spouses or between parents and children, the disturbance of possession, lease of immovables and nearly all matters of non-contentious jurisdiction.

Regional courts as courts of first instance are competent with regard to financial disputes involving values exceeding 130000 Austrian Schillings and certain matters irrespective of the value in litigation such as public liability, declaration of invalidity of lost documents and proceedings concerning declaration of death.

Remedies available in non-contentious jurisdiction consist of two forms of appeal against decisions rendered by courts of first instance, viz.: *Vorstellung* and *Rekurs* and one form of appeal against decisions of courts of second instance, viz.: *Revisionsrekurs.* In contentious jurisdiction there are two forms of appeal against decisions by courts of first instance, viz.: *Berufung* and *Rekurs* and three forms of appeal against decisions by courts of second instance, viz.: *Revision, Revisionsrekurs* and *Rekurs.*

5. System of legal recourse, sphere of activity in criminal matters

Criminal courts, as a rule, exercise their activities in two instances:

The judicial authorities acting in the first instance are:

– district courts which are responsible for conducting criminal proceedings concerning any misdemeanours (*Vergehen*) punishable by a sanction involving pecuniary penalties or deprivation of liberty not exceeding one year; they co-operate in preliminary inquiries and preliminary investigations in cases of crimes (*Verbrechen*) and misdemeanours (*Vergehen*) punishable by deprivation of liberty exceeding one year;

– the courts of first instance acting as:

i. investigating courts (*Untersuchungsgerichte*) which are generally responsible for conducting preliminary investigations or preliminary inquiries into all crimes and misdemeanours;

ii. judges' chambers (*Ratskammern*) which decide on complaints against decisions of investigating judges except decisions concerning detention;

iii. jurors' courts (*Schöffengerichte*), courts composed of judges and lay assessors, and single-judge tribunals (magistrates) (*Einzelgerichte*) in simplified proceedings in cases of crimes and misdemeanours;

– courts of assize (*Geschworenengerichte*) which decide on all charges of certain crimes and misdemeanours enumerated in the Code of Criminal Procedure such as high treason, rioting and insurrection, and incitement to hostilities; furthermore, they decide on charges of all other crimes liable to punishment of more than ten years' imprisonment provided that further conditions as described in the law are given (as a rule, most serious criminality).

The courts acting in the second instance are:

– the courts of first instance which decide on remedies taken against judgments (as regards conviction and sentence) and against orders passed by district courts in cases of contraventions;

– the courts of second instance (courts of appeal) which, in particular, decide on complaints raised against decisions of judges' chambers and decisions of investigating judges concerning detention, appeals against committal of an accused for trial and appeals against sentences from judgments rendered by courts of assize and jurors' courts as well as by magistrates in simplified proceedings;

– the Supreme Court, which is competent in particular to decide on all pleas of nullity (*Nichtigkeitsbeschwerde*) (against convictions) as well as on appeals connected with pleas of nullity. Since 1993 the Supreme Court is also competent to decide on appeals against decisions of criminal courts (allegedly) violating the constitutional right to (personal) liberty after all (other) remedies have been exhausted.

6. Persons or bodies exercising jurisdiction at ordinary courts

District courts exercise their judicial activities with respect to both civil and criminal matters through magistrates (*Einzelrichter*).

As for courts of first instance, a distinction has to be made between civil jurisdiction and criminal jurisdiction:

– In civil matters most cases are dealt with by magistrates, irrespectively of the value of the claim. However, if the claim exceeds 650000 Austrian Schillings the parties may apply for a panel of three judges (*Dreiersenat*). In commercial matters the panel of three judges comprises two professional judges and an expert lay judge. A panel of three judges also sits in matters of public liability and disputes arising from employment relations or social insurance matters. When acting in these matters two professional judges are replaced by expert lay judges.

Acting as the second instance in civil matters, the courts of first instance sit generally in panels consisting of three professional judges. Solely for decisions on judgments rendered by district courts in commercial matters one professional judge is replaced by an expert lay judge.

– In criminal matters the courts of first instance act as investigating courts as well as through magistrates in simplified proceedings.

As courts of judge and lay assessors they sit in sections consisting of two professional judges and two lay assessors (*Schöffen*).

As courts of appeal they sit in sections of three professional judges.

As judges' chambers, and in all other cases, the courts of first instance exercise criminal jurisdiction in assemblies of three professional judges.

A court of assize consists of the judges of assize (*Schwurgerichtshof*) and the jury (*Geschworenenbank*). The judges of assize are three professional judges, one of whom acts as the chairman; the jury is formed of eight jurors. As a rule, the jurors alone decide on the question of guilt, while the question of punishment is decided upon jointly by the professional judges and the jurors.

The courts of appeal sit both in civil and in criminal matters in panels consisting of three professional judges.

If a court of appeal has to decide on an appeal in commercial matters one of the professional judges is replaced by an expert lay judge. If it has to decide in labour disputes or in social insurance matters, the panels are composed of three professional judges and two expert lay judges. The court of appeal acts in cartel matters as a court of first instance. It consists of one professional judge and two expert lay judges.

At the Supreme Court jurisdiction in civil and in criminal matters is generally exercised by panels of five professional judges. In special cases, however, matters are handled by panels of three members or by enlarged panels of 11 professional judges. For decisions on appeals concerning an alleged violation of the constitutional right to (personal) liberty the panels are composed of three professional judges. When deciding on a "Revision" entered against a judgment of a court of appeal in labour disputes or social insurance matters, the panels of the Supreme Court as a rule are composed of three professional judges and two expert lay judges. In cartel matters the Supreme Court decides in panels of one professional judge and four expert lay judges.

B. Extraordinary courts

The Austrian court system includes, beside ordinary courts, other courts which are referred to in the literature as extraordinary courts or special courts. These are, in particular, the following:

– The Courts of Arbitration set up in accordance with the rules of the Austrian Code of Civil Procedure are special courts; on the basis of a valid arbitration agreement the authority to decide on disputes which may be settled by compromise may be transferred to such arbitration tribunals as are created under the provisions of the arbitration agreement; arbitration tribunals do not have executive power. Their awards are enforceable by ordinary courts only if they are signed by all arbitrators and their enforceability is certified.

– The Arbitration Tribunals for Stock Exchange Matters have a double function. They are public courts in the case of disputes which they are competent to decide upon by operation of law notwithstanding an arbitration agreement, and in this respect, they are authorised both to render decisions and to issue orders. But they are deemed private tribunals of arbitration if their competency is based on an arbitration agreement. In any case, however, they do not have any executive power. Their awards are enforceable and, if required, must be executed by ordinary courts. The terms of reference of the arbitration tribunals for stock exchange matters are laid down in the statutes of the respective stock exchanges.

C. The Public Prosecutor's Office

The Public Prosecutor's Office is organised as a judicial administrative authority. It is competent in general to institute proceedings in the case of offences subject to public prosecution and, in particular, to represent the Public Prosecutor's Office.

The functions of the public prosecutor are executed by the agents of public prosecutor's offices at district courts, by public prosecutors at courts of first instance, by senior public prosecutors at courts of second instance and by the Attorney General and his deputies at the Supreme Court.

In the fulfilment of their functions, the members of the public prosecuting authorities are independent of the courts where they are appointed.

Public prosecutors at courts of first instance are subordinate to senior public prosecutors, the latter and the Attorney General at the Supreme Court are subordinate to the Federal Ministry of Justice.

In fulfilling their functions, public prosecutors are authorised to contact directly and enlist the support of police authorities, other authorities of the *Bund* and the *Bundesländer* as well as local authorities.

Public prosecutors have an important sphere of action beyond criminal proceedings. They represent, for instance, the prosecution in a number of disciplinary matters. In the field of civil jurisdiction their *Cupertino* is necessary, among other things, in proceedings concerning legitimacy, matters of marriage and proceedings concerning declarations of death.

D. Statistical data

In Austria there are the following courts:
- the Supreme Court;
- four courts of appeal (courts of second instance) (*Oberlandesgerichte*);
- 20 courts of first instance (*Landesgerichte*); and
- 190 district courts (*Bezirksgerichte*).

The following numbers of cases were submitted to ordinary courts of all instances in 1996:

litigations	856444
appeal proceedings in civil matters	42698
enforcement cases in civil matters	1236553
non-litigious civil cases	177693
criminal cases (appeals included)	182727
matters of judicial administration	352722
other matters	1111084
Total number of cases	3959921
Land register extracts	643951
Total	4603872

In July 1997, altogether 1 677 judges were appointed:
- 57 at the Supreme Court;
- 169 at the Courts of Appeal;
- 718 at the Regional Courts; and
- 733 at the District Courts.

There were 206 posts in the public prosecuting authorities, including the Office of the Attorney General at the Supreme Court, in July 1997:
- 14 at the Office of the Attorney General;
- 17 at the offices of senior public prosecutors; and
- 175 at the offices of public prosecutors.

III. Court of public law

A. The Administrative Court and the Constitutional Court – common principles

The Administrative Court and the Constitutional Court (*Verwaltungsgerichtshof, Verfassungsgerichtshof*) are provided for in the 6th part (*Hauptstück*) of the Federal Constitutional Act of 1920 as amended in 1929 under the heading "guardians of the constitution and the administration" (Articles 129 to 148). They are called "Courts of Public Law". In the same part of the Constitution, the Independent Administrative Boards are regulated. They function as a "guardian of the administration" in addition to (and as a kind of first instance below) the Courts of Public Law.

The Administrative Court and the Constitutional Court are "genuine courts" as all of their members enjoy the judicial privilege of independence and immunity from being removed or transferred.

Both the Administrative Court and the Constitutional Court are "supreme courts" as they are independent from, and neither superior nor subordinate to one another. The same is true in relation to the Supreme Court.

Only one Administrative Court and one Constitutional Court exist (principle of concentration); their jurisdiction extends over the whole of the Austrian territory and both have their seat in Vienna (principle of centralisation).

The above principles have been weakened by the amendment to the 1988 Constitution. As the Independent Administrative Boards serve the function of an appeal instance against administrative decisions, they fulfil the task of a "first instance" with respect to court protection by the Courts of Public Law, although strictly speaking they cannot be qualified as courts. As they are composed of independent members that are appointed for at least six years according to the Constitution and can only be removed for the same reasons as judges, they can be seen as tribunals in the sense of Article 6 of the European Convention on Human Rights.

B. The Administrative Court

The Administrative Court decides on:

– official appeals (Amtsbeschwerden);

– appeals by private parties (*Parteibeschwerden*): appeals against administrative decisions (*Bescheidbeschwerden*); complaints against an administrative authority's failure to render a decision (*Säumnisbeschwerden*).

1. Official appeals

Such appeals may be lodged by certain public agencies as authorised under federal constitutional or "simple" acts (that is, acts which may be passed by a simple majority) on the grounds of violation of the public law; they are also called "objective" appeals.

In matters where, under the distribution of competences as provided in the Austrian Federal Constitution, legislation is the responsibility of the *Bund* and execution is incumbent upon the *Bundesländer* (Article 11 and Article 14, paragraph 2, of the Federal Constitutional Act) or where the legislation laying down general principles comes within the competency of the *Bund* while the *Bundesländer* are responsible for the enactment of executive laws and the operation of the laws (Article 12 and Article 14, paragraph 3, of the Federal Constitutional Act) as well as in those matters where an administrative decision of a *Bundesland* or district school authority is based on a board decision, the Federal Minister concerned may lodge an appeal with the Administrative Court provided that the parties in the administrative proceedings cannot lodge a further appeal against the decision under the administrative system of recourse (Article 131, paragraph 1, sub-paragraph 2, of the Federal Constitutional Act).

Pursuant to Article 81.*a,* paragraph 4, of the Federal Constitutional Act, the school boards of the *Bund,* which are organised in accordance with the principle of collective responsibility, may appeal to the Administrative Court against orders issued to them which prohibit the execution of a board's decision or order the repeal of an order issued by such a board on the grounds of unlawfulness.

In matters coming within their autonomous sphere of competence, local authorities have a right to lodge with the Administrative Court complaints against the control board of the local authority (*Gemeindeaufsichtsbehörde*) [Article 119.*a*, paragraph 9, of the Federal Constitutional Act].

Moreover, by virtue of Article 131, paragraph 2, of the Federal Constitutional Act, the legislator (of the *Bund* or of several *Bundesländer*) is empowered under certain circumstances to admit appeals to the Administrative Court by way of an authorisation under a "simple" act. Such an authorisation has been given in the following cases:

– Pursuant to Article 292 of the Federal Tax Code (*Bundes-Abgabenordnung*), *Federal Law Gazette* No. 194/1961, the Presidents of the Boards of Revenues of the *Bundesländer* (*Finanzlandesdirektionen*) are authorised to appeal, for the benefit and at the expense of the taxpayers concerned, against decisions of the appeal panels (*Berufungssenate*) established within these boards;

– Article 11 of the Act on Public Liability (*Amtshaftungsgesetz*) *Federal Law Gazette* No. 20/1949, as amended by the Federal Act, *Federal Law Gazette* No. 60/1952, provides that whenever a decision on a claim for damages is dependent on the question of whether an administrative decision is unlawful, the court rendering judgment shall interrupt the proceeding and request, by way of a complaint to the Administrative Court, that the administrative decision be declared unlawful.

2. Appeals by private parties

Appeals against administrative decisions

After exhaustion of the administrative system of recourse, every party to a preceding administrative proceeding may, within six weeks, lodge with the Administrative Court an appeal against a decision of an administrative authority on the grounds of alleged unlawfulness of that decision. Such an appeal is also called "subjective appeal". It, now, can also be lodged against a decision of an Independent Administrative Board; in cases falling within its responsibility the "exhaustion of the system of recourse" therefore also requires that an appeal to the Independent Administrative Board has been launched.

An administrative decision against which an appeal is lodged must be set aside by the Administrative Court on account of the following reasons:

– unlawfulness of its contents;

– unlawfulness because of the authority's incompetence;

– unlawfulness because of violation of rules of procedure, in particular on the grounds that:

i. the facts on an essential point as assumed by the authority concerned are in contradiction to what is on record; or

ii. the facts need to be supplemented on an essential point; or

iii. rules of procedure have been disregarded and the authority concerned might have arrived at another decision if it had proceeded in line with these rules.

Complaint against an administrative authority's failure to render a decision

A complaint against an administrative authority's failure to render a decision may be lodged by anyone who under a preceding administrative procedure was entitled to claim observance of the obligation to render a decision. It may be lodged by the party concerned with the Administrative Court only if the highest authority which could be applied to under the administrative proceeding (either under the system of recourse or by way of an application for transfer of the obligation to render a decision) was applied to by that party and did not decide on the matter within six months.

In the case of such a complaint the Administrative Court may decide on the matter as such.

C. The Constitutional Court

The Constitutional Court is competent to act as a:

– so-called *Kausalgerichtshof;*

– tribunal for deciding disputes about jurisdiction or competences:

i. decisions on so-called *Organstreitigkeiten;*

ii. decisions on conflicts of competence or jurisdiction;

iii. advance determination of competence;

– tribunal for deciding on the existence of and compliance with a treaty between the *Bund* and one or more *Länder* according to Article 15.*a* of the Constitution on the request of the federal government or of one of the provincial governments concerned (Article 138.*a*). The same competence exists with regard to treaties between the *Länder,* when this competence is fixed in the treaty;

– tribunal for examining orders (*Verordnungsprüfungsgericht*);

– tribunal for examining laws (*Gesetzesprüfungsgericht*);

– tribunal for examining international agreements (*Staatsvertragsprüfungsgerich*);

– election court (*Wahlgerichtshof*);

– high court of state (*Staatsgerichtshof*);

– special administrative court (*Sonderverwaltungsgerichtshof*);

– tribunal for international law (*Völkergerichtshof*).

*1. The Constitutional Court (*Kausalgerichtshof*) (Article 137 of the Federal Constitutional Act)*

The Constitutional Court decides on financial claims against the *Bund,* the *Bundesländer,* local authorities and municipal corporations, which cannot be settled either by due process of law or by a decision of an administrative authority.

Under this supplementary jurisdiction of the Constitutional Court, claims have to be asserted by way of an action for performance or a declaratory action; the execution of judgments concerning performance is incumbent upon the ordinary courts.

2. Tribunal for deciding disputes about jurisdiction or competence

The Constitutional Court is competent:

– to decide on *Organstreitigkeiten* (Article 126.*a* and 148.*f* of the Federal Constitutional Act);

– to decide on conflicts of competence or jurisdiction (Article 138, paragraph 1, of the Federal Constitutional Act);

– to determine competences in advance (Article 138, paragraph 2, of the Federal Constitutional Act).

Decisions on Organstreitigkeiten:

At the instigation of the federal government, the government of a *Bundesland* or of the Audit Court (*Rechnungshof*), the Constitutional Court decides on (concrete) disputes arising between the Audit Court on the one hand, and the federal government, a federal minister or the government of a *Bundesland* on the other hand, concerning the interpretation of the legal rules governing the competences of the Audit Court.

In the case of different opinions between the ombudsman and the federal government on the competences of the ombudsman, the Constitutional Court decides on the question upon request of the government or the ombudsman (Article 148.*f* of the Constitution).

Decisions on conflicts of competence or jurisdiction:

The Constitutional Court furthermore decides on (positive and negative) conflicts of competence or jurisdiction:

– between tribunals and administrative authorities;

– between the Administrative Court and all other tribunals and in particular between the Administrative Court and the Constitutional Court itself as well as between ordinary and other courts;

– between the *Bundesländer* among themselves as well as between a *Bundesland* and the *Bund.*

In the case of a negative conflict of competence an appeal may be lodged with the Constitutional Court only by the parties concerned.

A positive conflict of competence between tribunals as well as between tribunals and administrative authorities can be brought before the Constitutional Court only as long as no final judgment has been pronounced by the court. The proceedings before the Constitutional Court are instituted:

– in the case of conflicts of competence between tribunals and administrative authorities, at the request of the highest competent administrative authority within four weeks after the case has become known or, as a subsidiary possibility, at the request of a party after another four weeks;

– in the case of conflicts of jurisdiction between tribunals, *ex officio* by the Constitutional Court as soon as it obtains knowledge about the existence of a conflict (from a notice by a tribunal or the parties concerned or *ex officio*);

– in the case of conflicts of competence between the *Bundesländer* among themselves as well as between a *Bundesland* and the *Bund,* at the request of one of the governments concerned within four weeks after the case has become known.

In its decision the Constitutional Court determines the competences and cancels contradictory acts of authorities.

Advance determination of competence:

At the request of the federal government or the government of a *Bundesland,* the Constitutional Court determines whether under the rules of the Federal Constitution on competence an (envisaged) act of legislation or execution comes within the competence of the *Bund* or the *Bundesländer.* The decision is taken in the form of a (legislative) regulation, which has to be promulgated immediately by the Federal Chancellor in the *Federal Law Gazette* and has the same authority as the provisions of the Constitution.

3. Tribunal for examining the existence of treaties between the Bund *and the* Länder *and compliance with such treaties (Article 138.*a *of the Federal Constitutional Act).*

Article 15.*a* of the Federal Constitutional Act provides for the conclusion of treaties between the *Bund* and the *Länder.* In addition to Article 15.*a*, Article 138.*a* enables the *Bund* and the *Länder* to lodge an appeal with the Constitutional Court on the question whether such a treaty exists and whether a party to the treaty has fulfilled its obligaitions under the treaty.

Such treaties are used, for example, to fix the way the responsibilities of *Bund* and *Länder* are exercised or for financial matters. So far there has been no dispute on compliance with such treaties and as a consequence there has not yet been a decision of the court based on Article 138.*a* of the Federal Constitution Act.

4. Tribunal for examining orders (Article 139 of the Federal Constitutional Act)

The Constitutional Court decides:

– at the request of a court, on the question whether orders issued by an agency of the *Bund* or a *Bundesland* are unlawful. If such an order, however, is the basis of a judgment to be rendered by the Constitutional Court, it takes such a decision *ex officio;*

– at the request of the federal government, on the question whether orders issued by an agency of a *Bundesland* are unlawful;

– at the request of the government of a *Bundesland,* on the question whether orders issued by an agency of the *Bund* are unlawful;

– at the request of the local authority concerned, on the unlawfulness of an order issued by a control board of local authorities which sets aside an order passed by the local authority within its autonomous sphere of action;

– at the request of the federal ombudsman as well as the ombudsman of a *Land,* on the question whether an order of a federal authority or an authority of a *Land* is unlawful.

If the Constitutional Court finds an order to be unlawful, it rescinds by its judgment the order as a whole or specific parts thereof. The rescission has to be immediately promulgated. Exceptionally – exclusively at the request of a court – the Constitutional Court may also decide that an order, which has already ceased to have effect, was unlawful.

5. Tribunal for examining laws (Article 140 of the Federal Constitutional Act)

The Constitutional Court decides:

– at the request of the Supreme Court, a court of second instance, an Independent Administrative Board, the Administrative Court, one third of the members of the National Diet, one-third of the members of the Federal Diet, or a government of a *Land,* on the question whether a federal act is unconstitutional. Such a request can be made by a court or an Independent Administrative Board only in cases where the act forms the basis for a judgment to be rendered by the court submitting the request. In the other cases there is no such requirement ("abstract control"). It furthermore takes such a decision if such an act forms the basis for a judgment to be rendered by the Constitutional Court itself;

– at the request of the Supreme Court, a court of second instance, an Independent Administrative Board, the Administrative Court, one-third of the members of a provincial parliament (if this is provided for in the Constitution of the *Land*) or the federal government, on the question whether an act of the *Land* is unconstitutional;

– at the request of a private person, on the question whether a federal act or an act of the *Land* is unconstitutional when the act produces direct effect on the rights of the citizen (no decision of a court or an administrative authority on the basis of the act is necessary; the effect follows from the existence of the law itself; *Individualantrag – individual action*).

If the Constitutional Court finds an act to be unconstitutional, it rescinds by its judgment the respective act as a whole or specific parts thereof. The rescission has to be immediately promulgated. The rescission enters into force the day after its promulgation unless the court fixes another date for the entry into force (the court in doing so can choose a time period of up to two years, beginning with its ruling; within this period the rescinded law is still in force and has to be applied!).

6. Tribunal for examining international agreements (Article 140.a of the Federal Constitutional Act)

The Constitutional Court decides on the question whether an international agreement is unlawful. In this connection Article 140 of the Federal Constitutional Act (see Item 4 above) is applicable to all international agreements (political conventions, agreements modifying or supplementing the law) concluded with the approval of the *Nationalrat* in accordance with Article 50 of the Federal Constitutional Act. Article 139 of the Federal Constitutional Act (see Item 3 above) is applicable to all other international agreements, with the result that international agreements found to be unlawful or unconstitutional by the Constitutional Court shall not be applied by the agencies competent for their execution as of the date of the promulgation of the judgment, unless the Constitutional Court prescribes a period within which such international agreements may still be applied. This period must not exceed two years for international agreements concluded with the approval of the *Nationalrat* and one year for all other international agreements.

If an international agreement which must be implemented by national acts or orders is found to be unlawful or unconstitutional by the Constitutional Court, the respective acts and orders cease to be valid.

7. Election court (Article 141 of the Federal Constitutional Act)

The Constitutional Court decides:

– on petitions contesting the validity of an election of the federal President as well as of elections to parliamentary bodies of all levels and to the regulatory bodies (representative bodies) [*Vertretungskörper*] of legally instituted industrial associations;

– on petitions contesting elections to the government of a *Bundesland* and to the executive bodies of a local authority;

– at the request of a parliamentary body, on the forfeiture of the mandate of one of its members;

– at the request of a regulatory body (representative body) of a legally instituted industrial association, on the forfeiture of the mandate of one of the members of such a body;

– insofar as the federal acts or the acts of the *Bundesländer* governing elections provide that forfeiture of a mandate shall be declared by a decision of an administrative authority, it decides on appeals against such decisions declaring forfeited a mandate in a parliamentary body, in an executive body of a local authority or in a regulatory body (representative body) of a legally instituted industrial association after exhaustion of the system of recourse.

The contestation (petition) (*Anfechtung*) may be based on the alleged unlawfulness of the mode of election or on any reason prescribed by the law entailing forfeiture of membership in a parliamentary body, in an executive body of a local authority or in a regulatory body (representative body) of a legally instituted industrial association. The Constitutional Court must grant an election petition if the alleged unlawfulness of a mode of election has been proved and had influenced the election results.

Under similar conditions and with the same power to declare the contested acts void the court decides on petitions contesting the result of initiatives, plebiscites (referenda) and popular votes (the relevant steps of the initiative, plebiscite (referendum) or popular vote have to be repeated as a consequence of the ruling insofar as they have been set aside).

8. High court of state (Article 142, 143 of the Federal Constitutional Act)

The Constitutional Court decides on charges concerning the constitutional responsibility of the highest authorities of the *Bund* and the *Bundesländer* for culpable violations of the law in their official activities.

Charges may be brought:

– against the federal President, on the grounds of violation of the federal constitution (by a decision of the *Bundesversammlung* [joint meeting of the *Nationalrat* and the *Bundesrat*]);

– against the members of the federal government and the authorities with equal responsibility, on the grounds of violation of the law (by a decision of the *Nationalrat*);

– against the members of the government of a *Bundesland* and the authorities with equal responsibility under the federal constitution or the constitution of the *Bundesland,* on the grounds of violation of the law (by a decision of the competent *Landtag* [*Bundeslandparlament*]);

– against a *Landeshauptmann* (governor of a *Bundesland*), his deputy or a member of the government of a *Bundesland,* on the grounds of violation of the law and non-compliance with orders of other directives of the *Bund* in matters of indirect federal administration, and in the case of a member of a *Bundesland* government, also on the grounds of non-compliance with the directives of the *Landeshauptmann* in such matters (by a decision of the federal government);

– against authorities of the federal capital of Vienna, insofar as they fulfil within their autonomous sphere of activity functions coming within the scope of the federal executive authorities, on the grounds of violation of the law (by a decision of the federal government);

– against a *Landeshauptmann,* on the grounds of non-compliance with an order directing the *Landeshauptmann* to remedy a fault in matters of schools, which come within the responsibility of the *Bundesländer* as regards execution and within the responsibility of the *Bund* as regards legislation or legislation laying down general principles (*Grundsatzgesetzgebung*) (by a decision of the federal government);

– against a President or an acting President of the school board of a *Bundesland,* on the grounds of violation of the law or non-compliance with the orders or other directives issued by the *Bund* (by a decision of the federal government).

Charges may also be brought against the aforementioned authorities on the grounds of criminal acts connected with their official activities. In this event the Constitutional Court is exclusively competent to deal with the case. Any proceedings with ordinary criminal courts are taken over by it.

9. Special Administrative Court (Article 144 of the Federal Constitutional Act)

The Constitutional Court decides on appeals against decisions of administrative authorities if the applicant alleges violation of his constitutional rights by the decision. The appeal can be lodged only after exhaustion of the regular system of recourses.

It is, therefore, necessary to launch an appeal to an Independent Administrative Board before addressing the Constitutional Court.

If the Constitutional Court finds that no constitutional right has been violated by the contested decision of the administrative authority and if the matter concerned is not excluded from the jurisdiction of the Administrative Court, the Constitutional Court is held to cede, at the applicant's request, the appeal to the Administrative Court. Simultaneously with rendering a decision rejecting the appeal, the Administrative Court has to decide whether any other right of the applicant has been violated by the administrative decision.

10. Tribunal for international law (Article 145 of the Federal Constitutional Act)

The Constitutional Court decides on violations of international law in accordance with the rules of a special federal act, however, has not yet been passed.

D. Independent Administrative Boards

The Independent Administrative Boards are competent to decide upon:

– appeals against administrative decisions in administrative criminal matters;

– appeals against other administrative measures directly infringing the rights of citizens without a formal decision according to the Act on

Administrative Procedure (measures exercising administrative power directly: *Ausübung unmittelbarer verwaltungsbehördlicher Befehls- und Zwangsgewalt* – "exercise of direct administrative power");

– appeals in other administrative matters where it is provided for by law (not compulsory under the Constitution; an Act of Parliament can vest the boards with this responsibility; such laws have been issued in only a few cases so far);

– complaints against the breach of the obligation to take a decision by an administrative authority in those cases where an appeal to the board is possible against the decision that should be taken.

E. Statistical data

According to the annual reports of the Administrative Court, it received 11 132 appeals in 1995 and 12 790 appeals in 1996. Due to a large amount of appeals in matters of the law concerning aliens recently a board especially dealing with asylum matters was established (*Bundesasylsenat*).

The court took the following number of decisions between 1992 and 1996:

1992:	5715
1993:	5364
1994:	7841
1995:	7823
1996:	8903

The court has 60 judges at this time. It sits in sections composed of five members; in some cases – especially in criminal administrative matters – there are chambers of three members (composed of the members of a section). Responsibility for preparation of the decision lies with one member of the section or chamber (called the "reporting member"). According to the figures in the annual reports (see above) each reporting member prepares approximately 185 decisions a year (at present there are 21 sections and 48 reporting members).

The Constitutional Court received 4029 petitions and decided 14868 cases in 1997.

The court took the following number of decisions in 1997:

Kausalgerichtsbarkeit	26
Disputes on jurisdiction or competence	22
Examination of orders	165
Examination of acts	388
Elections	6
Forfeiture of the mandate	18
Special administrative court (11 167 of these appeals were special appeals concerning corporation income tax)	14243
Total:	**14868**

BELGIUM

I. Introduction

Under the Constitution sovereign power is shared between the legislature, the executive and the judiciary, which are separate and independent of one another. The courts therefore constitute an individual branch of power, distinct from the other two (Articles 33 and 40 of the Constitution). By virtue of the authority vested in them by the nation, the courts have unfettered discretion to apply the law to disputes brought before them and impose the penalties prescribed for each particular breach of the law (Articles 144, 145 and 146 of the Constitution). As their guiding criterion is the law, the courts apply orders, regulations and other similar decisions only in so far as these are in accordance with statute law (Article 159 of the Constitution).

They do not have jurisdiction to submit legislation to constitutional review, as that is to some extent the preserve of the Administrative Jurisdiction and Procedure Court (*Cour d'Arbitrage*) (see below). A court may only be established by law, and no tribunal or court other than the regular courts of law may be set up under any name whatsoever (Article 146 of the Constitution).

The judicial system is organised on four levels: national, judicial regions (*ressorts*), judicial districts (*arrondissements*) and judicial cantons.

At national level there is a Court of Cassation.

At regional level there are five courts of appeal and five labour courts of appeal. Assizes are held in the ten Belgian provinces and in the administrative district of Brussels-Capital.

At district level there are 27 courts of first instance, 27 commercial courts, 27 labour courts and 32 police courts.

It should be noted that within each court of first instance there is an attachments judge (*juge des saisies*) who examines all applications for preventive attachment measures and enforcement measures, and that a measure to preserve rights may be ordered in any legal matter and in respect of any kind of property, with the result that immovables can be attached as a preventive measure.

At cantonal level there are 225 magistrates' courts (for 186 cantons).

II. Information concerning the various types of court

The members of the courts are career judges, who have the title of *juge* in a district court (a *tribunal*) and *conseiller* in a regional one (a *cour*). They are appointed for life by the Crown. However, the Commercial Courts, the Labour Courts and the Labour Courts of Appeal constitute an exception, in that the career members of those courts are assisted by lay judges, appointed for a limited term of office.

At district level Belgium also has substitute judges, likewise appointed to that office for life by the Crown. These are not career judges but people with experience of judicial matters (such as legal practitioners (*avocats* or *notaires*)), authorised to replace a career judge who is sick or absent for other reasons, so as to avoid any disruption in the administration of justice. This system was recently extended to the Courts of Appeal at regional level.

The function of supplementary judge has long existed in the Magistrates' Courts and the Police Courts. These are career judges, usually appointed to sit in a given judicial district, whose role is to second judges in the Magistrates' Courts and the Police Courts with a view to reducing their workload. An Act of February 1998, extending this system to the district level, established the office of supplementary judge appointed by the Crown to sit, as needed, in one or more courts of first instance, one or more commercial courts or one or more labour courts. A system of this kind makes it possible, firstly, to deal with a temporary additional case-load and, secondly, to replace an incumbent judge of the above courts, for instance one temporarily assigned to other duties.

Article 151 of the Constitution, which was amended on 20 November 1998, makes provision for a Judicial Service Commission (*Conseil Supérieur de la Justice*), composed of members of the courts and of the Crown Counsel's Department and of an equal number of representatives of civil society, appointed by the Senate.

This body, which cannot be considered to belong to any of the established branches of power, is a unique institution with authority for the following matters:

– proposing candidates for appointment as judges or members of the Crown Counsel's Department;

– access to the above offices;

– training of judges and members of the Crown Counsel's Department;

– issuing opinions and proposals concerning the general functioning and organisation of the courts;

– general supervision and promotion of use of internal control methods;

– receiving and following up complaints concerning the functioning of the courts and initiating inquiries into such matters, without being empowered to take disciplinary measures or institute criminal proceedings.

A. Magistrates' Court (*Justice de paix*)

Jurisdiction:

– General jurisdiction: Magistrates' Courts deal with all claims not exceeding 75 000 Belgian Francs, except for those which, by law, lie outside their jurisdiction.

– Special jurisdiction: In addition, they have sole jurisdiction to deal with certain categories of disputes, regardless of the amount of the claim, including those concerning family affairs or real property.

Composition: Single judge

Appeals:

– in civil matters to the Court of First Instance;

– in commercial matters to the Commercial Court;

– on points of law to the Court of Cassation.

B. Police Court (*Tribunal de police*)

Jurisdiction: Police Courts deal with all minor offences (*contraventions*) and with certain more serious ones (*délits*), in particular traffic offences. They also examine claims for damages in connection with traffic offences.

Composition: Single judge

Appeals:

– on the merits to the Court of First Instance;

– on points of law to the Court of Cassation, where no appeal on the merits lies against the Police Court's decision.

C. Court of First Instance (*Tribunal de première instance*)

*First Section: Civil Court (*Tribunal civil*)*

Jurisdiction:

– General jurisdiction: The Courts of First Instance deal with all civil disputes concerning amounts in excess of 75 000 Belgian Francs, except in commercial or labour matters.

– Special jurisdiction: They also have sole jurisdiction to deal with certain categories of disputes, in particular those concerning the law of persons (nullity of marriage, divorce, descent), property rights (matrimonial property ownership, successions), expropriations, intellectual property rights, civil society, execution of judgments, and disputes regarding the application of tax law.

– Appellate jurisdiction: These courts examine appeals against decisions taken by the Magistrates' Courts at first instance and by the Police Courts in civil matters.

– Special jurisdiction of the President: The President may examine any application for an urgent, provisional decision in a matter coming within the court's jurisdiction and also, on a direct *ex parte* application (*requête*), in certain other matters provided for by law.

Composition: One or three judges. Certain matters must be dealt with by a bench of three. There is also a single judge, the attachments judge (*juge des saisies*), with jurisdiction for preventive attachment measures and enforcement measures.

Appeals:

– on the merits to the Court of Appeal;

– on points of law to the Court of Cassation.

*Second Section: Criminal Court (*Tribunal correctionnel*)*

Jurisdiction:

– more serious offences (*délits*);

– serious crimes reduced to lesser offences in view of extenuating or mitigating circumstances;

– minor offences connected with more serious ones;

– appellate jurisdiction to examine decisions taken by the Police Courts.

Composition: Usually a single judge; three judges in cases specified by law.

Appeals:

– on the merits to the Court of Appeal;

– on points of law to the Court of Cassation, against judgments given on appeal (that is concerning decisions by the Police Courts).

*Third Section: Youth Court (*Tribunal de la jeunesse*)*

Jurisdiction:

– proceedings concerning minors' civil rights: emancipation, adoption, guardianship and administration of minors' property, exercise of parental authority;

– measures to protect minors;
– measures in respect of parents, ordered on an application from the Crown Counsel's Department, including administration of family allowances, orders concerning a child's welfare and upbringing, and deprivation of parental authority;
– measures in respect of minors, ordered on an application from the Crown Counsel's Department or where a complaint has been laid by a person exercising parental authority or caring for a minor under the age of 18, including reprimands, supervision, placing in a home, and preventive detention combined with conditional release (*mise à la disposition du gouvernement*).
Composition: Single judge
Appeals:
– on the merits to the Court of Appeal;
– on points of law to the Court of Cassation.

D. Labour Court (*Tribunal du travail*)
Jurisdiction:
– all labour disputes, including those relating to employment contracts;
– proceedings relating to industrial injuries and occupational diseases;
– all social security disputes;
– all disputes relating to the establishment and functioning of works councils and health, safety and workplace improvement committees.
Special jurisdiction of the President: similar to that of the President of the civil section of the Court of First Instance.
Composition: A presiding career judge assisted by two lay judges (one appointed as an employer representative and the other as an employee representative).
Appeals:
– on the merits to the Labour Court of Appeal;
– on points of law to the Court of Cassation.

E. Commercial Court (*Tribunal de commerce*)
Jurisdiction:
– General jurisdiction: disputes between business parties relating to transactions which the law deems to be commercial in nature and which lie outside the general jurisdiction of the Magistrates' Courts.
– Special jurisdiction: disputes in the fields of trade registration, company law, bankruptcy, maritime law, trade bills, etc.; appellate jurisdiction to examine decisions taken by the Magistrates' Courts in commercial matters.
– Special jurisdiction of the President: Similar to that of the President of the civil section of the Court of First Instance.
Composition: A presiding career judge assisted by two lay judges from the business community.
Appeals:
– on the merits to the Court of Appeal;
– on points of law to the Court of Cassation.

F. District Court (*Tribunal d'arrondissement*)

The District Court does not really exist in its own right as it consists of the Presidents of the Court of First Instance, the Commercial Court and the Labour Court.

Its role is to settle jurisdictional disputes between those three courts.

Appeals: On points of law to the Court of Cassation.

G. Court of Appeal (*Cour d'appel*)

Jurisdiction:

– Appellate jurisdiction: The court examines appeals against first-instance decisions by all sections of the Courts of First Instance, by the Commercial Courts and by the Presidents of those courts.

– At first and last instance: In matters concerning loss or deprivation of citizenship, discharge of bankrupts, and elections.

Composition: In the three divisions of the Court of Appeal (which deal with civil and commercial, criminal, and youth matters) cases are heard either by a bench of three judges, including the President, or, where provided by law, by a single judge, who may or may not be the President of the division.

Appeals: On points of law to the Court of Cassation.

H. Labour Court of Appeal (*Cour du travail*)

Jurisdiction: The court examines appeals against first-instance decisions by the Labour Courts and their Presidents.

Composition: A presiding career judge assisted by two or four lay judges, depending on the circumstances.

Appeals: On points of law to the Court of Cassation.

I. Assize Court (*Cour d'Assises*)

Jurisdiction:

– serious crimes;

– political offences and most offences concerning the press;

– lesser offences (*délits* and *contraventions*) connected with serious crimes.

Composition: A President, who is a judge of the Court of Appeal, two assessors, who are judges of the Court of First Instance, and twelve jurors, chosen by lot from among the general public.

Appeals: On points of law to the Court of Cassation.

J. Court of Cassation (*Cour de cassation*)

Jurisdiction: The court's principal role is to examine appeals against last-instance decisions, entered on grounds of errors of law or of failure to comply with essential formal requirements or with requirements' failure to observe which makes the decision void. The Court of Cassation therefore has a regulatory role, ensuring consistency in interpretation of the law.

Composition:

– The Court of Cassation consists of a First President, a President, four Section Presidents and 24 judges.

– It has three divisions. The first deals with civil and commercial matters, the second with criminal proceedings and the third with cases coming within the jurisdiction of the Labour Courts. Each division is divided into two sections, one French-speaking and the other Dutch-speaking. Each section includes five judges. Cases are decided by a bench of five judges, including the President. However, in certain cases, provided for by law, the bench may consist of only three judges.

Note on the officers and the courts responsible for criminal investigations

Investigating judges (*juges d'instruction*) are judges of the Court of First Instance appointed to that office by the Crown. The principal investigatory methods employed by investigating judges are questioning the accused, visits to the site of an offence, house searches, obtaining expert opinions, examining witnesses, confrontations, and obtaining evidence on commission.

Since investigating judges' jurisdiction extends only to conducting an investigation, they are not competent to assess the consequences and results thereof. This is the role of the Investigating Courts: the Court of First Instance sitting in chambers (*chambre du conseil*) and the Indictments Division (*chambre des mises en accusation*) of the Court of Appeal.

Their task is to assess the evidence gathered by the investigating judge, establish the nature of the charge or charges, determine which criminal court has jurisdiction and refer the case to it, and decide whether the accused is to be detained pending trial.

K. Military courts

With certain exceptions, members of the armed forces who have committed a criminal offence are subject to the jurisdiction not of the ordinary courts but of special courts: the Court Martial (*Conseil de Guerre*) and the Courts-Martial Appeal Court (*Cour Militaire*).

This jurisdiction covers both breaches of the Military Criminal Code and of ordinary law.

Organisation: There is one Court Martial for the entire country, having its seat in Brussels. It includes a number of divisions. Where an offence has been committed abroad, one or more divisions may constitute a field court martial outside national territory. The Court Martial consists of four military members, including the President, and one judge of the Court of First Instance. Against decisions by the Court Martial an appeal lies to the Courts-Martial Appeal Court, which is made up of four military members and one presiding civilian judge.

Appeals: On points of law to the Court of Cassation.

III. The Crown Counsel's Department (*Ministère Public*)

Members of the Crown Counsel's Department are at the same time representatives of the executive and members of the judiciary. In this dual capacity, they share in the exercise of both executive and judicial power.

A. Functions

– uncovering offences, evidence thereof and their perpetrators;
– bringing prosecutions;
– enforcing decisions in criminal matters;
– issuing opinions in civil matters; in certain cases, specified by law, this opinion is mandatory;
– *ex officio* action in cases specified by law and wherever necessary for reasons of public policy;
– *ex officio* enforcement of court decisions wherever this is a matter of public policy;
– supervision of the proper functioning of the courts.

Principal Crown Counsel (*procureur général*) at the Court of Cassation does not act as a prosecuting authority except in cases where he or she institutes proceedings in which the decision on the merits falls to the Court of Cassation.

B. Organisation

Principal Crown Counsel at the Court of Cassation is assisted by advocates general (*avocats généraux*).

Principal Crown Counsel at the Court of Appeal fulfils all the functions inherent in that office in respect of the Court of Appeal, the Labour Court of Appeal, the Assize Courts and all the District Courts coming within the relevant regional jurisdiction. In proceedings before the Court of Appeal Principal Crown Counsel is assisted by advocates general and by Assistant Principal Crown Counsel (*substituts du procureur général*).

At each labour court of appeal there is a Principal Crown Counsel's office for labour matters (*auditorat général du travail*), placed under the control and supervision of Principal Crown Counsel at the Court of Appeal. It is staffed by one or more advocates general and Assistant Principal Crown Counsel.

Each judicial district has a Crown Counsel (*procureur du Roi*) who, under the supervision and control of Principal Crown Counsel at the Court of Appeal, fulfils the functions inherent in that office in respect of the district court, the Court of First Instance, the Commercial Court and the Police Courts within the district. Crown Counsel is assisted by one or more Assistant Crown Counsel (*substituts*).

At each labour court there is a Crown Counsel's office for labour matters (*auditorat du travail*). The relevant functions are fulfilled by a Crown Counsel for labour matters (*auditeur de travail*), under the supervision and control of Principal Crown Counsel at the Court of Appeal and with the assistance of one or more Assistant Crown Counsel.

Police courts do not have a prosecutor's office as such. It is the district Crown Counsel who is responsible for bringing prosecutions before these courts.

C. The Board of Principal Crown Counsel (*collège des procureurs généraux*)

Together, the Principal Crown Counsel at the Courts of Appeal form a board, placed under the authority of the Minister for Justice

This board decides on any measure necessary to:

– the coherent implementation and co-ordination of the crime policy defined by the Minister for Justice;

– the proper functioning and co-ordination of the Crown Counsel's Department.

The board is also responsible for informing the Minister for Justice of any matter of relevance to the role of the Crown Counsel's Department and for giving the Minister opinions on such matters, either of its own initiative or at the Minister's request. The board submits an annual report to the Minister, in which it assesses crime policy implemented over the past year and addresses priorities for the coming year. The Minister for Justice submits this report to parliament. It is made public.

The board is assisted by three members of the national legal service – known as *magistrats nationaux* – whose jurisdiction extends to the entire country. They are responsible for:

– co-ordinating the way in which prosecutions are conducted and facilitating international co-operation, in consultation with one or more Crown Counsel;

– taking any urgent measures needed to bring about a prosecution, as long as Crown Counsel has not exercised the authority conferred on him or her by law.

IV. The administrative courts

A. The *Conseil d'état* (Administration section)

Anyone who can establish a legitimate, personal interest is entitled to file an application (*recours en annulation*) with the administration section of the *Conseil d'Etat* to have it set aside an order, regulation or other decision by any Belgian administrative authority, including an administrative decision taken by the legislative assemblies or their organs, by the Audit Court, by the Administrative Jurisdiction and Procedure Court or by the ordinary courts in respect of a public works or supply contract or of their own staff. The *Conseil d'Etat* therefore submits administrative decisions to non-judicial review and at the same time acts as a Court of Cassation in respect of the lower Administrative Courts, despite the many exceptions provided by law.

Any institution fulfilling a public-interest role and/or exercising some degree of public authority qualifies as an administrative authority subject to the jurisdiction of the *Conseil d'Etat*. An application of the above kind may also be filed where an administrative authority which is required to take a decision fails to do so (by implication a decision of refusal). There is also a procedure of urgent application to the *Conseil d'Etat* (known as *référé administratif*), whereby it is possible to request a stay of execution of a disputed administrative decision, provided that the grounds relied on are sufficient to justify the decision's annulment and that immediate execution of the decision might cause virtually irreparable damage.

Moreover, where there is no other competent court, the administration section has jurisdiction to examine claims for compensation of exceptional damage caused by an administrative authority. It also settles disputes concerning the respective powers of the provincial and the municipal authorities or the powers of public establishments. Lastly, the administration section of the *Conseil d'Etat* deals with applications aimed at preventing or settling conflicting decisions by the Administrative Courts subject to its jurisdiction and with certain other kinds of application provided for by law, in particular in electoral matters.

No appeal lies against judgments of the *Conseil d'Etat,* which can be overturned only by the Court of Cassation should the *Conseil d'Etat* infringe the jurisdiction of an ordinary court.

Composition: Taking all the sections together, the *Conseil d'Etat* consists of a First President, a President, ten Division Presidents and 24 members. It also has a corps of legal assistants (the *auditorat*), a co-ordination office and a registry.

B. The Audit Court (*Cour des comptes*)

Jurisdiction: Examines and closes the accounts of the general administrative authorities and monitors the activities of all accounting officers answerable to the Treasury.

It has sole jurisdiction to try and convict these accounting officers for acts relating to their financial management.

Composition: The Audit Court has two divisions, each of which is made up of a President, four judges and a registrar.

Appeals: On points of law to the Court of Cassation against a decision convicting an accounting officer.

C. Other administrative courts

These are to be found at all levels and do not form an organised whole. Some decide at first instance, others on appeal.

Appeals against their decisions lie to the *Conseil d'Etat* or the Court of Cassation.

V. Administrative Jurisdiction and Procedure Court (*Cour d'arbitrage*)

The Administrative Jurisdiction and Procedure Court, which is neither an ordinary nor an administrative court, decides appeals or preliminary questions concerning disputes over jurisdiction between the various legislative bodies (at federal, regional and community level). It also examines appeals concerning violations of constitutional provisions relating to education, the equality of all Belgians before the law and the prohibition of discrimination. It therefore has limited powers of constitutional review.

An application may be made to the court by any authority specified by law, any individual who can establish an interest in a case, and, on a preliminary question, by any court.

VI. Statistical data

A. Number of members of the Judiciary and of the Crown Counsel's Department as at 20 July 1998

Court	Judiciary	Crown Counsel's Department	Total
Court of Cassation	30	13	43
Courts of Appeal	216	99	315
Labour Courts of Appeal	51	26	77
Courts of First Instance	613	592	1205
Commercial Courts	111	-	111
Labour Courts	138	101	239
Supplementary judges at district level	84	13	97
Magistrates' Courts	187	-	187
Supplementary judges in the Magistrates' Courts	5	-	5
Police Courts	83	-	83
Supplementary judges in the Police Courts	17	-	17
Magistrats nationaux	0	3	3
Courts-Martial Appeal Court	1	9	10
Court Martial	-	42	42

B. Number of cases brought and decided

1997	Cases brought	Decisions
Magistrates' Courts	259 700	312 740
Police Courts	174 575	167 683
Courts of First Instance	187 119[1]	322 431[2]
Labour Courts	Not available	Not available
Commercial Courts	146 657	108 019
District Courts	Not available	Not available
Courts of Appeal	20 094[3]	25 870[4]
Labour Court of Appeal	Not available	Not available
Assize Courts	Not available	Not available
Military Courts	Not available	Not available
Court of Cassation	Not available	Not available

1. Cases brought before the civil and youth sections. No information available concerning criminal cases.
2. Decisions by the Civil, Youth and Criminal Courts.
3. Excluding criminal cases.
4. Including criminal cases.

Croatia

ENACTMENT of the Constitution of the Republic of Croatia in December 1990 marks the beginning of the development of the new legal system in the Republic of Croatia.

According to the Constitution of the Republic of Croatia, the organisation of state authority is based on the principle of division of power between legislative, executive and judicial powers. Consequently, the principle of division of powers has been implemented establishing each of the three powers as mutually independent, with its constitutionally defined powers and competencies.

Judicial power is exercised by courts. It is autonomous and independent, and the courts make their judgments on the basis of the Constitution and the law.

The Constitution of the Republic of Croatia contains fundamental provisions on the organisation of judicial power. The Law on the Courts (*Narodne novine/Official Gazette* No. 3/94, 100/96 and 131/97) regulates in more detail the organisation, scope of operation and competence of courts, internal organisation of courts as well as the conditions for appointment of judges and lay judges together with their rights and responsibilities.

Judicial power is carried out by the following courts: municipal courts (the law envisages 115 municipal courts; at the moment there are 99 municipal courts), county courts (the law envisages 21 county courts; at the moment there are 17 county courts), commercial courts (the law envisages 13; at the moment there are eight commercial courts), and the High Commercial Court of the Republic of Croatia and the Administrative Court of the Republic of Croatia.

The highest court in the Republic of Croatia is the Supreme Court of the Republic of Croatia, which, as the highest court, ensures the uniform application of laws and the equality of its citizens.

A separate law may establish special courts for certain legal fields. Consequently, the Law on the Amendments and Supplements of the Law on Misdemeanours established misdemeanour courts for first instance misdemeanour proceedings, while the High Court for Misdemeanours decides second instance misdemeanour cases.

I. The jurisdiction of courts[1]

A. Municipal courts

In criminal cases

– they make judgments in first instance cases involving crimes for which a punishment of up to ten years' imprisonment is prescribed, if the law does not grant jurisdiction for certain crimes to another court;

– carry out other tasks as prescribed by law.

In civil cases they decide on the following cases:

– maintenance;

– existence or non-existence of marriage or divorce;

1. According to the Law on Courts (*Narodne novine* No. 3/94, 100/96, 131/97).

– establishment or rebuttal of paternity or motherhood;
– legal custody and upbringing of children;
– easements appurtenant and easements in gross;
– possessor's and property cases;
– landlord-tenant suits;
– labour cases;
– suits for correction of information and suits for damages caused by the publishing of information;
– other civil cases which are not within the jurisdiction of commercial courts;

In other cases they decide on the following:

– *ex parte* and execution of judgments cases, if they are not within the jurisdiction of another court;
– cases on inheritance and cases related to the keeping of land-registers;
– recognition and enforcement of foreign judgments;
– carrying out tasks related to international legal assistance;
– carrying out tasks related to the provision of legal assistance.

Municipal courts decide all cases which do not fall within the jurisdiction of any other court or a public notary.

Municipal courts decide and have full jurisdiction in criminal cases against military persons, military officials and military employees in service in the armed forces for crimes committed during service or in connection with service.

Municipal courts shall establish a special division or a panel for deciding cases outlines in the paragraphs above.

In counties in which more than one municipal court is established, a law may prescribe that only one of those municipal courts shall decide certain type of cases falling within the jurisdiction of all the municipal courts.

B. County courts

County courts:

– decide cases in the first instance for crimes punishable by imprisonment for more than 10 years;
– carry out investigations and other actions, decide appeals from decrees and proposals of the investigative judge;
– carry out the proceedings for the extradition of accused and convicted persons when the law does not prescribe the jurisdiction of the Supreme Court of the Republic of Croatia;
– decide on conflicts of jurisdiction between municipal courts, if it is their common court of immediately higher instance;
– decide appeals from first instance decisions of municipal courts;
– carry out investigative proceedings against public notaries for violations of discipline and pass first instance decisions in these proceedings when prescribed by law;
– decide appeals of decisions passed in disciplinary proceedings for disorderly conduct of public notaries when so prescribed by law;
– carry out enforcement of foreign criminal judgments;
– decide cases in the second instance in all civil cases and in criminal cases which passed in the first instance;

– carry out other tasks as prescribed by law.

County courts shall establish a special division or a panel for deciding criminal cases against military persons, military officials and military employees in service in the armed forces for crimes committed during the service or in connection with the service.

C. Commercial courts

These decide in the first instance:

– disputes originating from commercial agreements and claims for compensation of damages resulting from such agreements entered into by persons or entities which carry out commercial activities;

– disputes relating to ships and navigation at sea and internal waters, and disputes to which maritime law applies (maritime disputes), except disputes concerning transport of passengers;

– disputes relating to aeroplanes and disputes to which air navigation law is applied, except disputes concerning transport of passengers;

– disputes relating to the protection and use of inventions, trademarks and technical improvements, copyright disputes, except when otherwise provided in a separate law;

– disputes relating to unfair competition, monopolistic agreements and violation of equality on the integral market of the Republic of Croatia;

– disputes in which, in addition to the cases listed under a) above, also participate, as co-litigators, the persons who are in legal community with respect to the object of the dispute or if their rights or obligations stem from the same factual or legal basis,

– proceedings for commercial infractions.

They also decide cases relating to establishment, operation and termination of corporations, carry out liquidation and bankruptcy proceedings of juridical persons and decide all cases in which juridical persons against which liquidation or bankruptcy proceedings are pending are a party, regardless of the nature of the opposite party and the time of the commencement of the proceedings.

They keep court registers.

In *ex parte* proceedings they decide:

– registration of ships and rights on ships, limitations of liability of ship operators, objections against a final basis for the division in the case of common average adjustment into ship register, if not otherwise prescribed in a law for certain type of cases,

– proposals related to establishment, operation and termination of corporations.

These courts decide and carry out execution of decisions which they passed in the first instance, as well as disputes which occur during or because of the execution of these decisions. They may also assign the carrying out of execution against non-monetary funds of execution creditor to a municipal court, carry out the proceedings for the securing of evidence in proceedings over which they otherwise have jurisdiction, and carry out proceedings for the recognition and execution of foreign judicial decisions as well as arbitration decisions in commercial disputes;

They order and carry out execution of decisions on the basis of a credible document in legal matters from Point 1, Paragraph 1.

They carry out other tasks as prescribed by law.

D. The High Commercial Court of the Republic of Croatia

This court decides appeals against decisions passed in the first instance by commercial courts;

It decides conflicts of venue between commercial courts;

It also carries out other tasks as prescribed by law.

E. The Administrative Court of the Republic of Croatia

This court decides disputes on administrative acts;

It carries out other tasks as established by law.

F. The Supreme Court of the Republic of Croatia

The Supreme Court ensures uniform application of the law and the equality of its citizens, as well as equality of all before the law;

It considers current issues of judicial practice;

It decides legal remedies against final decisions of the courts in the Republic of Croatia;

It decides appeals from decisions of county courts passed in the first instance;

It decides appeals from decisions of the High Commercial Court of the Republic of Croatia and the Administrative Court of the Republic of Croatia, as well as other courts where provided by law;

The court also decides conflicts of jurisdiction between the courts on the territory of the Republic of Croatia as their immediately higher court;

It carries out other tasks as established by law.

G. The Constitutional Court of the Republic of Croatia

Although it is not a part of its judicial power, we deem it necessary to mention the role of the Constitutional Court of the Republic of Croatia in this report. The Constitution of the Republic of Croatia established this court as a special body which primarily decides on the comformity of laws and other regulations with the Constitution. Namely, according to Article 125 of the Constitution, the Constitutional Court does the following:

– decides on the conformity of laws with the Constitution;

– decides on the conformity of other regulations with the Constitution and the law;

– protects the constitutional freedoms and rights of the person and the citizen;

– decides conflicts of jurisdiction between legislative, executive and judicial authorities;

– decides, in comformity with the Constitution, on the impeachability of the President of the Republic;

– supervises the constitutionality and legality of elections and national referenda and decides electoral disputes which are not within the jurisdiction of courts;

– carries out other tasks as provided in the Constitution.

However, in addition to these competences, the Constitutional Court has another important task, related to judicial power. Namely, this court carries out the control of judicial decisions by means of constitutional complaints. Any person who believes that his or her constitutional right or freedom has been violated by a decision of a court (or another state body) has the right to file a complaint with the Constitutional Court for the protection of these rights (the constitutional complaint).

II. Appointment of judges

In order to provide for the most consistent implementation of the principle of division of power and to ensure the independence of judicial power in relation to legislative and executive powers, the Constitution has prescribed that a separate body, namely the High Council of Justice, appoints judges and decides on their responsibility and removal from office. It is composed of lawyers from the ranks of distinguished judges, state attorneys, practising lawyers and law school professors.

According to the Law on Courts (Article 46), the number of judges in a court is determined by the Minister of Justice in accordance with the framework criteria for the work of judges.

An appointed judge can be any citizen of the Republic of Croatia who has graduated from a law school and who has passed the bar exam, who has worked on certain legal affairs, who has professional ability and has demonstrated working abilities.

An appointed judge of a municipal court may be any person who has passed the bar exam as a judicial, state attorney's, practising attorney's, public notary's or misdemeanours courts' apprentice or any person who after having passed the bar exam has been working for two years on other legal tasks.

An appointed judge of a commercial court may be any person who, after having passed the bar exam, has worked for at least two years as a municipal or county court judge, or four years as a judicial adviser or an adviser in a state attorney's office or as a state attorney or deputy state attorney, misdemeanours court judge, practising attorney or notary public or who has worked on other legal tasks in corporations.

An appointed county court judge may be any person who, after having passed the bar exam, has worked for a minimum of six years as a judge, state attorney, deputy state attorney, judge of a court for misdemeanours, practising attorney or notary public or who worked the minimum of eight years as a judicial adviser of such a court or of the Supreme Court of the Republic of Croatia, or for ten years on other legal tasks.

An appointed judge at the Supreme Court of the Republic of Croatia may be any person who, after having passed the bar exam, worked for a minimum of twelve years as a judge, state attorney or deputy state attorney, a judge at the High Court for Misdemeanours, practising attorney, judicial adviser or a senior judicial adviser at the Supreme Court of the Republic of Croatia, senior lecturer or law school professor.

The Constitution of the Republic of Croatia prescribes that judicial office shall be permanent. The permanent judicial office will contribute to the professional security of judges as one of the guarantees of their independence, which is the guarantee of the protection of human rights.

Another contribution to the professional security of judges is the fact that a judge may be relieved of his or her judicial office only in the cases provided in the Constitution, namely:

- at his or her own request;
- if he or she has become permanently incapacitated, unable to perform his or her office;
- if he or she has been sentenced for a crime which makes him or her unworthy to hold judicial office;
- if he or she commits a serious disciplinary violation. A separate law defines serious disciplinary violations.

This list of reasons is exhaustive. (Therefore the Law on Courts, which prescribes the conditions for appointment of judges does not contain special provisions on their removal from office.)

Judges and lay judges who take part in trials and deliberations may not be called to account for an opinion given in the process of judicial decision-making. Judges enjoy, in conformity with the law, the same immunity as members of the Croatian National Parliament.

III. Statistical data

A. Overview of human resources in courts

According to the Law on Courts (Article 47) the Minister for Justice prescribes framework criteria for the number of judges in courts, upon the proposal from an extended general session of the Supreme Court of the Republic of Croatia.

Judicial body	According to systematisation	Appointed	To be appointed	% appointed in relation to systematisation
Municipal courts	946	716	230	-24.3
County courts	343	279	64	-18.7
Commercial courts	175	95	80	-45.7
Supreme Court of the Republic of Croatia	38	26	12	-31.6
Administrative Court of the Republic of Croatia	33	21	12	-36.4
High Commercial Court of the Republic of Croatia	20	19	1	-5.0
Total:	1 555	1 156	399	-25.7

1. Overview of appointed judges according to sex

Judicial body	Women	Men
Municipal courts	452	264
County courts	105	174
Commercial courts	47	48
High Commercial Court of the Republic of Croatia	5	14
Administrative Court of the Republic of Croatia	15	6
Supreme Court of the Republic of Croatia	11	15
Total:	635	521

B. Statistical overview of number of cases by courts and types of procedures

1. Municipal courts

a. Number of new cases according to type

Type of case	1997	% in relation to 1996
Pre-trial criminal proceedings	810	72.0
Criminal proceedings	27683	13.3
Civil proceedings	94731	16.8
Inheritance	60765	4.6
Executions	167138	15.0
Ex parte proceedings	49595	-4.4
Total:	400722	10.9
Other cases	340560	28.6
Total:	741282	18.4

b. Resolved cases according to type

Type of case	1997	% in relation to 1996
Pre-trial criminal proceedings	804	67.5
Criminal proceedings	25055	25.6
Civil proceedings	74841	12.9
Inheritance	53861	3.5
Executions	167855	3.8
Ex parte proceedings	48057	-8.0
Total:	370473	5.0
Other cases	260067	14.4
Total:	630540	8.7

c. Pending cases according to type

Type of case	1997	recent occurrence ratio	% in relation to 1996
Pre-trial criminal proceedings	12	0.2	100.0
Criminal proceedings	43946	19.0	6.4
Civil proceedings	184233	23.3	12.1
Inheritance	44601	8.8	18.3
Executions	84144	6.0	-0.8
Ex parte proceedings	15993	3.9	10.6
Total:	372929	11.2	8.8
Other cases	324481	11.4	33.0
Total:	697410	11.3	18.9

2. County courts

a. new cases according to type

Type of case	1997	% in relation to 1996
Pre-trial criminal proceedings	26780	28.9
First instance criminal	1850	112.2
Criminal panel deciding in chambers	6120	79.7
Second instance criminal	5181	6.0
Second instance civil	25161	11.5
Total:	65092	24.0
Other cases	2159	78.3
Total:	67251	25.2

b. Resolved cases according to type

Type of case	1997	% in relation to 1996
Pre-trial criminal proceedings	24265	24.6
First instance criminal	1288	78.9
Criminal panel deciding in chambers	5929	73.9
Second instance criminal	4590	-2.3
Second instance civil	25465	14.6
Total:	61537	21.8
Other cases	2115	71.7
Total:	63652	23.0

c. Pending cases according to type

Type of case	1997	recent occurrence ratio	% in relation to 1996
Pre-trial criminal proceedings	12204	5.5	26.0
First instance criminal	1626	10.5	52.8
Criminal panel deciding in chambers	313	0.6	156.6
Second instance criminal	1271	2.9	86.9
Second instance civil	11358	5.4	-2.6
Total:	26772	4.9	15.3
Other cases	94	0.5	88.0
Total:	26866	4.8	15.5

3. Commercial courts

a. New cases according to type

Type of case	1997	% in relation to 1996
Commercial disputes	11950	-14.3
Executions	43953	-7.8
Ex parte proceedings	76923	35.7
Regular liquidations and bankruptcy	2097	-85.8
Commercial infractions	1345	-50.3
Total:	136268	0.3
Other cases	55	-74.5
Total:	136323	0.2

b. Resolved cases according to type

Type of case	1997	% in relation to 1996
Commercial disputes	24521	-5.4
Executions	54502	-25.9
Ex parte proceedings	81172	11.5
Regular liquidations and bankruptcy	8647	97.2
Commercial infractions	3921	31.7
Total:	172763	-3.8
Other cases	44	-80.2
Total:	172807	-3.9

c. Pending cases according to type

Type of case	1997	% in relation to 1996
Commercial disputes	35956	-25.9
Executions	8579	-55.1
Ex parte proceedings	62417	-6.4
Regular liquidations and bankruptcy	14040	-31.8
Commercial infractions	5046	-33.8
Total:	126038	-22.5
Other cases	163	7.2
Total:	126201	-22.4

4. High Commercial Court of the Republic of Croatia

a. New cases according to type

Type of case	1997	% in relation to 1996
Commercial disputes, executions, bankruptcies and second instance *ex parte* proceedings	3786	6.9
Second instance commercial infractions	467	1.3
Total:	4253	6.2

b. Resolved cases according to type

Type of case	1997	% in relation to 1996
Commercial disputes, executions, bankruptcies and second instance *ex parte* proceedings	3969	0.3
Second instance commercial infractions	315	-19.6
Total:	4284	-1.5

c. Pending cases according to type

Type of case	1997	% in relation to 1996
Commercial disputes, executions, bankruptcies and second instance *ex parte* proceedings	2593	-6.6
Second instance commercial infractions	605	33.6
Total:	3198	-1.0

5. Administrative Court of the Republic of Croatia

a. New cases according to type

Type of case	1997	% in relation to 1996
Administrative disputes	12636	30.0
Retrials in administrative disputes	36	-2.7
Total:	12672	29.8

b. Resolved cases according to type

Type of case	1997	% in relation to 1996
Administrative disputes	6727	-11.3
Retrials in administrative disputes	17	-51.4
Total:	6744	-11.5

c. Pending cases according to type

Type of case	1997	% in relation to 1996
Administrative disputes	16655	55.0
Retrials in administrative disputes	67	39.6
Total:	16722	54.9

6. Supreme Court of the Republic of Croatia
a. New cases according to type

Type of case	1997	% in relation to 1996
Second instance criminal	712	-23.6
Second instance civil	9	-35.7
Third instance criminal	1	-
Protection of legality in criminal cases	22	-31.3
Protection of legality in civil cases	42	-31.1
Protection of legality in commercial disputes	9	12.5
Protection of legality in administrative disputes	11	22.2
Protection of legality in misdemeanour cases	1	-
Extraordinary reduction of punishment	243	-25.5
Revision	2645	1.3
Extraordinary review of judicial decisions in criminal cases	47	-26.6
Extraordinary review of judicial decisions in administrative disputes	2	-
Judicial protection in misdemeanour cases	50	163.2
Total:	3794	-6.9

b. Resolved cases according to type

Type of case	**1997**	**% in relation to 1996**
Second instance criminal	709	-21.0
Second instance civil	6	-60.0
Third instance criminal	1	-
Protection of legality in criminal cases	25	47.1
Protection of legality in civil cases	60	30.4
Protection of legality in commercial disputes	13	225.0
Protection of legality in administrative disputes	5	66.7
Protection of legality in misdemeanour cases	5	-
Extraordinary reduction of punishment	259	-22.5
Revision	1 808	-15.4
Extraordinary review of judicial decisions in criminal cases	38	-25.5
Extraordinary review of judicial decisions in administrative disputes	83	196.4
Judicial protection in misdemeanour cases	-	-
Total:	3 102	-14.7

c. Pending cases according to type

Type of case	1997	% in relation to 1996
Second instance criminal	860	0.4
Second instance civil	4	300.0
Third instance criminal	31	-8.8
Protection of legality in criminal cases	17	-51.4
Protection of legality in civil cases	1	-
Protection of legality in commercial disputes	56	12.0
Protection of legality in administrative disputes	3	-57.1
Protection of legality in misdemeanour cases	44	-26.7
Extraordinary reduction of punishment	-6 504	14.8
Revision		
Extraordinary review of judicial decisions in criminal cases	40	29.0
Extraordinary review of judicial decisions in administrative disputes	15	15.4
Judicial protection in misdemeanour cases	-	-100.0
Total:	7 575	11.5

CYPRUS

I. Judicial organisation

Under the Constitution of the Republic of Cyprus its judicial power is exercised by the Supreme Constitutional Court and the High Court of Justice and such inferior courts as may be provided by law.

The Supreme Constitutional Court used to be composed of a neutral President, one Greek judge and one Turkish judge; and it exercised exclusive jurisdiction in certain specified matters, most of which related to the interpretation of the Constitution and the declaration of laws, subsidiary legislation and acts of executive organs as unconstitutional. Furthermore, jurisdiction was conferred on the court by Article 146 of the Constitution for the judicial review of administrative acts, similarly to that exercised in France by the *Conseil d'Etat*.

Under the Electoral Law (see especially section 4(2) (d) of Law 71 of 1963), the Supreme Constitutional Court was the Electoral Court for trying election petitions.

The High Court of Justice was composed of one neutral President, two Greek judges and one Turkish judge and was the highest appellate court in the Republic, hearing and determining all appeals from any court in the Republic other than the Supreme Constitutional Court. It also exercised exclusive jurisdiction as an admiralty court and as a court of first instance to try the President or the Vice-President of the Republic for high treason or for any offence involving dishonesty or moral turpitude under Article 45 of the Constitution. It also exercised exclusive revisional jurisdiction by issuing orders in the nature of habeas corpus, *mandamus,* prohibition, *quo warranto* and *certiorari.*

Owing to the events which occurred after 31 December 1963, the functioning of the Supreme Constitutional Court and the High Court of Justice, as described above, was rendered impossible and as it was imperative that the administration of justice should continue by the Administration of Justice (Miscellaneous Provisions) Law 1964 (Law 33 of 1964) the two aforementioned courts were amalgamated in a new court established thereby – the Supreme Court. The new court exercises the jurisdiction formerly exercised in the aforesaid two Supreme Courts.

The constitutionality of Law 33/64 was tested in the case of Attorney-General of the Republic v. Ibrahim (1964) C.L.R. 195. The Supreme Court found that the law was justified by necessity and on that account not inconsistent with the Constitution. Consequently the law was declared to be constitutional.

The Supreme Court is composed of a President and 12 judges.

II. Jurisdiction of the Supreme Court

Under the Constitution of the Republic of Cyprus and the Administration of Justice (Miscellaneous Provisions) Law, 1964 (33/64) the Supreme Court is established;

a. as the Constitutional Court;

b. as the court vested with jurisdiction to review administrative action;

c. as the Appellate Court;

d. as a court with exclusion original jurisdiction to issue orders to the nature of habeas corpus, *mandamus,* prohibition, *quo warranto* and *certiorari.* It also has original jurisdiction in admiralty matters;

e. as a court of admiralty; and

f. as the Court of First Instance to try the President or the Vice-President of the Republic for high treason or for any offence involving dishonesty or moral turpitude under Article 45 of the Constitution.

In the exercise of its competence as the Constitutional Court and the court vested with jurisdiction to review administrative actions, it is vested with exclusive jurisdiction:

i. to declare laws and regulations unconstitutional;

ii. to resolve conflicts between organs of the state;

iii. to provide an authoritative interpretation of the Constitution;

iv. to act as an electoral court with regard to the elections of the President, the Vice-President and Members of the House of Representatives;

v. to exercise administrative jurisdiction with power to review, with a view to annulment of administrative and executive acts, decisions and omissions of the Administration. The administrative jurisdiction of the court is modelled on the continental pattern of administrative justice;

vi. to exercise appellate jurisdiction to hear appeals against decisions coming under v above.

The jurisdiction outlined above is exercised by the full bench of the court. The jurisdiction under v above is exercised by a single judge of the court and an appeal lies before a bench of five or more judges (see vi above).

In exercise of its competence under *c* above, the Supreme Court is vested with exclusive jurisdiction to hear and determine all appeals from any inferior court, in both civil and criminal matters.

This jurisdiction is exercised by a bench of at least three judges.

The jurisdiction under *d* and *e* above is exercised in the first instance by a single judge and an appeal lies before a bench of five or more judges.

The Supreme Court also exercises disciplinary jurisdiction over members of inferior courts. Moreover it may:

a. retire judges of the Supreme Court on account of mental or physical incapacity or infirmity; or

b. dismiss for misconduct.

The jurisdiction can only be exercised in the context of judicial proceedings and the judge concerned is entitled to be heard and to present his case before the court.

The judicial power, other than the one exercised by the Supreme Court, is exercised by the inferior courts. Cyprus is divided into six districts and there are functioning inferior courts in each district. Regrettably since July 1974 the District Courts of Famagusta and Kyrenia have stopped functioning in their districts due to the Turkish invasion. The territorial jurisdiction of each district court is prescribed by law.

Justice at first instance is administered by:

a. district courts which try civil cases (general jurisdiction) and non-serious criminal cases;

b. assize courts which try serious criminal cases;

c. family courts which try cases relating to family matters and person status;

d. Industrial Disputes Court which tries cases relating to matters of employment, including redundancy;

e. rent control courts which try cases relating to the Rent Control Law;

f. Military Court which tries cases relating to the Military Criminal Code;

An appeal lies to the Supreme Court from any judgment of all the above courts.

The total number of judges of all the inferior courts is now 60.

The independence and impartiality of the Cyprus judiciary is fully guaranteed by the Constitution.

Judges of inferior courts are appointed, promoted and disciplined by the Supreme Council of Judicature which is composed of all the judges of the Supreme Court. After their appointment they enjoy full security of tenure until retirement, which is prescribed by law, and they may be dismissed after judicial proceedings by the Supreme Court on the grounds of misconduct. Also they may be retired by the Supreme Court on account of such mental or physical incapacity or infirmity as would render them incapable of discharging the duties of their office either permanently or for such period of time as would render it impracticable for them to continue in office.

There are certain boards exercising professional disciplinary jurisdiction in respect of advocates, architects, dentists, medical practitioners, veterinary surgeons, pharmacists, nurses and midwives. An appeal lies to the Supreme Court from the Disciplinary Council of Advocates and a recourse to the revisional jurisdiction of the Supreme Court in all other cases.

The Public Service Commission and the Public Education Service Commission are two independent authorities dealing with matters relating to appointments, promotions, etc. and disciplinary control of public officers and teachers respectively. Recourse lies with the revisional jurisdiction of the Supreme Court.

III. The Attorney-General of the Republic

The Attorney-General of the Republic is an independent officer, appointed by the President and serving on the same terms and conditions as the judges of the Supreme Court of Cyprus until he attains the age of 68. His functions emanate from the Constitution itself. He is the head of the Law Office of the Republic and he acts as the legal adviser of the Republic, the President, the Council of Ministers and the Ministers. Furthermore, under Article 113.2 of the Constitution, the Attorney-General is vested with the power, exercisable upon this discretion in the public interest, to institute, conduct, take over and continue or discontinue any proceeding for an offence against any person in the Republic. The Attorney-General also represents the Republic in any judicial proceeding and all actions by, or against, the Republic are brought by, or against, the Attorney-General.

Czech Republic

I. Introduction

The Czech Republic is a unitary state. It is divided into regions, districts and municipalities; the municipalities constitute the basic territorial administrative entities. The capital of Prague has a special position; it is divided into ten districts. There are no public administration bodies on the level of regions; however, there are regional courts.

The Czech Constitution provides for the division of power into the legislative, executive and judicial branches and governs the mutual relations between these three powers.

Judicial power is exercised in the name of the Republic by the independent judiciary. The Constitution guarantees the protection of the judiciary against pressures menacing the judge's independence and impartiality (lifetime appointment, incompatibility of functions, etc.). The judge's major role is to protect the rights in the manner stipulated by law. It is only the judge that decides on the guilt and punishment in case of a criminal offence.

The judges are bound by law; should they believe that a piece of legislation is contrary to the Constitution, they must refer the case to the Constitutional Court.

The court system is composed of the Supreme Court, the Supreme Administrative Court, superior courts, regional and district courts, which are general courts. The Constitutional Court is an autonomous body and thus does not constitute another instance of the court system. The Supreme Administrative Court has not been established yet.

The competence and organisation of the courts are defined by law.

The territorial competence of the District and Regional Courts and their locations copy the administrative structure of the state. In addition, some regional and district courts have their branch offices. The regional competence in the capital of Prague is exercised by the City Court and the district competence is exercised by the Prague District Courts. In Brno, the competence of the District Court is exercised by the City Court of Brno.

Arbitration proceedings are conducted by the Arbitration Courts.

Commercial cases are handled by the general courts. Regional commercial courts have been established in Prague, Brno and Ostrava in order to deal with commercial cases pertaining to the competence of the Regional Courts. They have the "causal competence of *rationae materiae*". In other regions, these cases are handled by the Regional Courts. In commercial cases, the Regional Courts act as the Courts of First Instance.

Administrative matters are handled by general courts. Based on actions or appeals, the courts examine decisions issued by the state administration authorities, local government bodies, self-government bodies and other entities empowered by law to decide on rights and duties of individuals and corporations in the area of public administration.

The courts takes decisions based on:

– actions which can be made against all the final administrative decisions after the ordinary means of remedy have been exhausted except for the decisions excluded by law;

– means of remedy which can be lodged against administrative decisions as specified by law.

II. Constitutional Court

The Constitutional Court is a judicial authority protecting constitutionality. The Constitutional Court decides on:

– annulment of laws contrary to the Constitution or to a ratified and published international instrument on human rights and fundamental freedoms binding on the Czech Republic;

– annulment of other legal regulations contrary to the Constitution, an Act of Parliament or an international treaty;

– constitutional complaints lodged by local government bodies against an illegal intervention by the state;

– constitutional complaints against final decisions and other acts of public authorities interfering with constitutionally guaranteed fundamental rights and freedoms;

– remedies against decisions relating to the election of a deputy or senator;

– doubts in case of loss of eligibility or incompatibility to exercise the functions of a deputy or senator;

– constitutional petitions made by the Senate against the President of the Republic, should the President be prosecuted for high treason based on an action brought by the Senate;

– motions made by the President of the Republic to annul a resolution adopted by the Chamber of Deputies and the Senate which grant some Presidential functions to the Prime Minister;

– measures necessary to enforce a decision of an international court binding on the Czech Republic, unless the enforcement can be performed otherwise;

– whether the decision to dissolve a political party or another decision relating to the activities of a political party is in compliance with constitutional or other laws;

– disputes relating to the scope of powers granted to central government bodies and local government bodies unless otherwise provided by law.

The law may establish that the Supreme Administrative Court shall decide, in lieu of the Constitutional Court, on annulment of legal regulations, which are contrary to law, on disputes relating to the scope of powers of the central government bodies and local government bodies, unless otherwise provided by law.

The Constitutional Court is composed of 15 judges who take decisions at plenary sessions or in three-member panels.

III. General courts

A. District Courts

The District Courts issue judgments as the First Instance Courts unless the first instance competence pertains by law to higher degree courts.

With respect to civil cases, the District Courts decide matters which arise from civil, labour, family, co-operative and commercial relations. They deal with other matters only if provided by law.

With respect to criminal matters, the District Courts act as first instance courts with the exceptions mentioned hereinafter.

District Courts are competent to handle administrative cases and examine the decisions on minor administrative offences and other administrative decisions as provided by law.

District Courts are competent for the enforcement of proceedings.

The decisions of the District Courts are taken by panels of judges or by a single judge. The panels are composed of one professional judge and two lay judges.

Appeals against the decisions of the District Courts are heard by regional courts. In criminal proceedings, it is possible to lodge a complaint for violation of law at the Supreme Court. The application for a new trial must be made at the court that has decided the case in the first instance.

B. Regional Courts

Regional Courts act as second instance courts in cases that have been decided in the first instance by district courts.

Regional Courts take decisions in the civil proceedings in non-commercial matters as first instance courts:

i. in matters relating to the protection of personality and against disclosure of information which constitute the abuse of freedom of expression, speech and the press;

ii. on claims resulting from the Copyright Act;

iii. on actions relating to industrial property rights;

iv. on actions relating to social insurance claims between the employer and the benefit recipient according to the legislation on pension and social insurance;

v. on actions for damages due to wrong health insurance proceedings;

vi. on actions relating to the illegality of strikes or lock-outs,

vii. on actions for annulment or termination of a labour or civil service contract pursuant to Act No. 451/1991, which defines the criteria of some civil service positions in public bodies and organisations in the Czech and Slovak Federal Republic, the Czech Republic and the Republic of Slovakia;

viii. in disputes relating to a foreign country or persons having diplomatic status;

ix. on actions for bankruptcy proceedings, should the debtor be an individual or a legal entity which is not registered in the Commercial Register including all related disputes;

x. on actions to determine whether an application for registration of a political party or a political movement includes any irregularities inhibiting the registration.

Regional Courts represent the main degree of justice in commercial matters when they act as first instance courts. They decide disputes between businesses, should both parties be registered in the Commercial Register or should at least one of them be registered in the Commercial Register and the claim is at least 50000 Czech Republic Korunas.

Regional Courts then act as first instance courts in commercial matters, should the parties be businesses or not, with respect to the disputes arising from legal relations concerning establishment of companies or co-operatives, from contracts to operate a means of transport, from patent rights, protected utility models and industrial designs including non-commercial deals, and other matters defined by law.

Regional Courts acting as first instance courts in all commercial matters dealing with bankruptcy proceedings, should the debtor be an individual or a legal entity registered in the Commercial Register; they also decide on dissolution of a company and closing its books.

With respect to criminal proceedings, regional courts act as first instance courts in cases of offences for which the minimum imprisonment sentence is five years or for which the exceptional sentence can be imposed; they also deal with terrorism, subversion, sabotage and all cases governed by the Act on Protection of Peace.

With respect to administrative actions, Regional Courts are competent to examine administrative decisions, unless otherwise provided by law.

Regional Courts administer the Commercial Register.

Regional Courts take decisions in panels of judges. The panels are composed of one professional judge and two lay judges if they act as first instance courts in criminal matters. In other matters, the panels are composed of one presiding judge and two professional judges.

The ordinary means of remedy against first instance decisions delivered by the Regional Courts may be lodged at the Superior Court, extraordinary means of remedy (appeal for review in civil cases and complaint for violation of law in criminal matters) are lodged at the Supreme Court. The request for a new trial must be made at the court which decided the case in the first instance.

C. Superior Courts

Superior Courts act as second instance courts in case of appeals against the decisions of the Regional Courts acting as first instance courts.

With respect to civil proceedings, the Superior Court deals with the competence disputes between judicial bodies and public bodies. The Superior Court is competent to examine the administrative decisions issued by central government bodies except for the pension and health insurance cases, pension schemes and unemployment benefits. It is also competent to hear appeals against regional court decisions in all pension insurance cases.

The Superior Court makes decisions in panels composed of one presiding judge and two professional judges.

The extraordinary means of remedy against the decisions issued by the Superior Court may be lodged at the Supreme Court.

D. The Supreme Court

The Supreme Court sees to the legality of the court decisions through extraordinary means of remedy, that is, the appeal for review in civil cases and the complaint for violation of law in criminal cases.

The Supreme Court decides on recognition and enforceability of foreign judgments.

The Supreme Court monitors final judgments and ensures uniformity through its opinions. Such opinions are taken at plenary sessions or by the criminal, civil or commercial chambers of the Supreme Court.

The Supreme Court acts as the first instance court in election cases.

The Supreme Court takes decisions in panels composed of one presiding judge and two professional judges. Panels composed of the President of the court and four judges decide on the extraordinary means of remedy against decisions of the Superior Courts.

IV. Prosecution

The prosecution is part of executive power. This is a system of prosecution offices which represent the state in cases defined by law. The prosecution brings charges on behalf of the state in criminal proceedings and performs other duties imposed by the Code of Criminal Procedures.

The prosecutor may be involved in the civil proceedings in cases of legal capacity, validation of death and in cases of registration in the Commercial Register. The prosecutor is then authorised to act as a party to the proceedings, unless specific acts can be performed solely by the parties to the legal relationship concerned.

Pursuant to the Family Act, the Supreme Prosecutor may act in the interest of society and bring actions for denial of paternity against the father, mother and the child in the event that the period for denial of paternity has elapsed for either of the parents. In the event that the father, mother or the child is not alive, the Supreme Prosecutor may bring an action for denial of paternity against the surviving persons; in the event that none of them is alive, the Supreme Prosecutor may bring an action against the guardian appointed by the court.

The locations and territorial competence comply with the locations and districts of the courts. The prosecution system includes the Supreme Prosecution Office, two superior prosecution offices in Prague and in Olomouc, the regional prosecution and district prosecution offices. The capital has its city prosecution and Prague district prosecution offices.

V. Permanent Arbitration Courts

The Permanent Arbitration Courts operating in the Czech Republic are as follows:

– The Stock Exchange Arbitration Court established by the Stock Exchange Chamber which is competent to judge disputes arising from stock exchange trades. The parties must foresee the involvement of the Arbitration Court in a written contract;

– The Stock Exchange Arbitration Court, pursuant to Act No.222/1992 Coll. on the Commodities Stock Exchange in terms of its amendments, decides the disputes arising from Stock Exchange trades and out of Stock Exchange trades with commodities traded in the Stock Exchange with the proviso that the parties to the dispute agree on such a dispute solution;

– The Arbitration Court of the Czech Economic Chamber and the Czech Agricultural Chamber.

The Permanent Arbitration Courts can hear property disputes except for disputes arising from enforcement of a judgment and disputes due to bankruptcy proceedings, which would otherwise be subject to the competence of the Judicial Courts. The parties must sign a written arbitration agreement.

The arbitration award can be invalidated by the court based on an action brought by either party.

VI. Statistics

1. Number of courts

– Constitutional Court
– Supreme Court
– seven Regional Courts, City Court of Prague and three regional commercial courts
– 75 District Courts, City Court of Brno and 10 Prague District Courts
– three Permanent Arbitration Courts.

2. Number of judges: 2 149

3. Number of prosecutors: 860

Court system of the Czech Republic

Constitutional Court: three member panels, 15 administrative judges, plenary session.

Supreme Court: Supreme Administrative Court: five-member panels, plenary session.

Superior Courts: three-member panels, plenary session.

Regional courts/regional commercial courts:
– three-member panels
– three-member panels with single judge
– two lay judges in criminal matters in the first instance
– single judge.

District Courts:
– three-member panels (from which two lay judges)
– single judge.

Permanent arbitration courts:
– Stock Exchange Arbitration Court
– Stock Exchange Arbitration Court of the Commodities Stock Exchange
– Arbitration Court of the Czech Economic and Agricultural Chamber.

Denmark

I. Information on the different courts

A. District Courts (*Byretter*)

1. Competence

The vast majority of civil cases are brought before the District Courts as courts of first instance. The powers of the District Court include – besides the actual administration of justice – the functions of bailiff (*foged*), probate and bankruptcy court (*skifteret*) and notary (*notar*), together with responsibility for certain records and registrations, particularly in regard to real estate (*tinglysningsvæsenet*).

Only a very few categories of criminal cases are tried before one of the High Courts as courts of first instance (see below, B. 1). All other criminal cases are brought before the District Court.

2. Composition

Denmark is divided into 82 court districts. In comparison the total number of local government areas (*borroughs*) is 275. Thus most court districts cover more than one *borrough*.

Most District Courts have only one professional judge, but in some larger District Courts there are two or three professional judges. In Copenhagen the District Court is known as the Copenhagen City Court, which is made up of a Chief Justice and 42 other judges. A similar organisation is found in Aarhus (a Chief Justice and 15 other judges), Odense (a Chief Justice and 10 other judges), Aalborg (a Chief Justice and 10 other judges) and Roskilde (a Chief Justice and seven other judges). Finally the District Court in Randers is made up of four judges.

Regardless of the number of judges appointed to a particular District Court, only one professional judge tries each case. Thus District Courts with more than one judge are divided into an equal number of chambers.

Civil cases are as a general rule heard by the professional judge with no lay judges taking part in the proceedings.

Civil cases (and criminal cases) in which special knowledge of maritime affairs is regarded as essential are heard by the district court supplemented by two assessors. In commercial cases the District Court may rule that the court be supplemented by two assessors. This option is very rarely used in commercial cases. The assessors are chosen from a list of maritime and commercial assessors appointed by the Chief Justice of the competent High Court after consultation with the appropriate organisations. (In the Greater Copenhagen area these cases are heard by the Maritime and Commercial Court. This court may also hear cases from court districts outside the Greater Copenhagen area if the parties agree. But as a general rule suits where the amount in dispute does not exceed 100 000 Danish Kroner will be heard by the District Court, also in the Greater Copenhagen area (see below, C)).

All suits dealing with renting of houses or other accommodation covered by the Lease Act are heard by the Rent Tribunals as courts of first instance. These tribunals are made up of the District Court judge and two assessors appointed by the judge from two lists drawn up by the Chief Justice of the High Court after consultation with the major associations of real estate owners on the one hand and the tenants' associations and business organisations in the district on the other.

When trying *criminal cases* the District Court is composed of the District Court judge and two lay judges, except in cases where the accused has pleaded guilty, and in minor cases where a fine will be the highest sentence. In these cases no lay judges take part. However, in cases where the accused has pleaded guilty, lay judges do sit if special sanctions are claimed, such as preventive detention in an institution for psychopathic criminals, and the like.

3. Legal remedies

Appeals from judgments rendered by the District Court, whether in civil or criminal cases, lie to the competent High Court. This is also the case in regard to the local Maritime Courts and Commercial Courts and in regard to the Rent Tribunals.

B. High Courts (*Landsretter*)

1. Competence

The High Courts are courts of appeal in regard to judgments rendered by the District Courts (see above, A.3). In civil cases, suits, where the amount in dispute is below 10 000 Danish Kroner, can only be tried before the High Court on appeal with leave from the Board of Appeal Permission (*Procesbevillingsnævnet*). As regards criminal cases, the accused can only bring the case before the High Court if the judgment rendered by the District Court exceeds a fine of 3 000 Danish Kroner or confiscation of property of a similar value or 20 day fines, and the accused has been present during the legal proceedings. (These cases can however be appealed to the High Court with leave from the Board of Appeal Permission.)

The High Courts are also courts of first instance in more important civil cases (for example, suits where the amount in dispute exceeds 500 000 Danish Kroner and most actions for declaratory judgments against administrative agencies), and in those criminal cases which under Danish law are tried by jury (such as prosecution in regard to crimes which under the law may be punished with imprisonment for four years or more, and cases where a judgment for placement in an institution or deprivation of liberty for an unlimited period is involved, and the accused has pleaded not guilty).

2. Composition

There are two High Courts, the High Court for the Eastern Region (*Østre Landsret*), having jurisdiction in the counties of the islands and located in Copenhagen, and the High Court for the Western Region (*Vestre Landsret*), having jurisdiction in the counties of Jutland and located at Viborg. *Østre Landsret* is made up of a Chief Justice and 61 other judges. *Vestre Landsret* is made up of a Chief Justice and 38 other judges. Each of the High Courts is divided into a number of chambers consisting of three judges.

Civil cases are as a general rule heard by three professional judges with no lay judges taking part in the proceedings, regardless of whether the case is brought before the High Court on appeal or as a court of first instance.

Certain decisions made by the Tribunal of Appeal in Social Affairs, for example decisions on removal of children from their home, may be brought before the High Court. In the hearing of these cases, the High Court is composed of three judges and two assessors, one being an expert in child welfare and the other in children's psychiatry or psychology. The assessors are chosen from a list drawn up by the Minister for Justice after consultation with the Minister for Social Affairs.

When maritime cases are brought before the High Court, two assessors shall participate in the proceedings; in commercial cases the court may so rule. The assessors are chosen from a list drawn up by the Chief Justice of the High Court after consultation with the appropriate organisations.

Criminal cases brought before the High Court as a court of first instance are tried by three judges and a jury of twelve.

Criminal cases brought before the High Court on appeal are tried by three professional judges and three lay judges, if lay judges also assisted in the District Court, or if the case involves a more severe punishment than a fine, or in cases that are otherwise considered to be especially punitive for the indicted or of special interest to the public.

In other cases only the professional judges sit.

3. Legal remedies

Appeals from judgments in civil cases heard by the High Court as a court of first instance lie to the Supreme Court. As regards judgments in cases heard on appeal, a further appeal is possible only in cases involving matters of principle and after special permission by the Board of Appeal Permission.

Appeal against judgments in criminal cases heard by the High Court as a court of first instance lie to the Supreme Court except as regards questions of evaluation of evidence. In cases heard by the High Court on appeal, this remedy lies only if the case involves a matter of principle or if special reasons speak in favour thereof and after special permission by the Board of Appeal Permission.

C. Maritime and Commercial Court (*Sø- og Handelsretten*)

1. Competence

The court has jurisdiction in civil cases (and criminal cases) from the Greater Copenhagen area in which special knowledge of maritime and commercial affairs is regarded as essential. If the parties agree the case can instead be brought before the District Court. In cases of this kind outside the Greater Copenhagen area the parties may agree that the case be brought before the Maritime and Commercial Court (of Copenhagen).

2. Composition

The court is made up of a Chief Justice, two Deputy Chief Justices, and one judge, all being graduates in law, and a number of assessors in commercial and maritime affairs, appointed by the Chief Justice after consultation with the appropriate organisations.

Cases are heard by the Chief Justice, one of the Deputy Chief Justices or the judge and a number of experts.

3. Legal remedies

Appeals from judgments rendered by the Maritime and Commercial Court (of Copenhagen) lie to the Supreme Court.

D. The Supreme Court (*Højesteret*)

1. Competence

The Supreme Court has jurisdiction only as a court of appeal in regard to judgments passed by the High Courts, the Maritime and Commercial Court (of Copenhagen), and the Special Court of Revision (when exercising disciplinary authority over judges, see below).

2. Composition

The Supreme Court is made up of a Chief Justice and at present 17 other Supreme Court judges.

At least five judges must sit in a case. The court usually sits in two chambers each comprising at least five judges. In cases involving issues of major importance, however, more than five judges sit, and in outstandingly important cases the court sits as a full court.

There are no cases where lay judges take part in the proceedings.

3. Legal remedies

There is no appeal from the Supreme Court. Petitions for re-opening of criminal cases decided by the Supreme Court on appeal may, however, be brought before the Special Court of Revision, see below.

E. The Special Court of Revision (*Den Særlige Klageret*)

1. Competence

The court has jurisdiction as a disciplinary body in regard to judges. Cases are brought before the court by the Director of Public Prosecution on complaints from private citizens or the Minister for Justice. The court may reprimand the judge, issue a fine or in severe cases suspend the judge.

The court also has jurisdiction to hear petitions for the re-opening of criminal cases, for example when new evidence has been found in favour of the sentenced.

Interlocutory appeals concerning the disqualification of a counsel for the defendant also lie under the jurisdiction of the Special Court of Revision.

2. Composition

When exercising its disciplinary powers the court is composed of one Supreme Court judge, one high court judge, and one district court judge. In other cases the court consists of the above-mentioned three members and, in addition, a practising lawyer and a lawyer with a special scholarly education.

Members of the court are appointed for ten years at a time.

3. Legal remedies

The courts' exercise of disciplinary powers is subject to appeal to the Supreme Court.

II. The Office of the Attorney of State

The Public Prosecution (*anklagemyndigheden*) comes under the Ministry of Justice.

The supreme prosecution authority for the country as a whole is the Director of Public Prosecution (*rigsadvokaten*), who, except for the powers of the Minister for Justice which are rarely applied has the final decision as to whether proceedings should be instituted. In addition, he (assisted by one or more assisting procecutors) pleads all criminal cases before the Supreme Court on behalf of the public.

In criminal cases brought before the High Court as the court of first instance or on appeal, and in cases concerning certain criminal offences, the decision to prosecute is made by one of the seven district attorneys (*statsadvokater*). The district attorney also pleads the cases in the High Court, on behalf of the public, either in person or through a number of full-time and part-time assistants.

In most criminal cases the decision to prosecute is made by one of the 54 local chiefs of police (*politimestre*), who also plead the cases before the District Courts and the Maritime and Commercial Court on behalf of the public.

All preliminary inquiries are carried out under the authority of one of the local chiefs of police (*politimestre*). The court takes no active part in this inquiry.

Besides being subordinate prosecuting authorities, the chiefs of police discharge a number of administrative functions as local representatives of central government authorities. The chiefs of police are assisted by deputies.

Criminal cases against military personnel for violation of the Military Penal Code are handled by a special Military Prosecution which comes under the Ministry of Defence. However, these cases are however, tried by ordinary courts.

III. Statistical data

A. Number of courts

There is one Supreme Court and there are two high courts. As of 1 January 1998 the number of district courts is 82.

B. Number of cases and judicial decisions

1. Civil cases

In 1996, 99 140 civil cases were concluded by the District Courts. This number does not include probate and bankruptcy cases, enforcement proceedings, records and registration and notary cases. 1 395 civil cases were concluded by the High Courts as courts of first instance and 4 805 civil cases were concluded by the High Courts on appeal. 389 civil cases were concluded by the Supreme Court.

2. Criminal cases

In 1996, 84 386 criminal cases were concluded by the District Courts. Some 89 cases were brought before the High Courts as courts of first instance, and 6886 criminal cases were decided by the High Courts on appeal. There were 96 cases decided by the Supreme Court.

C. Number of judges

At present there are 18 Supreme Court judges (including the President of the court) and 101 High Court judges. As of 1 January 1998, the number of District Court judges is 206.

ENGLAND AND WALES

THE different types of court and the court structure in England and Wales have evolved over many centuries. The present structure is shown in the diagram later in this section.

I. Magistrates' courts

Magistrates' courts deal mainly with criminal matters. The less serious cases are usually tried by lay magistrates who can fine and imprison those who have been convicted. More serious cases are passed to the Crown Court for trial. Magistrates' courts also deal with some civil cases such as certain family law matters, the recovery of debts such as unpaid council tax, and the granting of licences to businesses such as betting shops, pubs and restaurants.

Appeals against conviction or sentence go to the Crown Court. Appeals on points of law or procedure are referred to the Queen's Bench Division of the High Court. Appeals in family matters can be made to the Family Division of the High Court.

Most cases in magistrates' courts are heard by lay magistrates (also known as Justices of the Peace or JPs) who have not been legally trained. There are some 30000 lay magistrates – ten times as many as all the professional judges put together. The magistrates usually sit in threes and are advised on matters of law by legally qualified clerks. There are also Stipendiary Magistrates who are full-time members of the judiciary, and Acting Stipendiary Magistrates who sit part-time, who hear the more complex matters in magistrates' courts in London and the other main urban areas in England and Wales.

II. County courts

County courts were first established in the mid-nineteenth century and they deal with the majority of civil cases in England and Wales. Put in the simplest terms, the less complicated civil cases are heard in the county courts while the more complex cases are heard in the High Court. The largest number of cases handled by county courts relate to debt recovery, but property repossession, family, adoption and bankruptcy matters are also heard in county courts. Divorce work in Central London is dealt with by the Principal Registry of the Family Division and not the county courts.

Small claims for debt or damages are usually dealt with under a special small claims procedure. There is a monetary limit for small claims cases which is reviewed from time to time. The procedure is meant to be a low cost and informal way of resolving disputes without the need to use a solicitor, but both the plaintiff (the person making the claim) and the defendant (the person against whom the claim is made) are allowed to take someone with them to the hearing to speak on their behalf. The judge acts as an arbitrator and helps both the plaintiff and the defendant to explain their case.

Most appeals from county courts are heard in the Court of Appeal but appeals in bankruptcy matters are heard in the High Court.

County Courts are presided over by Circuit Judges and District Judges. Circuit Judges hear the larger, more complicated cases and can also hear some appeals from decisions of District Judges. Part-time judges – Recorders, Assistant Recorders and Deputy District Judges – also sit in county courts.

III. The Crown Court

The Crown Court was created in 1972. It is one national court which sits at different centres in England and Wales. It deals with all serious criminal cases passed from the magistrates' courts. Contested cases are heard by a judge and a jury or 12 lay people selected at random. The Crown Court also deals with appeals from the magistrates' courts.

Appeals from the Crown Court go to the Criminal Division of the Court of Appeal.

Circuit Judges hear the majority of cases in the Crown Court, but the most serious or sensitive cases are tried by High Court Judges or specially designated Circuit Judges. Part-time Recorders and Assistant Recorders also sit in the Crown Court, typically dealing with less serious cases. In appeals from a magistrates' court a judge hears the case together with a bench of up to four lay magistrates and without a jury.

IV. The High Court

The High Court is based at the Royal Courts of Justice in London, although its business is also dealt with at over 100 district registries which are located in county courts outside London. The High Court can hear almost any civil action, although in practice it deals mainly with the larger or more complex cases. It is organised into three divisions, which correspond to some of the ancient courts which it replaced in the nineteenth century.

A. Queen's Bench Division

This is the largest of the three divisions of the High Court and is presided over by the Lord Chief Justice. It deals with a wide range of civil matters including actions for damages arising from breaches of contract and libel, commercial disputes and Admiralty cases (civil actions relating to ships, for example collision, damage to cargo and salvage).

B. Chancery Division

The Lord Chancellor is the President of this division, although in practice his deputy, the Vice-Chancellor, acts as the Head of Division. The Chancery Division is particularly concerned with property matters including the administration of the estates of people who have died, the interpretation of wills, insolvency, and disputes about companies and partnerships.

C. Family Division

This is headed by the President of the Family Division and deals with divorce and matrimonial matters, cases concerning children, such as adoption, uncontentious wills and the distribution of estates of people who have died without making a will.

The High Court has an additional supervisory function over a wide range of courts, tribunals and bodies or individuals performing public functions including Government Ministers. This function, known as "judicial review", is designed to ensure that decisions made by these bodies or individuals do not go beyond the powers given to them by Parliament.

Appeals from lower courts are heard in Divisional Courts of the High Court. Appeals from county courts in bankruptcy cases are heard by a Divisional Court of the Chancery Division; Divisional Courts of the Queen's Bench Division hear appeals on points of law from magistrates' courts; and a Divisional Court of the Family Division hears appeals against decisions about family matters made by magistrates' courts.

Appeals from the High Court are heard in the Civil Division of the Court of Appeal.

V. The Court of Appeal

The Court of Appeal is divided into two Divisions, Criminal and Civil. Its courtrooms and offices are based in the Royal Courts of Justice and it normally never sits outside London. The Criminal Division, presided over by the Lord Chief Justice, hears appeals against conviction and sentence from the Crown Court. The Civil Division, presided over by the Master of the Rolls, hears appeals mainly against decisions of the High Court and the county courts. In doing so, its judges may make any order which they decide ought to have been made in the court below. In some cases a re-trial is ordered. Witnesses are rarely heard in the Court of Appeal. Decisions are usually based on documents, transcripts of the previous hearings and the arguments of the lawyers appearing for the parties.

VI. The supreme Court

The Crown Court, the High Court and the Court of Appeal are collectively referred to as the Supreme Court.

VII. The House of Lords

In addition to its function as the upper House of Parliament, the House of Lords is the final court of appeal for both criminal and civil cases. Leave to appeal to the House of Lords must be granted by the Court of Appeal or the Appeal Committee of the House of Lords and leave will be granted only if the case raises a point of law of general public importance.

Cases are heard by the Lords of Appeal in Ordinary, also known as the Law Lords.

VIII. Other courts

The above are the main courts in England and Wales, but there are others, including:

– Coroners' courts, where coroners, sometimes with a jury, investigate violent, unnatural and suspicious deaths or sudden deaths where the reason for death is unknown;
– Courts martial where cases subject to military law are brought against members of the armed forces; and
– Ecclesiastical courts where matters relating to the Church of England and ecclesiastical law are decided.

IX. Tribunals

In addition, there are many tribunals which deal with varied subjects such as immigration, tax, mental health, land and property, welfare benefits, transport, industry and employment. The procedure in tribunals tends to be less formal than in the other courts. Members of tribunals can include specialists or experts, such as doctors, and lay people, although the chairperson is almost always legally qualified. Depending on the type of tribunal, appeals against decisions made by a tribunal can be made to a higher tribunal, the High Court or the Court of Appeal.

Outline of court structure in England & Wales

House of Lords
appeals from Court of Appeal and High Court (also Scotland and Northern Ireland)

Judicial Committee of the Privy Council
appeals from the Commonwealth, etc

Court of Appeal

Civil Division
appeals from High Court and county courts

Criminal Division
appeals from Crown Court

High Court

Chancery Division
equity and trusts, contentious probate, tax, partnerships, bankruptcy

Companies Court
Patents Court

Divisional Court:
appeals from county courts re. bankruptcy and land registration

Family Division
dissolution of marriage, matrimonial proceedings, proceedings relating to children

Divisional Court:
appeals from county courts and magistrates' courts on family matters

Queen's Bench Division
Contract and tort, etc
Commercial Court
Admiralty Court

Divisional Court:
appeals from Crown Court and magistrates' courts by way of cases stated and judicial review

county courts
majority of civil litigation subject to nature of claim

magistrates' courts
trials of summary offences committals to the Crown Court, family proceedings courts, youth courts

Crown Court
trials of indictable offences, appeals from magistrates' courts

This diagram is, of necessity, much simplified and should not be taken as a comprehensive statement on the jurisdiction of any specific court

Estonia

THE Estonian court system is governed by Chapter 13 of the Constitution, as well as the Courts Act and the Status of Judges. Justice is solely administered by courts of law. The courts are independent in their work and administer justice in accordance with the Constitution and the laws. The Ministry of Justice is, according to the Government of the Republic Act, only responsible for the management and financing of the Courts of First and Second Instance. The Supreme Court is both legally and financially independent.

The Estonian court system comprises the following three levels:

– county and city courts, and administrative courts;
– circuit courts; and
– the Supreme Court

The Estonian Constitution provides for the creation of specialised courts with specific jurisdiction.

I. The County and City Court (*Maa-ja Linnakohtud*) and the administrative courts (*Halduskohtud*)

These courts are the Courts of First Instance. The County and City Courts deal with all civil and criminal cases, while the administrative courts investigate cases which the court has been specially empowered to deal with. Administrative courts are usually attached to county or city courts.

At present, there are 21 county and city courts with one judge hearing administrative cases in each of them. Special administrative courts have been established in Tallinn and Tartu.

The administrative courts:

– give judgment on complaints concerning legislation (only individual pieces of legislation) and activities of the institutions of executive state power, local government and the election committee;
– give judgments on disputes concerning administrative agreements; and
– gives judgments on cases of administrative offences.

If any case is linked with a civil dispute, the case will be heard by a city or county court.

II. Circuit courts

Circuit courts (*Ringkonnakohtud*) are the Courts of Second Instance and hear appeals of decisions from the First Instance Courts. Circuit courts are divided into panels according to the type of case under consideration (civil, criminal or administrative) and decisions are reached after panel discussion.

There are three circuit courts: the Circuit Court of Tallinn, the Circuit Court of Tartu and the Circuit Court of Viru.

III. The Supreme Court

The Supreme Court (*Riigikohus*) is the final appeal court in Estonia. It hears appeals of decisions from the circuit courts and may also, in cases specified by law, change a lower court decision or correct a miscarriage of justice. The work of the Supreme Court is carried out by the following bodies:

- the Civil Panel;
- the Criminal Panel;
- the Administrative Panel;
- the Constitutional Review Panel; and
- the Supreme Court in full session, comprising all members of the court.

The Supreme Court cannot rule on an issue of fact but may decide an issue of law concerning a judgment of a circuit court.

Appeal to the Supreme Court in the case of cassation may be submitted by the accused, the victim or the public prosecutor in criminal cases, by the plaintiff or the defendant in civil cases, and by the complainant or the institution who adopted the piece of legislation in dispute in administrative cases.

An appeal must be submitted within one month to the circuit court which made the decision in dispute, which must then transmit the complaint to the Supreme Court. The basis of the appeal must be a violation of substantive or procedural law.

The Appeals Panel of the Supreme Court grants leave to appeal, if at least one of the three members of the Panel finds that an appeal contains sufficient reason for granting leave. In order to start a proceeding, security for costs must be paid in the court. Such security will be refunded if the appeal is fully or partly satisfied.

A constitutional review is conducted by the Supreme Court Constitutional Review Panel. The Panel consists of five members who are elected by the Supreme Court in full session. The duties of the chairman of the Supreme Court Constitutional Review Panel is fulfilled by the Chief Justice of the Supreme Court. If any law or other legislation is in conflict with the provisions and spirit of the Constitution, such law will be declared null and void by the Supreme Court. A proposal to review the conformity of a law or other legislation with the Constitution may be made by the President of the Republic, the Legal Chancellor or the courts.

The Supreme Court is situated in Tartu and consists of 17 judges.

IV. Judges

Most cases in the Courts of First Instance are heard by a single judge. Two lay justices may assist the judge, if the parties so request in civil proceedings, and in criminal proceedings in the case of a serious offence or if the accused is under age. Lay justices are elected by local government councils.

In circuit courts, decisions are reached after panel discussion.

The work of the Supreme Court is also carried out by the way of panels.

Judges are appointed for life. In Estonian practice however, appointment for life means a possible tenure up to five years beyond pension age. Judges may be recalled only by a court order.

The Chief Justice of the Supreme Court is appointed by the Parliament (*Riigikogu*), on the proposal of the President of the Republic. Justices of the Supreme Courts are appointed by the *Riigikogu,* on the proposal of the Chief

Justice of the Supreme Court. All other judges are appointed by the President of the Republic on the proposal of the Chief Justice of the Supreme Court.

While in office, judges may be charged with a criminal offence or arrested only on the proposal of the Chief Justice of the Supreme Court, and with the consent of the President of the Republic. The Chief Justice and other justices of the Supreme Court may be charged with a criminal offence only on the proposal of the Legal Chancellor, and with the consent of the majority of the *Riigikogu*.

FINLAND

I. Introduction

The Finnish Constitution guarantees everyone the right to have his case heard appropriately and without undue delay by a court or other public authority. Everyone also has the right to have a decision affecting his rights and duties reviewed by a court or other judicial organ.

In addition the Constitution contains the basic provision on good government. The main guarantees of good government are the publicity of proceedings, the right to be heard, the right to receive a decision with stated grounds, and the right to appeal against the decision.

The independence of the judiciary is constitutionally guaranteed. Professional judges must have a higher university degree in law. They are appointed by the President of the Republic. Most appointments are made upon nomination by the judiciary. The courts of first instance also have some locally elected lay judges.

II. Jurisdiction in constitutional matters

At present the Finnish Constitution consists of four separate acts. The most important are the Constitution Act of Finland of 1919 and the Parliament Act of 1928. These acts are, however, to be replaced by a single act during the first half of 2000. A bill to effect this amendment was presented to Parliament in early spring 1998.

The constitutionality of laws is supervised in advance. It mainly takes place in Parliament, and especially in its Constitutional Committee. The goal of this parliamentary control is to prevent in advance laws which are in conflict with the Constitution from being enacted in the ordinary legislative procedure. A specific feature of the Finnish system is that exceptions to the Constitution may be enacted in the order prescribed for the enactment of constitutional legislation, and thus the wording of the Constitution may be left untouched.

No constitutional court exists in Finland. According to an established interpretation, the courts are not permitted to examine the constitutionality of legislation or choose not to apply an act in a certain case because it is in conflict with the Constitution. A court shall, however, not apply provisions in legislation of a lower order than acts if they conflict with the Constitution.

The government bill now under consideration in Parliament does not contain a proposal for a constitutional court. According to the bill the courts should, however give preference to the Constitution when they decide a case, if the application of the act should be in a manifest conflict with the Constitution.

According to the proposal the Constitutional Committee would continue to supervise the constitutionality of laws.

III. General courts in civil and criminal matters

Finland is divided into a number of court districts, each with a district court (*karajaoikeus*) The actual number of districts is 68. They vary greatly in size, both in terms of population and of area. A district court is made up of a Chief Judge (*laamanni*) and a number of other professional judges.

In ordinary civil cases the court consists of three professional judges. One judge, however, presides over the preparation of a civil case. In criminal cases (and in some cases concerning family law) the court is composed of one presiding professional judge and three lay assessors. Some minor cases may be tried by one judge alone.

The second instance in an ordinary case is the Court of Appeal (*hovioikeus*). There are six courts of appeal in Finland; the oldest is the Turku Court of Appeal founded in 1623. These courts hear civil and criminal appeals regardless of the importance of the case.

There are certain criminal cases that a Court of Appeal hears as the first instance. These include treason and certain offences in public office.

The Court of Appeal is divided into divisions. The cases are heard by three judges (all professionals). However, minor cases may also be dealt with by three judges.

The last instance is the Supreme Court (*korkein oikeus*) which has its seat in Helsinki. The Supreme Court hears civil and criminal appeals, but cases are admitted only under certain conditions. As the word appeal indicates, the Supreme Court may deal not only with questions of law but also with questions of fact.

The Supreme Court is the third and final instance in the country. Its most important task is to hand down precedents, thus giving directions on the application of the law to the lower courts.

The Supreme Court may grant a leave to appeal in cases in which a precedent is necessary for the correct application of the law, a serious error has been committed in the proceedings before a lower court or another special reason exists in law.

Normally two members decide whether leave should be granted. If leave is granted the case is decided in a composition of five members. If the matter is principally important and has far-reaching consequences it is decided in plenary session or in a reinforced composition of eleven members.

Cases which the Court of Appeal considers as the first instance are subject to appeal in the Supreme Court without restriction.

IV. Special courts

The High Court of Impeachment (*valtakunnanoikeus*) which has seldom been convened hears criminal cases relating to offences in office allegedly committed by a member of the Council of State, the Chancellor of Justice, or a member of either the Supreme Court or the Supreme Administrative Court. In such cases the prosecution is taken care of either by the Chancellor of Justice or the Parliamentary Ombudsman.

There are four land courts (*maaoikeus*) in Finland. These hear disputes and appeals relating to the demarcation of plots of real estate. The decisions of the land courts are subject to appeal in the Supreme Court.

Finland also has three water courts (*vesioikeus*) and the Water Court of Appeal (*vesiylioikeu*). These consider permit cases, disputes and appeals relating to the use of and legal title to waters, as well as certain criminal cases. The decisions of the Water Court of Appeal are subject to appeal in the

Supreme Court or the Supreme Administrative Court depending on the subject matter of the case.

The Market Court (*markkinatuomioistuin*) can prohibit misleading or improper advertising and unreasonable contractual terms. Its decisions are not subject to appeal.

The Labour Court (*työtuomioistuin*) hears disputes relating to collective agreements on employment relationships and on civil service relationships. Its decisions are not subject to appeal. Disputes relating to individual employment relationships are heard by the general courts and individual civil service relationships by the general administrative courts.

The Insurance Court (*vakuutusoikeus*) considers certain cases falling within the field of social insurance, for example accident insurance and pensions. Such cases are usually first heard by an appellate board whose decisions are then subject to appeal in the Insurance Court. The decisions of the Insurance Court are not subject to appeal.

The Prison Court (*vankilaoikeus*) considers the incarceration of dangerous recidivists and the enforcement of sentences involving the deprivation of liberty of young offenders.

V. Administrative jurisdiction

A general right of administrative appeal exists in Finland. This right can only be restricted with a specific legislative provision to that effect. The administrative courts hear appeals of private individuals and corporate bodies against the acts of the authorities. In certain cases the state and municipal authorities also have a right of appeal.

An appeal is usually first heard by a County Administrative Court (*lääninoikeus*); there are 11 such courts in Finland. In the autonomous province of Åland there is no county administrative court, but instead an administrative court attached to the Åland District Court.

These courts hear tax, municipal, construction, social welfare, and health care cases as well as other administrative cases. In certain of these the appeal must be preceded by a complaint to a separate lower appellate body.

The Supreme Administrative Court (*korkein hallinto-oikeus*) is the final arbiter of the legality of the acts of the authorities. The bulk of its caseload consists of appeals against the decisions of the County Administrative Courts.

Usually no leave to appeal is required. The main exception to this rule is an appeal against a decision in a tax case for which leave is required. It is the Supreme Administrative Court itself that grants the leave.

In addition to its purely judicial tasks, the Supreme Administrative Court supervises the lower judicial authorities in the field of administrative law and participates in the development of the administrative court system.

VI. Office of the Prosecutor General

The highest prosecuting authority in Finland is the Prosecutor General (*valtakunnansyyttäjä*). As the director of the prosecution service the Prosecutor General manages and supervises its operation and work. The state prosecutors (*valtionsyyttäjä*) who work in the Office of the Prosecutor General appraise the evidence and decide whether charges should be brought in cases with wider national significance. The state prosecutors have the right to act throughout the country.

The local prosecuting authorities in Finland, the district prosecutors (*kihlakunnansyyttäjä*), are appointed by the Prosecutor General.

The prosecutors make their decisions to bring charges on the basis of preliminary investigations carried out by the police; it is their duty to appraise the available evidence and determine whether there is a *prima facie* case. If the evidence is deemed to be insufficient, prosecution will be declined. Prosecution may similarly be refused, for example, in cases in which the alleged offence is of minor significance.

VII. Advocates and legal aid

A party to proceedings before a court usually uses the services of a counsel, even though this is strictly speaking not required by law. The duties of counsel are most often performed by an advocate, a legal aid counsel, or another lawyer. Legal aid counsels are employed by the state to assist people in their legal affairs.

A person of limited means may also be granted cost-free proceedings. These are applied for from the court and usually cover the main proceedings only. In a criminal case it is, however, possible to be granted a public defender already for the preliminary police investigation.

VIII. Supervision of the administration of justice

The Chancellor of Justice of the Council of State (*oikeuskansleri*) monitors the legality of the operations of the Council of State and other authorities, as well as of other public agencies. The Chancellor of Justice is appointed by the President of the Republic.

The Chancellor of Justice has access to the information and accounts held by the authorities in so far as he needs them for the performance of his duties. He conducts inquiries, for example on the basis of complaints by members of the public. He can issue admonitions to the authorities and public officials for errors in office, and lay down instructions for future conduct. In serious cases he may order charges to be brought. In addition, the Chancellor of Justice monitors the activities of the members of the Finnish Bar Association.

In addition to the Chancellor of Justice, the Finnish administrative machinery is overseen by the Parliamentary Ombudsman (*eduskunnan oikeusasiamies*). In practical terms the duties of these senior authorities differ only in that the overseeing of the legality of the activities of the Council of State is mainly entrusted to the Chancellor of Justice, and that matters pertaining to conscripts and convicts are within the ambit of the Ombudsman. If the same complaint has been addressed to both authorities only one of them will deal with it.

The overseers of legality have no jurisdiction to alter the decisions of other authorities, nor to award damages. Their rulings are not subject to appeal.

IX. Statistical data

A. Number of cases and of judicial decisions

1. Civil cases

In 1997 approximately 136 500 civil cases were brought before the District Courts, and judgment was delivered in 139 000 cases. About 5 000 cases were brought before the Appellate Courts which delivered judgment in 5 400 cases. The Supreme Court received 2 153 new civil cases and delivered judgment in 2 393 cases.

2. Criminal cases

In 1997 about 52 000 criminal cases were brought before the District Courts, and judgment was delivered in 49 000 cases. About 7 400 cases were brought before the Appellate Courts which delivered judgment in 7 200 cases. The Supreme Court received 1 212 new criminal cases and delivered judgment in 1 057 cases.

3. Administrative cases

In 1997 approximately 19 700 cases were brought before the County Administrative Courts, and judgment was delivered in 20 200 cases. The Supreme Administrative Court received 3 900 cases on appeal, and judgment was delivered in 3 852 cases.

B. Number of judges

At present there are 21 justices at the Supreme Court (including the President of the Court) and 163 justices at the Courts of Appeal. The number of district court judges is 455. There are 121 judges in the County Administrative Courts. The number of justices at the Supreme Administrative Court is 25 (including the President of the Court).

France

FOR historical reasons, there are two types of court in France: ordinary and administrative courts.

After the Revolution, an attempt was made – rightly or wrongly – to put an end to the situation that had arisen under the monarchy whereby it was the prerogative of the royal courts (*parlements*) to intervene in the administrative, financial or even political affairs of the state. The Act of 16-24 August 1790 was therefore passed, prohibiting the courts from intervening in disputes to which the administrative authorities were party. Jurisdiction in such matters was given to the administrative tribunals, the ordinary courts being responsible for settling disputes between private individuals.

A further distinction is drawn between general courts – that is, those with general jurisdiction – and special courts – that is, those whose jurisdiction is limited to particular matters.

This text will deal with the two types of court separately, even though recent developments in the court system have brought the organisation of the administrative courts similar to that of the ordinary courts, and will describe the organisation of a typical institution, the Public Prosecutor's Office (*ministère public*), and the principal officers engaged in the administration of justice (*auxiliaires de justice*).

I. Courts with administrative jurisdiction

The system of courts with administrative jurisdiction comprises administrative courts, administrative courts of appeal and, at the top, the Council of State (*Conseil d'Etat*), which, for both historical and legal reasons, continues to be at the same time a court of first instance, a court of appeal and a court of cassation, the latter being its main judicial function today. However, it remains a court of first instance and a court of final decision for certain other cases, such as matters concerning the careers of officials appointed by decree or the legality of regulations. The administrative authorities must comply with the decisions of these administrative courts.

A. Administrative courts

The administrative courts are courts of first instance with general jurisdiction in disputes concerning administrative issues. There are currently 36 of them, each serving several *départements*. They deal with such cases as those involving the responsibility of the public authorities or with fiscal matters. However, cases relating to indirect taxation, customs and excise duties, and so on, come under the jurisdiction of the ordinary courts.

Appeals against the decisions of the administrative courts are lodged with one of the Administrative Courts of Appeal, except for certain categories of litigation for which appeals lie to the Council of State.

B. The Administrative Courts of Appeal

There are currently six Administrative Courts of Appeal, which were set up under a law of 31 December 1987. They are competent to hear appeals against most of the judgments delivered by the administrative courts.

C. The Council of State

As the successor to the former Royal Council, the Council of State is the highest administrative court.

Apart from its judicial functions briefly described above, it still performs administrative functions and advises the government.

It is divided into four specialised administrative sections: interior (public order), finance, public works and social affairs. A section responsible for reports and studies has been set up to carry out studies commissioned by the government or ordered by its Vice-President and to deal with difficulties in implementing decisions of the administrative courts.

Government bills, orders and decrees are submitted by the government before their promulgation to the appropriate section of the Council. It revises the text in co-operation with the ministry concerned before it is finally adopted by the full bench of the Council.

The adoption of the text does not, however, prevent decrees – or any other administrative measures – from subsequently being challenged on the grounds of *ultra vires* before the judicial section, which may annul them in full or in part on such grounds after the *Commissaire du Gouvernement* (who, despite the title, does not represent the government at all) has presented his or her observations.

The Council's function is thus to protect the citizens against any encroachment upon their rights by the administrative authorities and to ensure that the action of the latter is lawful.

The Council of State consists of the Prime Minister (or in his or her absence the Minister for Justice) as President (in a purely formal capacity), a Vice-President, the Presidents of the sections, the members of the Council and junior judges (*maîtres des requêtes* and *auditeurs*), plus extraordinary members appointed for a specific period by reason of their eminence and their specialised knowledge of relevance to the state's affairs.

D. The Court of Audit

The Court of Audit (*Cour des comptes*) occupies a special position in the judicial system in the broad sense. It is an ordinary court responsible for examining the accounts drawn up by the public accountants, while regional bodies (*Chambres régionales des comptes*) are responsible for checking the accounts of the public authorities and their institutions.

The Court of Audit hears appeals against decisions of the *Chambres régionales des comptes.*

The Council of State acts as a court of cassation in cases of appeals against decisions of the Court of Audit.

Moreover, the Court of Audit assists the government and Parliament by supervising the execution of the state budget. It also examines the efficiency of the administrative bodies of the state and ascertains whether they have followed the proper procedures. Its observations are contained in a summary published in an annual report to the President of the Republic.

The Court of Audit consists of seven chambers and is presided over by a First President. The Public Prosecutor's Office is represented by a Chief Public Prosecutor (*procureur général*) appointed by the government. The judges at the Court of Audit – but not the members of the prosecution service (*parquet*) – cannot be removed from office.

II. The Jurisdiction Disputes Court (*Tribunal des conflits*)

The Jurisdiction Disputes Court, which links the two types of court, is responsible for settling disputes as to jurisdiction that may arise between ordinary and administrative courts, that is to say it decides whether a case is of an administrative nature and should be heard by the administrative courts or whether it comes under the jurisdiction of the ordinary courts.

Cases are referred to the Jurisdiction Disputes Court either by the Court of Cassation or the Council of State when a dispute raises a question of jurisdiction involving the separation of powers or by the administrative authorities when they believe they have been wrongly sued in an ordinary court. The Jurisdiction Disputes Court is also asked to resolve disputes in which neither of the two types of court considers it has jurisdiction in a case brought first before one and then before the other.

The court is presided over *ex officio* by the Minister for Justice who, apart from exceptional cases, does not deliberate with the other eight regular members. It consists of an equal number of judges from the Court of Cassation and the Council of State. The Public Prosecutor's Office is represented by four government commissioners (*Commissaires du Gouvernement*), two chosen from among the advocates-general (*avocats généraux*) at the Court of Cassation and two from among the members of the Council of State. In fact, they do not actually represent the government and are absolutely independent in reaching their conclusions.

III. Ordinary courts

A. Courts with general jurisdiction

These consist of 181 regional courts (*tribunaux de grande instance*), ordinary courts of first instance, 33 courts of appeal, as well as two higher courts of appeal, 99 assize courts and the Court of Cassation, which sits in Paris. The work of these courts is governed by the general principle applying to the non-specialised courts that the administration of civil and criminal justice forms a single unit, so that they are able to try both civil and criminal cases.

*1. The Regional Courts (*tribunaux de grande instance*)*

There must be at least one Regional Court in each *département,* its composition varying according to the economic importance of the area and the size of its population. The Paris Regional Court thus comprises 31 chambers, each divided into two or three sections.

Since 1995, it has been possible for a Regional Court to have separate chambers located closer to where the public needs them.

This court has general jurisdiction in civil cases. Subject to appeal, it tries all cases that do not expressly fall within the jurisdiction of another court. In some matters (nationality, personal status and capacity, actions to establish the ownership of, and executions against, real property, patents, trademarks, orders to enforce foreign judgments, liquidation of the assets of private, non-commercial corporate bodies, and so on) it has sole jurisdiction for claims not exceeding 13 000 French Francs, its decisions being final. Since 1970, cases have either been decided by a single judge (if the presiding judge so rules) or by a bench. The latter is obligatory when a party so requests (without having to state its reasons) or if a single judge refers a matter to the court. The exception here is cases concerning civil status that come under the jurisdiction of the family judge (*juge aux affaires familiales*).

As well as exercising general jurisdiction, single judges of the Regional Court also deal with specific types of dispute (such as road accidents or applications for recognition and enforcement of decisions by foreign courts).

The Regional Courts also have specialised single judges attached to them, for example:

– the *juge de l'exécution,* who has jurisdiction when difficulties arise with writs of execution and when objections are raised to the execution of a judgment;

– the *juge aux affaires familiales,* an office instituted in 1993. He or she has jurisdiction over all family disputes, with the exception of guardianship for minors deprived of legal capacity and care measures.

– Finally, each *département* has a Regional Court judge specialising in expropriation cases (*juge de l'expropriation*) and responsible for assessing the compensation payable by the state or the public authorities to persons whose real estate has been expropriated in the public interest.

In addition to functioning as head of a panel of judges and of the court administration, the presiding judge has judicial powers of his or her own. First of all, he or she deals with unilateral applications for the court to order certain types of measure or authorisation. He or she also rules on applications for a provisional order to be issued in urgent cases or when the facts are clear or delegates this power to a judge. This is a rapid summary procedure (known as *référé*) that involves both parties and leads to an immediately enforceable decision without prejudice to the merits of the case.

As a criminal court, the Regional Court, consisting of either a single judge or, in the case of more serious crimes, a panel of judges, tries offenders charged with *délits* (offences punishable with up to ten years' imprisonment or a fine exceeding 10 000 French Francs) brought before it directly by the prosecution service (*ministère public*) or a civil plaintiff or referred to it by an investigating judge (*juge d'instruction*).

The *juge d'instruction* is a regional court judge charged with investigating the most serious criminal cases. He or she constitutes a single-judge court, but several *juges d'instruction* may be appointed to handle the more complex cases. The *juge d'instruction* has various means available to establish the truth (means of transport, the right to search premises, to seize property, to hold hearings, to commission expert reports, and so on) and possesses judicial powers, notably the ability to place a person in custody or under court supervision and to commit an offender for trial.

The *juge de l'application des peines* is responsible for ensuring that convicted persons are treated in prison in a manner conducive to their reformation, for co-ordinating aid to released prisoners and for monitoring persons serving non-custodial sentences.

In civil cases, the *juge des enfants,* who is also a member of the Regional Court, is responsible for taking all educational measures necessary for the protection of children whose health, safety, moral welfare or upbringing are endangered. He or she is also the guardianship judge in cases involving family and social benefits. In criminal cases, he or she tries persons under 18 who have committed minor offences (*délits*) and those under 16 charged with more serious offences (*crimes*) and orders any measures necessary for their reformation. This judge sits either alone or, in the more serious cases, as head of the Juvenile Court (*tribunal pour enfants*), which also includes two lay assessors.

2. Courts of Appeal and Assize Courts

Since 1958, the Courts of Appeal (*cours d'appel*), which are distant descendants of the pre-revolutionary *parlements,* have been the only appellate courts competent to hear (as a bench) appeals against decisions of all the civil and criminal courts given at first instance within their area of jurisdiction (which usually coincides with the geographical boundaries of a *région*). They are separated into chambers, each with a presiding judge. Special mention should be made of the Indictment Chamber (*Chambre d'accusation*), which reviews cases of detention on remand, hears appeals against orders made by the investigating judge and decides whether to refer cases to the Assize Court. It is also the disciplinary court for police officers and has certain other responsibilities (extradition, rehabilitation, amnesties).

The Assize Court (*cour d'assises*) tries *crimes* (the most serious offences, punishable with imprisonment for either a specific term or life) referred to it by the Indictment Chamber. Each *département* has one Assize Court, which has special characteristic features of its own. Firstly, it sits for only two weeks in every quarter and, secondly, it consists of three professional judges, who constitute the court proper, and, with the exception of trials for certain offences (such as crimes against the state or military, terrorist or drugs-related offences), of a lay jury of nine citizens appointed by lot according to a complex procedure. They deliberate together on the defendant's guilt and on the sentence to be passed by replying to questions put to them. A decision against the defendant must be reached by a majority of at least eight, which ensures the jury's predominance. The court's judgments, for which no reasons are given, are not subject to appeal but may be referred to the Court of Cassation. A reform aimed at providing for an appeal against its decisions is likely to be adopted in the near future.

3. The Court of Cassation

This is the highest ordinary court, with five civil chambers (including one for commercial and financial cases and one for social cases) and one criminal chamber. It is not a third tier of jurisdiction. Rather, its function is to ascertain that any final decision in a civil or criminal case referred to it is in conformity with the law.

If it sets the judgment aside, the case is sent to another court of the same level of jurisdiction as the one whose decision has been annulled. Should the new judgment be referred to it for identical reasons, the plenary court may reach a decision without remitting the case to another court. Alternatively, it may again remit the case to another court, but in this case its judgment is binding on the court in question. In this way, the Court of Cassation serves to unify case law and to create new law. Since 1991, it has also been possible for any ordinary civil court to ask for its opinion.

B. Special courts and tribunals

The increase in the number and powers of special courts necessarily limits the general jurisdiction of the Regional Courts. Their basis is either historical (in the case of the Commercial Courts and to a certain extent also the District Courts, or social, as in the case of the industrial conciliation tribunals (*conseils des prud'hommes*). In criminal cases, certain distinctions between types of offender have proved unavoidable and have led in the recent past to the setting up of new courts, the most typical example being the juvenile courts. A reform carried out in 1958 abolished the special courts for civil appeals. With the exception of the *Haute Cour de Justice,* their decisions are all subject to review by the Court of Cassation.

*1. The District/Police Courts (*tribunaux d'instance et de police*)*

The District Court (formerly the *justice de paix*), whose jurisdiction normally covers an *arrondissement,* sits with a single judge and rules on all claims involving persons or movable property up to 30000 French Francs, with decisions on claims up to 13000 French Francs not being subject to appeal. In addition, it has special jurisdiction in a limited number of specified matters (all types of lease, seizures, actions to recover possession, disputes arising from the application of provisions relating to consumer credit, disputes concerning the drawing up of electoral rolls, and so on). Finally, the judge also performs numerous extra-judicial functions (issuing *actes de notoriété* [documents stating a matter of common knowledge], issuing an authority to vote by proxy, and so on). He or she is also the guardianship judge (*juge des tutelles*) and, as such, supervises statutory representation and guardianship within the court's area of jurisdiction in the case of adults and minors without legal capacity.

In criminal cases the court, known as the *Tribunal de police,* rules as a court of ordinary law on contraventions (minor offences subject to a fine not exceeding 10000 French Francs). The judges of the *Tribunal d'instance* are drawn from the *Tribunal de grande instance.*

*2. Commercial jurisdiction (*juridiction consulaire*)*

The unusual feature of the Commercial Courts (*tribunaux de commerce*), numbering 228, which were known in the Middle Ages as *juges-consuls,* is that, with the exception of Alsace-Lorraine, they are made up entirely of persons engaged in commerce and elected by their peers. They settle claims concerning commercial transactions up to 13 000 French Francs and their decisions are not subject to appeal. They have sole jurisdiction over class actions (settlements with creditors, receivership) and over disputes between business persons and partners of commercial firms. The presiding judge has judicial powers similar to those of the presiding judge of the Regional Court, especially in the case of applications (*référés*) for the court to make a provisional order. In places without a commercial court, commercial disputes are heard by the Regional Court.

Disputes concerning leases for commercial premises do not come under the jurisdiction of the Commercial Courts. This responsibility is shared between the Regional Court and its presiding judge, depending on the subject-matter of the application.

As far as rural premises (farm tenancies) are concerned, jurisdiction lies with the Agricultural Land Tribunal (*tribunal paritaire de baux ruraux*), 413 in number, presided over by the district court judge (*juge d'instance*), normally assisted by two landlords and two tenants.

3. Social tribunals

Whereas the Commercial Courts were set up to provide for trial by members of the same occupation, the Industrial Conciliation Tribunals (*conseils des prud'hommes*), numbering 270, came into being in the nineteenth century, mainly as a result of a desire for conciliation and for the equal representation of wage earners and employers.

For this reason, two of their members are elected by the employers and two by the workers, with the *juge d'instance* holding a casting vote.

These tribunals have jurisdiction over individual disputes arising from contracts of employment or apprenticeship in firms belonging to the branches of industry specified in the order setting them up. The tribunal and each of its occupational sections have a conciliation panel, before which the case must be brought in the first instance, and a judgment panel, as well as a *référé* panel common to all sections to hear urgent applications for provisional orders.

On the same principle, disputes relating to general social security matters (membership and benefits) are submitted to a Social Security Tribunal (*tribunal des affaires de sécurité sociale*), of which there are 116, presided over by a judge of the Regional Court accompanied by lay assessors representing the groups involved (wage earners, employers or self-employed persons).

4. Commercial maritime courts

These courts (5 in number) sit temporarily at merchant seamen's registration offices. Their function is to try certain breaches of the merchant navy's Penal Code.

5. Courts martial

The organisation of these courts is fairly complex and varies between peacetime and wartime.

The courts of the armed forces are now competent only to try breaches of the Code of Military Justice in wartime and breaches of the ordinary law committed by military personnel or comparable persons. There are also military tribunals that have been set up to try offences committed by members of the armed forces stationed abroad.

In peacetime, military offences and breaches of the ordinary law committed by military personnel come under the jurisdiction of ordinary criminal courts made up of judges specialising in military matters.

6. Political courts – the Haute Cour de Justice *and the* Cour de Justice de la République

The *Haute Cour de Justice* has 15 judges, 12 parliamentary judges elected in equal numbers by the Senate and the National Assembly from among their members and three judges at the seat of the Court of Cassation.

It has sole jurisdiction to try the President of the Republic for high treason. It is made up exclusively of parliamentarians elected by their peers.

The *Cour de Justice de la République,* which was set up under a 1993 amendment to the Constitution, is also a political court. It tries members of the government for both minor and serious offences committed in their official capacity.

The prosecutors at these two courts are provided by the Office of the Chief Public Prosecutor (*procureur général*) at the Court of Cassation.

IV. The Public Prosecutor's Office

There is a representative of the Public Prosecutor's Office (*ministère public*) at most courts. Whereas the parties act on their own behalf and in the defence of their own interests, the *ministère public,* which is under the authority of the Ministry of Justice, is an agent of the executive and acts on behalf of the public.

The duties of the *ministère public* are carried out by the *procureurs généraux,* barristers (*avocats*) and *substituts généraux* at the Court of Cassation and the Courts of Appeal and by the *procureurs de la République* and their deputies at the Regional Courts, who have the status of *magistrats.* In criminal cases, the *ministère public* is a principal party, initiating and conducting the prosecution unless the victim of the offence has done this as a civil plaintiff. It has a monopoly both with regard to this duty and to the enforcement of sentences. It also directs and supervises the police, who are under the control of the Ministry of the Interior.

The *ministère public* initiates civil proceedings in exceptional cases only. It acts on its own initiative only where authorised to do so by law, for instance in cases concerning personal status and capacity or in the defence of public policy. Usually, it is no more than an associated party to proceedings, where its function is confined to giving opinions (in the form of written or oral submissions) as to what it considers to be most in accordance with the law and natural justice. It also performs administrative functions, such as exercising supervision over the registration of births, marriages and deaths and over the *auxiliaires de justice* (see below).

V. *Magistrats*

The professional *magistrats* (6287 in number), although technically civil servants, were given separate status under an institutional law of 22 December 1958 in accordance with the principle of separation of powers and the special nature of judicial work.

The 1958 reform also had a considerable effect on their recruitment and training as it provided for the setting up at Bordeaux of the National Legal Service Training College (*Ecole Nationale de la Magistrature*), where admission for training as an *auditeur de justice* is normally by means of three competitive examinations of the same level of difficulty, one open to higher education graduates, the second to certain civil servants and the third to persons with the relevant professional experience or experience of holding local political office.

In exceptional circumstances, certain categories of people (professors of law, civil servants, *officiers de justice* or *auxiliaires de justice*) may be appointed directly on the basis of their qualifications if they hold a master's degree in law.

Magistrats include judges and members of the *ministère public* at the Court of Cassation, the courts and tribunals of first instance and the central administration, as well as the *auditeurs de justice.* Although forming a single body, they are divided into two distinct categories: judges (*magistrats du siège*) and prosecutors (*magistrats du ministère public* – also known as the *parquet*), who can readily move from one category to the other. Only the former benefit from the constitutional principle that they cannot be removed from office, which guarantees their independence of the political authorities. The latter do not have this right. They are subject to the orders and supervision of their superiors and are under the authority of the Minister for Justice (whose official title is *Garde des Sceaux*). Their superiors may give them instructions, which they have to follow in their written submissions, although – in theory at least – they enjoy freedom to speak as they wish at a hearing.

All appointments to the *magistrature* are made by order of the President of the Republic, but judges must be appointed on the basis of a favourable opinion (which binds the government) issued by the Legal Service Commission (*Conseil Supérieur de la Magistrature*) or even (in the case of the highest posts) on the basis of the latter's proposals. The *Conseil Supérieur de la Magistrature* is a constitutional body with two different sections (since 1993), one responsible for the judges and the other for prosecutors. It is made up of six *magistrats* elected by their peers, a member of the Council of State and three persons appointed by the President of the Republic, the President of the Senate and the President of the National Assembly. It is presided over by the Head of State, and its Vice-President is the Minister for Justice. The section with responsibility for judges also constitutes the latter's disciplinary body. It is presided over by the First Presiding Judge of the Court of Cassation.

All courts (with the exception of the Commercial Courts) must be assisted by a registry headed by a civil servant, the Chief Clerk of the Court or a clerk delegated by him or her, all of whom must be the members of the court and have retained particular rights enjoyed by public legal officers (*officiers publics* – see below for a definition).

VI. Court auxiliaries (*Auxiliaires de Justice*)

In addition to the *magistrats,* there are many professions that work to ensure the proper functioning of the administration of justice or serve as intermediaries between the courts and the public

These professions, which have inherited a centuries-old judicial tradition and have been inspired by a rigorous code of practice, have significantly modernised their statutes and practices in recent years. While staff of the registries of the civil and criminal courts were given civil service status in 1965, the liberal character of the other professions has become apparent and some have merged with others.

A. *Avocats*

This profession has been marked by two important developments. Firstly, the law of 31 December 1971 brought about the merger of the profession of lawyer (*avocat*) with that of the *avoué* at the Regional Courts and of the *agréé* at the Commercial Courts.

Subsequently, the law of 31 December 1990 modified that of 1971 by bringing about a new merger between the *avocats* and the legal advisers (*conseils juridiques*) to form the new profession of *avocat.* The latter's work now revolves around three different tasks: advice, assistance and legal representation.

The *avocats* possess a monopoly with regard to assisting and representing parties before the courts and the various judicial or disciplinary bodies.

By contrast, in the case of legal consultation and the drawing up of private documents they work alongside other professions authorised by law to act in this particular area.

The *avocats* belong to 183 bar associations (*barreaux*) in metropolitan France and its overseas territories and *départements* set up at the Regional Courts. Each *barreau* is headed by a chairman (*bâtonnier*) and administered by a council, whose responsibility is to consider all questions concerning the exercise of the profession and to ensure that the *avocats* carry out their duties and that their rights are protected.

The profession is characterised by the absence of a national association, since the *avocats* want to ensure the fair representation of all the *barreaux,* especially those of medium size, whose job is to defend litigants in two-thirds of French territory. However, the 1990 law created a national council charged with representing the profession before the public authorities, ensuring the harmonisation of rules and professional practices and carrying out professional training.

In order to be admitted to a *barreau,* it is necessary to have a master's degree in law and a qualifying certificate (*certificat d'aptitude à la profession d'avocat* – CAPA). The holder of the latter becomes a fully qualified *avocat* and is registered as a probationer for two years before being entered on the roll of a *barreau.* Those who have acquired a qualification equivalent to the *avocat* in their country of origin may, under certain conditions and after their knowledge of French has been verified, have themselves registered with a French *barreau.*

B. *Officiers Publics* and *Officiers Ministeriels*

Officiers ministériels may be defined as public office holders with the right to nominate their successors for approval by the government, which appoints them for the exercise of certain public functions.

In this capacity, they are subject to legal provisions and regulations that define the qualifications for their appointment, their eligibility, the area for which they are responsible, the manner in which they are to carry out their functions, and their system of disciplinary procedures. These provisions also lay down mechanisms for providing clients with a collective guarantee and an assurance of the quality of their work and determine the level of remuneration.

The following are *officiers ministériels: avocats* at the Council of State and the Court of Cassation, *avoués* at the Courts of Appeal, bailiffs, notaries, bailiffs and clerks at the Commercial Courts. Of these, the notaries, bailiffs and clerks at the Commercial Courts are, by reason of the authority conferred on them by the legislature to authenticate legal or judicial documents and to enforce judicial decisions, agents for the public authorities and, as such, also have the status of public legal officers (*officiers publics*).

C. Other court auxiliaries (*Auxiliaires de Justice*)

Here it is necessary to mention, on the one hand, the official receivers appointed to liquidate companies who, in co-operation with the Commercial Courts, act in proceedings to turn around companies in difficulties or close their books.

In addition, in order to obtain clarification of technical points raised in the course of various proceedings, the courts enlist the services of experts whose names are on lists drawn up by the Courts of Appeal or, in the case of the national list, by the bureau of the Court of Cassation.

Finally, the courts also engage social workers to supervise and reintegrate young or adult offenders and employ conciliators and legal assistants, who participate directly in the public administration of justice under the supervision of the judges.

VII. Statistical data[1]

A. Activities of the courts

1. Criminal

Number of decisions in 1996 (ordinary law)

Total:	10689466
by the Court of Cassation	5993
the Courts of Appeal	40508
the Assize Courts	2369
the Criminal Courts	397433
the Police Courts	803105
Juvenile Courts	56578
fixed penalties	9440058

1. Data from 1996.

2. Civil
Number of decisions in 1996

Total (decisions on the merits only)		2014203
proceedings on the merits (ordinary law)		1335813
référé proceedings		308196
Specialised courts[1] (excluding *référés*)		*678390*
Court of Cassation		20420
Courts of Appeal		203997
Regional Courts		655315
	(+ 124052 *référés*)	
Commercial Courts		263282
	(+ 51007 *référés*)	
District Courts		456081
	(+ 81911 *référés*)	
Industrial Conciliation Tribunals		159489
	(+ 51226 *référés*)	
Social Security Tribunals		116675
Juvenile Courts (care measures)		138944

1. Source: *Les chiffres clés de la Justice.* 1997, publication of the Ministry of Justice.

Germany

I. Introduction

The organisation of the judicial system of the Federal Republic of Germany is characterised by two criteria:

– the federal structure of the Federal Republic of Germany;
– the division into several branches of jurisdiction.

The federation is comprised of states, which have in principle autonomous statehood. These states are, according to the Preamble of the Basic Law: Baden-Württemberg, Bavaria, Berlin, Brandenburg, Bremen, Hamburg, Hesse, Mecklenburg-Western Pomerania, Lower Saxony, North-Rhine/Westphalia, Rhineland-Palatinate, Saarland, Saxony, Saxony-Anhalt, Schleswig-Holstein and Thuringia. This means that a distinction has to be made between the federation (*Bund*), with its parliament (*Bundestag*), its government and its courts on the one hand and the several states (*Länder*) with their own parliaments, governments and courts on the other.

The jurisdiction is divided into several branches. Apart from the constitutional jurisdiction, which has a specific and fundamental importance in the entire judicial and constitutional system, there are five main branches of jurisdiction: ordinary jurisdiction, administrative jurisdiction, finance jurisdiction, labour jurisdiction, social jurisdiction. In all branches of jurisdiction courts exist in the *Länder,* and in each case a federal court, which has final appellate jurisdiction. In other words, the structure of the German judicial system is both a vertical one (courts of the *Länder* and, on the highest level, a court of the *Bund*) and at the same time a horizontal one (courts in the several branches of jurisdiction).

Finally, the Parliament can establish, under the Constitution, courts for special fields of jurisdiction. It has done so in the case of the courts of honour for special professional groups like attorneys-at-law and chartered accountants.

II. Constitutional jurisdiction

The federal Constitutional Court (*Bundesverfassungsgericht*) sitting at Karlsruhe is an independent constitutional organ. It decides according to the Basic Law on, *inter alia:*

a. disputes on the rights and obligations of supreme federal organs;
b. differences of opinion on rights and obligations of the federation and of the federal states;
c. compatibility of federal or state (*Land*) law with the Basic Law; compatibility of state law with federal law;
d. constitutional complaint (*Verfassungsbeschwerde*);
e. unconstitutionality of political parties;
f. forfeiture of basic rights;
g. accusations raised by the federal Parliament or the federal Council (*Bundesrat*) against the federal President or accusations against judges on the ground of a violation of the Constitution;
h. validity of elections or of a seat in parliament.

Of special significance is the constitutional complaint. Anyone may lodge such a complaint with the federal Constitutional Court on the allegation that one of his fundamental rights has been violated by the public powers (an administrative authority, a court or the Parliament).

The Constitutional Courts of the federal states have similar tasks within the framework of state Constitutions.

III. Ordinary jurisdiction

Courts of ordinary jurisdiction are the Local Court (*Amtsgericht*), the Regional Court (*Landgericht*), the Higher Regional Court (*Oberlandesgericht;* in Berlin: *Kammergericht*), and the Federal Court of Justice in Karlsruhe. There are about 706 local courts, 116 regional courts and 24 higher regional courts. Only in Bavaria there is, in addition, the Supreme Regional Court of Bavaria (*Bayerisches Oberstes Landesgericht*). As a court of the federation, the Federal Court of Justice stands at the summit of courts of ordinary jurisdiction.

Ordinary jurisdiction includes civil and criminal matters. Jurisdiction in civil matters is divided into contentious and non-contentious jurisdiction.

The present Constitution of the courts of ordinary jurisdiction is based on the Constitution of the Courts Act of 27 January 1877, which has, however, undergone various amendments since. Rules on the Constitution of the courts in other branches of jurisdiction are contained in the respective court rules such as the Administrative Court Rules, the Finance Court Rules, the Labour Court Rules, and the Social Court Rules. In addition, to this, the Basic Law contains a number of essential principles for the Constitution of the courts. Articles 20, paragraph 3, and 28, paragraph 1, of the Basic Law, for instance, contain the principle of division of powers among the legislative, the executive and the judiciary. The judicial power is vested in the judges (Article 92 of the Basic Law) who are personally and objectively independent and only subject to the law (Article 97, paragraph 1, of the Basic Law). The judges, who are appointed on a permanent and full-time basis, cannot against their will be posted to another court or retired before the expiration of their term of office except by virtue of a judicial decision and only on the grounds and in the form provided by law. The Basic Law, furthermore, guarantees the right of recourse to the courts in all cases where a person's rights have been violated by public authorities (Article 19, paragraph 4, of the Basic Law). Article 101, paragraph 1, of the Basic Law, finally provides that no one may be removed from his "lawful judge". This entails the necessity of determining in advance, clearly and unequivocally – in accordance with the law and by the allocation of cases among the judges of the court – the judge who shall be competent for each given case. The judgment of a court whose composition has been determined in an arbitrary way and not in accordance with these requirements will not be upheld on appeal, regardless of its contents. What is decisive for the determination of the "lawful judge" is the allocation of cases made before the beginning of each business year by the "Präsidium" (judges' council) of a court. Under a Law of 26 May 1972, the judges of each court now elect a "Präsidium". Its composition – there can be up to 9 judges on it – depends, amongst other things, on the number of judges sitting in the respective court.

The public prosecutors are also organs who are responsible for the administration of justice. Every court has its public prosecutor's office. The public prosecutor's functions are exercised at the Federal Court of Justice (*Bundesgerichtshof*) by the Federal Prosecutor General (*Generalbundesanwalt*) and several federal prosecutors (*Bundesanwälte*); at the Higher Regional Courts (*Oberlandesgerichte*) and the Regional Courts (*Landgerichte*) by state prosecutors (*Staatsanwälte*), and at the Local Courts (*Amtsgerichte*) by state prosecutors and district prosecutors (*Amtsanwälte*). The Federal Prosecutor General and the federal prosecutors come under the control of the Federal Minister of Justice, the state prosecutors and district prosecutors under that of the Ministers for Justice of the individual federal states.

It is the public prosecutor's function to institute proceedings in all cases involving punishable acts. He or she is in charge of the investigation proceedings, preferring the public charge and at the trial representing before the court the state's right to prosecute. The police authorities have to follow the instructions of the public prosecutor. But, different from the public prosecutors of the federal states, the federal prosecutors are competent for investigations and for the preferment of charges only in certain cases coming under the law of treason.

The public prosecutors are entirely independent in relation to the courts, but, on the other hand, they must not take up a partial position against the accused either. Their duty is to assist the court in reaching a just decision. The law, therefore, makes it incumbent on the public prosecutor to investigate not only the circumstances that are liable to incriminate an accused, but also those that might serve to exonerate him. The public prosecutor's function of contributing to the finding of the truth becomes particularly apparent from the fact that he has to give an opinion on the appeals and petitions for review filed by an accused person.

The attorneys-at-law, too, although professionally independent, have the status of an organ of the administration of justice. They can, amongst other things, appear before all local courts in the Federal Republic of Germany, and in criminal matters – as defence counsel – also before any other court. But in civil matters they can appear before the Regional Court and the higher courts only if they are admitted to the court concerned in the individual case. In those matters, contrary to the proceedings before the Local Court, representation by counsel is *compulsory*. This so-called "compulsion to be represented by counsel" (*Anwaltszwang*) exists also in certain other branches of jurisdiction. In criminal proceedings – especially in cases involving serious crime – there are cases where defence by counsel is mandatory. The geographical restriction which applies only for court representation in civil matters was relaxed on 1 January 2000 (in the federal states Brandenburg, Mecklenburg-Western Pomerania, Saxony, Saxony-Anhalt and Thuringia this will only be relaxed on 1 January 2005). From this point in time, the restriction of the entitlement to representation to the attorneys-at-law who are admitted to the court will only apply in proceedings before the Higher Regional Courts and the Federal Court of Justice. Until 31 December 2004 representation in the aforementioned federal states is only possible by attorneys-at-law who are admitted to one of the Local Courts or Regional Courts in these federal states.

Not only professional judges, who have obtained their "qualification for the office of judge" by passing two state examinations, participate in the adjudicating process, but also, to a considerable extent, laymen (*Schöffen*) versed in the matter concerned, and also unversed ones, and this in particular in criminal matters in proceedings before the chambers for commercial matters, in proceedings under labour law and in proceedings before the Administrative Courts, the Finance Courts and the Social Courts.

To relieve the judges – especially in the field of non-contentious litigation – a special type of court officer, the *Rechtspfleger,* was introduced into the court system at the beginning of this century. The range of the functions exercised today by the *Rechtspfleger* within the entire administration of justice has become wider and wider over the years. Although not vested with judicial powers, he works independently in many fields, for instance in that of non-contentious litigation in land register matters and in authenticating matters. He undergoes special courses organised for the particular requirements of his office, including courses in legal theory; he is an appointed civil servant who, although not enjoying the constitutional privileges of a judge, is independent in his decisions on the matters dealt with by him.

A. Civil matters

In actions involving property disputes, the competence of the Court of First Instance is determined as a rule by the value of the matter in dispute, the so-called "disputed value" (*Streitwert*). But there are certain cases under civil law in which the Local Court or the Regional Court is the Court of First Instance regardless of the "disputed value". If in a given case a particular court does not have the exclusive local or material jurisdiction, an agreement among the parties as to jurisdiction is admissible.

The Local Court

All cases coming under the civil law jurisdiction of the Local Court are decided by the local judge. The only exception to this rule is the Agricultural Court which is competent for certain special matters and composed of a local judge and two lay judges. The Local Court has jurisdiction *ratione materiae* when the "disputed value" is not more than 10000 Deutschmarks at the present time. It is competent regardless of the value of the matter in dispute, *inter alia,* in matters involving rent, alimony and paternity matters and also in matrimonial matters and certain other special matters.

The Local Courts are also competent in the first instance in matters of non-contentious jurisdiction (including matters of guardianship, inheritance matters, land register, register of commercial enterprises, agricultural matters).

The remedies against a judgment given or order made by the Local Courts are the *Berufung* (appeal against a judgment) and the *Beschwerde* (appeal against orders and decisions which are not judgments). The court competent to decide on these remedies is the Regional Court. Only in paternity matters and in agricultural matters both these appeals lie to the Higher Regional Court. Where there is no remedy against the judgments made by the Regional Court on a *Berufung,* an order made by the Regional Court on a *Beschwerde* against a decision of the Local Court can, under certain circumstances, be appealed against by means of a *Weitere Beschwerde* to the Higher Regional Court.

The Regional Court

The Regional Court generally gives its decisions as a court of first instance and as a court of second instance by chambers composed of three professional judges. Where, however, a commercial matter has to be decided on, the chamber for commercial matters may be seized of the case on the application of one of the parties to the dispute. This chamber is composed of one professional judge and two lay judges versed in commercial matters. If the parties consent, it is possible for actions involving property claims to be decided upon in the first instance by a single judge.

Apart from being competent as a court of first instance in actions with a "disputed value" of more than 10000 Deutschmarks, the Regional Courts are competent, *inter alia,* for claims for compensation against the treasury, for patent disputes and for cartel matters.

The remedies against the judgment given and orders made by the Regional Court in its capacity as a court of first instance are the *Berufung* or the *Beschwerde.* The courts competent to decide on these are the Higher Regional Courts.

The Higher Regional Court

As far as matters under civil law are concerned, the Higher Regional Court is a mere court of appeal. It decides in a composition of three professional judges or, in agricultural matters, three professional judges and two lay judges.

The Federal Court of Justice

The Federal Court of Justice decides on the petitions for review lodged against the judgments of the Higher Regional Courts. In legal disputes involving property claims the admissibility of a petition for review is largely dependent on the value of the cause of complaint (*Beschwer*) which, for reasons of lightening the burden of the Federal Court of Justice, has to be at least 60000 Deutschmarks at the present time. The Court of Appeal does however have the option of refusing to accept the petition for review if there is no fundamental significance. In certain other cases it is necessary to file an application to the Higher Regional Court for leave to lodge a petition for review. The Higher Regional Court has to give leave regardless of the value of the cause for complaint in cases involving questions of law of fundamental importance and in cases where its own decision, the object of appeal, departs from a decision of the Federal Court of Justice.

Contrary to the remedy of *Berufung,* that of the petition for review can only be founded on the allegation that the decision is based on a violation of the law. The Federal Court of Justice does not review the facts. But under certain circumstances it can remit the case to the Higher Regional Court for that purpose.

The decisions of the Federal Court of Justice are given by chambers of five judges and in agricultural matters by chambers of three professional judges and two lay judges.

Number of cases filed in 1996 in proceedings of contentious civil jurisdiction:

- number of actions under civil law filed with the Local Courts,
  total: 2152095
  of which family matters: 465135
- number of actions under civil law filed with the Regional Courts
  in the first instance: 422995
  appeals: 101394
  number of actions under civil law filed with the Higher Regional Courts
  in their capacity as appeal courts, total: 90206
  of which family matters: 23510
  number of actions under civil law filed with the Federal Court of Justice
  (petitions for review), total: 3888

B. Criminal matters

The competence of the Criminal Courts as courts of first instance is determined mainly by the gravity and significance of the offence concerned. The competence of the Courts of Higher Instance is determined by the question of which court has been the Court of First Instance.

The Local Court

The Local Court is competent for offences of minor gravity and significance. It cannot impose higher sentences than four years' imprisonment nor preventive detention (*Sicherungsverwahrung*), nor confinement in a mental hospital. The Local Court's competence is distributed between the single judge and the so-called *Schöffengericht* (one professional judge, two lay judges). The single judge adjudicates on minor misdemeanours if the charge has been preferred by a private person or if a sentence of no more than two years' imprisonment is to be expected. The *Schöffengericht* tries and decides on cases where a sentence of not more than four years' imprisonment is expected and the public prosecutor did not prefer the charge to the Regional Court because of the special importance of the case. In special cases the *Schöffengericht* may act as *Erweitertes Schöffengericht* (two professional judges, two lay judges), namely, if owing to the volume of the matter the participation of a second professional judge is necessary.

The Regional Court

The Regional Court is competent for serious crime. The Courts of First Instance in such cases are the Great Criminal Chambers and the *Schwurgerichte* (three professional judges, two lay judges). The Great Criminal Chamber is competent for all crimes not coming within the competence of the Local Courts. It has jurisdiction, furthermore, for all cases of gross misdemeanours and felonies in respect of which the public prosecutor has preferred the charge to the Great Criminal Chamber because the sentence to be expected may be more than four years' imprisonment or because the case is of particular importance. The *Schwurgericht* has jurisdiction over crimes of the most serious kind, in particular, wilful homicide (murder, manslaughter and so on).

The Higher Regional Court

The Higher Regional Court is competent as a court of first instance in the case of certain grave offences against the laws of treason. The decision is made in those cases by a Chamber for Criminal Matters composed of three or five professional judges.

The judgment of a single judge and of the *Schöffengericht* can be appealed against by the remedy of *Berufung*. The court competent for deciding on the *Berufung* is the Small Criminal Chamber with the Regional Court (one professional judge, two lay judges). In both cases a petition for review may be lodged with the Higher Regional Court as a further remedy. Under certain conditions it is also admissible to file a petition for review to the Higher Regional Court directly instead of first filing a *Berufung*. If in a question of law the Higher Regional Court wishes to depart from a decision of another Higher Regional Court or of the Federal Court of Justice, it has to submit the questions of law to the Federal Court of Justice for the latter's decision. The Federal Court of Justice decides, moreover, on petitions for a review of the judgments given by the Great Criminal Chamber in its capacity as court of first instance of the *Schwurgericht* and of the Higher Regional Court.

The remedy of *Berufung* lodged against a judgment of the local judge or of the *Schöffengericht* leads to a re-hearing in which the entire circumstances of the case, that is to say, the facts and also the law applied, are heard and tried once more, but the *Berufung* may also be confined to certain specific points, such as the sentence.

The remedy of *Revision* (petition for review) lodged against a judgment of the Regional Court given on an appeal or against a judgment of the Regional Court in its capacity as court of first instance, gives rise to a review of the judgment as to the law. It can be founded on a violation of substantive law or on a violation of procedural provisions. If the court dealing with the petition for review is satisfied that the petition for review has merit, it sets aside the judgment appealed against and also the factual findings if they are affected by the violation of law. As a rule, it remits the case to the lower court; in exceptional cases it may also decide itself.

The office of *Schöffe* (lay assessor) is an honorary one. The *Schöffe* enjoys the full rights and has the same duties in the trial and in the deliberations for reaching a judgment as the professional judges. Lay assessors and professional judges therefore decide together on the guilt of an accused and on the sentence to be imposed in case of a conviction. In this way the participation of lay assessors in the administration of justice safeguards the direct influence of the people on the decisions of the courts. A verdict by jury alone does not exist in the Federal Republic of Germany.

Juvenile Courts

Within the framework of juvenile jurisdiction, special Juvenile Courts are competent for the adjudication of all offences committed by young persons between the age of 14 and 21 years. When imposing their sanctions, the Juvenile Courts are not bound by the levels of punishment provided by the general penal laws. For juveniles (14 to 18 years of age) and for those young adults (18 to 21 years of age) who have to be treated in the same way as juveniles because of the stage of their mental development or who have committed any such offences as are typical of juveniles, the Juvenile Courts first of all impose measures of education or correction. Only where these do not suffice because the dangerous tendencies of the accused concerned are too strong or because the guilt is too grave is a sentence of juvenile imprisonment imposed. This type of sentence is served in special juvenile prisons and organised in such a way as to mend the juvenile's ways. If a young adult is sentenced under general penal law it is possible to mitigate the sentence.

If, owing to a lack of maturity, a juvenile is not responsible criminally or if the sentence to be considered is only an educative one, the Juvenile Courts may leave the choice and the ordering of the necessary measures to the guardianship judge.

The juvenile judge sitting alone in the Local Court as court of first instance is competent in cases in which only measures of education, means of correction or additional penalties and consequences admissible under the Juvenile Court Act are to be expected. He is not competent for imposing juvenile imprisonment of more than one year. The Juvenile Court (*Jugendschöffengericht*), composed of one judge and two lay judges in the Local Court, is competent with regard to any offence not belonging to the jurisdiction of another juvenile court.

The Juvenile Chamber of the Regional Court is competent as court of first instance in matters which under general provisions fall within the jurisdiction of a Court of Assize, that is for certain very serious offences, in particular for offences of homicide committed with intent.

The Juvenile Chamber is competent as an appeal court also for hearing and deciding on appeals (*Berufungen*) against the judgments of the juvenile judges and those of the Juvenile Courts composed of judge and jury.

The Criminal Chamber of the Higher Regional Court is competent for hearing and deciding on petitions for a review of the judgments given by the Juvenile Judge or by the *Jugendschöffengericht* as court of first instance or those given by the Juvenile Chamber on an appeal. The court competent for deciding on petitions for the review of judgments given by the Juvenile Chambers in their capacity as courts of first instance is the Federal Court of Justice.

For certain serious offences under the laws of treason, the Ordinary Courts are competent, and not the Juvenile Courts.

If a person has filed an admissible *Berufung* he can no longer file a petition for review of the judgment obtained on *Berufung*.

The juvenile judges, juvenile prosecutors and lay judges with the Juvenile Courts are expected to have pedagogical abilities and experience in the treatment of juveniles.

In proceedings involving juveniles, the public is always excluded. In proceedings involving young adults, the public may be excluded if this is necessary for educative reasons. Persons responsible for the offender's education and legal representatives have far-reaching rights so as to be able to represent their educative interests.

The Juvenile Courts assistance organisation (*Jugendgerichtshilfe*) explores the personality of the accused and his development and surroundings and puts forth in the proceedings the educative, social and welfare points of view. Where necessary, expert opinions may also be called for.

C. Breaches of regulations (*Ordnungswidrigkeiten*)

Apart from offences, the German law knows breaches of regulations (*Ordnungswidrigkeiten*). These are violations of the law which, because of their small degree of moral demerit, are not regarded as criminal, although certain rights of others protected by the law are injured or endangered by them. The scale of such breaches of regulations is a wide one and includes, for instance, contraventions of road traffic rules as well as violations of the law on restrictive practices.

The sanction for a breach of regulation is a fine, which may be quite substantial in certain cases. It is an appeal to one's duties and is not accompanied by any grave injury to one's reputation. In addition to a fine, secondary measures can be ordered, for instance the confiscation of certain objects or the prohibition to drive a vehicle.

The law on breaches of regulations directly links the competences of administrative authorities and those of the courts of ordinary jurisdiction. The authorities primarily competent for the prosecution of breaches of regulations are the administrative authorities. The public prosecutor's office, however, can take over the prosecution. The administrative authority is also the authority imposing the fine, namely by way of an injunction (*Bußgeldbescheid*). This injunction can be challenged by a protest addressed to the administrative authority (*Einspruch*). The protest is decided on by a court of ordinary jurisdiction, that is to say, by a single judge of the Local Court (*Amtsgericht*) or, in cartel matters, by a Higher Regional Court. The judicial decision in its turn can be challenged by means of an objection (*Rechtsbeschwerde*). As in the case of a petition for review, it can be supported only by the allegation of a violation of the law. An objection filed against a decision of the Local Court is decided upon by the High Regional Court. In cartel matters it is the Federal Court of Justice which decides on an objection. The authority competent finally for enforcing the decision about the breach of regulation fine is, in principle, against the administrative authority.

D. Patents

The Ordinary Courts also include the Federal Patents Court (*Bundespatentgericht*), which acts in proceedings against decisions given by the Federal Patent Office. The appellate instance is the Federal Court of Justice.

IV. Administrative jurisdiction

In the Federal Republic of Germany there are general administrative courts and special administrative courts, the latter being the Finance Courts and the Courts for Social Affairs. Although the disputes on which these courts have to decide are to a great extent similar, each of the three branches of jurisdiction dealing with public law has its own procedure act: the Administrative Court Rules, the Finance Court Rules and the Act concerning the Courts for Social Affairs. Previous efforts on a legal policy level to unify the three sets of procedural rules are still being discussed but no specific efforts to pursue this are currently being made.

Courts with general administrative jurisdiction are: the Administrative Court (*Verwaltungsgericht*), the Higher Administrative Court (*Oberverwaltungsgericht*) and the Federal Administrative Court (*Bundesverwaltungsgericht*). In Germany there are 52 administrative courts, 16 higher administrative courts and, as the Court of Highest Instance, the Federal Administrative Court, which has its seat in Berlin (shortly to be in Leipzig).

The Courts of General Administrative Jurisdiction decide on all disputes under public law that are not of the kind as to come under constitutional law, unless jurisdiction of another court has been expressly provided for by federal law. By an action brought to the Administrative Court, a plaintiff can request the annulment of an administrative act (*Anfechtungsklage*) or apply for a judgment obliging the performance of an administrative act which had been refused or omitted (*Verpflichtungsklage*), or apply for an order requiring some other performance (*Leistungsklage*) or for a declaratory judgment (*Feststellungsklage*).

A. The Administrative Court

The Administrative Court decides as a court of first instance by chambers composed of three professional judges and two lay judges. The lay judges do not participate when orders are made outside an oral hearing and when court notices are issued (decisions in written proceedings in simple cases). If the matter does not show any particular problems of fact or law and the question of law does not have any fundamental significance, the chamber is usually expected to pass on the litigation to one of its members to decide as a single judge. The remedy against judgments of the Administrative Courts is the appeal on fact and law (*Berufung*) to the Higher Administrative Court; the Higher Administrative Court must give leave to appeal. An appeal on fact and law is only admissible if serious doubts as to the correctness of the judgment made by the Court of First Instance exist, if the case involves particular problems of fact or law, if the question of law is of fundamental significance, if the judgment differs from a decision of the Higher Administrative Court, the Federal Administrative Court, the Joint Panel of the Highest Federal Courts or the Federal Constitutional Court and is based on this differing view, or if the judgment of the Court of Appeal on fact and law is alleged to contain, and actually contains, a procedural error on which the decision may be based. In a number of cases, these being subject to separate statutory regulation, an appeal on fact and law is excluded; the remedy in such a case is a petition for review (*Revision*) to the Federal Administrative Court. In general, the option of a leap-frog review (*Sprungrevision*) also exists – that is, a review bypassing the instance of appeal, if those involved agree and the Administrative Court gives leave to appeal. Appeal against orders made by the Administrative Courts is made by way of an objection (*Beschwerde*) to the Higher Administrative Courts; just as for an appeal, leave must be given by the Higher Administrative Court for an objection.

B. The Higher Administrative Courts

The Higher Administrative Courts, known as administrative tribunals in some of the federal states, are in some cases courts of first instance, particularly in proceedings which involve the approval of large-scale technical projects. Furthermore, Higher Administrative Courts decide on the validity of building schemes as well as in some federal states on the validity of other legal provisions ranking lower than federal state law (*Normenkontrollverfahren*).

A judgment of the Higher Administrative Court can be challenged by those involved by means of a petition for review to the Federal Administrative Court, if leave is given by the Higher Administrative Court. A petition for review is only admissible if the question of law involved is of fundamental significance, if the judgment differs from a decision of the Federal Administrative Court, the Joint Panel of the Highest Federal Courts or the Federal Constitutional Court, or if a procedural error has been made. If the Higher Administrative Court does not give leave for the petition for review, this can then be contested by means of an objection.

A petition for review may only be based on the violation of federal law.

The panels of the Higher Administrative Court are composed of three professional judges; the federal state parliament may provide for adjudication by panels composed of five judges, of whom two may also be lay judges.

C. The Federal Administrative Court

The Federal Administrative Court (*Bundesverwaltungsgericht*) decides on petitions for review of judgments of the Higher Administrative Court and, if there is no appeal on fact and law, also of judgments of the Administrative Court. The Federal Administrative Court is, in addition to this, the Court of Appeal for judgments of the Federal Disciplinary Court (*Bundesdisziplinargericht*) and the Armed Forces Disciplinary Courts (*Truppendienstgerichte*). As a court of first instance, the Federal Administrative Court is competent in disputes between the federation and the federal states, in actions against prohibitions of associations declared by the Federal Minister of the Interior, as well in actions against the federation, which are based on operations under service regulations within the scope of the Federal Intelligence Service (*Bundesnachrichtendienst*). Furthermore, the Federal Administrative Court is the competent Court of First Instance under a number of specialist laws.

The panels of the Federal Administrative Court are composed of five judges and when orders are made outside an oral hearing they are composed of three judges.

V. Finance jurisdiction

In the field of finance jurisdiction there are only two instances: the Finance Courts (*Finanzgerichte*) and the Federal Finance Court (*Bundesfinanzhof*). In the Federal Republic of Germany there are a total of 19 Finance Courts. The Federal Finance Court has its seat in Munich.

A. The Finance Courts

The Finance Courts decide on matters concerning public charges, in particular, on disputes about taxes and customs duties. For some of these matters the Administrative Courts are competent (in particular, for disputes about local taxes). Actions can be brought before the Finance Courts to demand the annulment of an administrative act of the fiscal authorities, in particular, a notice of tax assessment; furthermore, an application can also be made to oblige an authority to perform an administrative act which had been refused or omitted, and an action for declaratory judgment is also admissible.

At Finance Courts (courts of first instance) panels are set up. The panels give their decisions composed of three professional judges and two lay judges. The lay judges do not participate when orders are made outside an oral hearing and when court notices are issued (decisions in written proceedings in simple cases). If the matter does not show any particular problems of fact or law and the question of law does not have any fundamental significance, the chamber may pass on the litigation to one of its members to decide as a single judge.

A petition for review against the judgment of a Finance Court can be lodged with the Federal Finance Court. Leave must be given to lodge a petition for review in the judgment by the Finance Court. The grounds for leave correspond to those which apply to a petition for review in administrative court procedure (petition for review for reasons of fundamental significance, on the grounds of divergence from another judicial decision, or for procedural reasons). If leave is not given by the Finance Court for a petition for review, an objection against refusal of leave (*Nichtzulassungsbeschwerde*) can be lodged within one month.

The remedy of the objection to the Federal Finance Court is possible against orders of the Finance Court.

B. The Federal Finance Court

The Federal Finance Court is competent for decisions on petitions for review of judgments and on objections. The Federal Finance Court decides by panels composed of five judges; orders made outside an oral hearing are made by three judges.

VI. Labour jurisdiction

A. Jurisdiction

Courts of labour jurisdiction are the Labour Courts (*Arbeitsgerichte*) – in all 124 labour courts – the Regional Labour Courts (*Landesarbeitsgerichte*) – in all 19 regional labour courts – and the Federal Labour Court (*Bundesarbeitsgericht*) at Kassel.

These courts for labour matters have independent civil law jurisdiction for settling:

a. in judgment proceedings (proceedings for securing a judgment): legal disputes under civil law arising:

– between the parties to a collective wage agreement or between any such parties and a third party, or about the existence or otherwise of a collective wage agreement, or from any tortious acts so far as any measures for the purpose of an industrial strike or any questions connected with the freedom to associate are concerned; or

– between an employer and an employee about the employment relationship or about the existence or otherwise of an employment contract, or from negotiations on the conclusion of an employment contract, or from the after-effects of such a contract, or from any tortious acts so far as they are connected with the employment contract; or

– between workers/employees from their common work, or arising from any tortious acts so far as these are connected with the employment relationship; or

– between workers and/or employees on the one hand and employers on the other if the exclusive subject of the action is a claim for payment of a fixed or assessed amount of remuneration for an invention:

b. in order proceedings (proceedings for securing a court order): disputes:

– arising from the Act on the Constitution of Business and Industrial Enterprises (*Betriebsverfassungsgesetz*); and

– arising about the capacity of an association to be a party to a collective wage agreement.

Civil actions between legal entities under private law and persons authorised by law to represent them, either alone or as members of the representative organ of the legal entity concerned, do not come within the competence of the Labour Courts, but they may be brought to these courts by virtue of an agreement to that effect. Other actions not normally dealt with by the Labour Courts can be filed with them in exceptional cases if the claim concerned is legally or economically connected with a civil action of the kind mentioned under *a* above and already pending with a labour court or being introduced simultaneously and if jurisdiction in the case concerned does not lie exclusively with any other court.

In matters which have to be decided by the Labour Courts it is impossible, in principle, to exclude the latter's jurisdiction by contract. The only exception is that in favour of the parties to a collective wage agreement who are allowed:

– in civil disputes between them about a collective wage agreement or about the existence or otherwise of a collective wage agreement, to exclude the jurisdiction of the Labour Courts generally or for a given case by an express understanding to the effect that the matter shall be decided by a court or arbitration;

– in civil disputes arising from an employment contract which is determined by the terms of a collective wage agreement, to exclude the jurisdiction of the Labour Courts by an express understanding to the effect that the matter in question shall be decided on by a court or arbitration, if the persons to whom the collective wage agreement applies are predominantly stage artists, persons engaged in the film industry, circus performers, or captains and crew members of the German merchant navy.

B. The Labour Courts

The Labour Courts (*Arbeitsgerichte*) are courts of the federal states; they are courts of first instance whose decisions are given by chambers (*Kammern*)

composed of one professional judge and one lay judge each from the workers'/employees' side and from the side of the employers.

The remedy admissible against the judgments of the Labour Courts is the appeal (*Berufung*) to the *Land* Labour Courts if the value of the matter as assessed by the Labour Court is 800 Deutschmarks or more and if that court has given leave to appeal because of the fundamental significance of the question of law involved. In special cases and under certain conditions the appeal instance can be skipped and a petition for review filed with the Federal Labour Court directly.

The orders of the Labour Court in order proceedings by which the proceedings are terminated can be appealed against by means of an objection (*Beschwerde*) to the *Land* Labour Court.

C. The Higher Labour Courts

The Higher Labour Courts (*Landesarbeitsgerichte*) – also courts of the federal states – are courts of second instance; their decisions both in judgment proceedings and in order proceedings are equally made by chambers (*Kammern*) which are composed, as a rule, of one professional judge and one lay judge each from the workers'/employees' side and from the side of the employers.

The legal remedy against a judgment of a Higher Labour Court is the petition for review to the Federal Labour Court if the former court has given leave in the judgment which is to be reviewed to file such a petition. Leave shall be given to lodge a petition for review if the question of law is of fundamental significance, or if the judgment differs from a decision of the Joint Panel of the Highest Federal Courts, from a decision of the Federal Labour Court, or, as long as a decision of the Federal Labour Court has not been given, from a decision of a different chamber of the same higher labour court or of a different higher labour court, and if the decision is based on that differing view. The divergence from the decision of another court means that a petition for review is thereafter no longer admissible on its own, although it does oblige the Higher Labour Court to give leave and it can be submitted along with the objection against refusal of leave (*Nichtzulassungsbeschwerde*) in a case of refusal of admission.

The decisions made by the Higher Labour Courts can be challenged by means of the so-called complaint (*Rechtsbeschwerde*), to be lodged with the Federal Labour Court. A precondition for admissibility is that the complaint is admitted by the Higher Labour Court, or, in the case of an objection against refusal of leave, that it is admitted by the Federal Labour Court. The preconditions for admission by the Higher Labour Court correspond to those which apply to leave for a petition for review.

D. The Federal Labour Court

The Federal Labour Court (*Bundesarbeitsgericht*) is a supreme court of the federation; it is a court of third instance which decides in judgment proceedings and in order proceedings by chambers (Senate) composed of one professional judge as presiding judge, two professional judges as assessors and one lay judge each from the workers'/employees' side and from the side of the employers. Apart from these, a Great Chamber is set up at the Federal Labour Court which is composed of the President of the Federal Labour Court as presiding judge, the senior among the Presidents of the chambers, four additional professional judges of the Federal Labour Court and two lay judges each from the workers'/employees' side and from the side of the employers. This chamber has to be seized of a case if in a question of law one of the chambers of the Federal Labour Court means to depart from the decision of another chamber of the Federal Labour Court or of the Great Chamber. In a case involving a question of law of fundamental significance, moreover, the chamber dealing with the case can ask for a decision on the matter by the Great Chamber if it is of the opinion that this is necessary for the development of the law or for safeguarding uniform decisions.

VII. Social jurisdiction

In the field of social jurisdiction there are, altogether, 69 social courts (*Sozialgerichte*) of first instance, 16 higher social courts (*Landessozialgerichte*) of second instance, and – as the Court of the Federation – the Federal Social Court (*Bundessozialgericht*) of last resort in Kassel.

A. The Social Court

The Social Court decides, as a court of first instance, by chambers composed of one judge and two lay judges. The remedy against a judgment of a Social Court is, on principle, the appeal (*Berufung*) to the Higher Social Court (*Landessozialgericht*), and that against an order of a Social Court is objection (*Beschwerde*) to the Higher Social Court. In certain cases of lesser importance, an appeal is only admissible if the Social Court has given leave to do so. An appeal has to be allowed, *inter alia,* if the case concerned involves a question of law of fundamental importance; if the contested judgment departs from a decision of the Superior Court, that is the Higher Social Court, or if an essential procedural defect is complained of. The plaintiff may skip the appeal instance and file a petition for review directly with the Federal Social Court if the respondent consents.

B. The Higher Social Court

The court of second instance, the Higher Social Court, decides on appeals (*Berufungen*) against judgments and on objections (*Beschwerden*) against orders made by the Social Courts. Its decisions are given by chambers composed of three judges and two lay judges.

The judgments of a Higher Social Court can be challenged by means of a petition for review if the Higher Social Court has given leave to do so. The grounds for leave correspond to those in Administrative Court and Finance Court procedure (petition for review for reasons of fundamental significance, on the grounds of divergence from another judicial decision, or for procedural reasons). Violations of federal law can be complained of by means of a petition for review only.

The orders of the Higher Social Courts cannot be contested by an objection

C. The Federal Social Court

The Federal Social Court decides as a court of both first and last instance on disputes between the federation and the federal states and also in disputes between the federal states. Apart from this, it decides on petitions for the review of judgments of the Higher Social Courts. The chambers of the Federal Social Court are composed of three judges and two lay judges.

VIII. Common Chamber of the Supreme Federal Court

In order to preserve the uniformity of jurisdiction, a Common Chamber of the Supreme Federal Courts has been established by virtue of a law of 1968.

The Common Chamber decides if and when a Supreme Federal Court intends to depart from a decision of another Supreme Federal Court or of the Common Chamber in a question of law.

The Common Chamber is composed of the Presidents of the Supreme Federal Courts, the Presidents of the Chambers of the Supreme Federal Courts involved, and an additional judge from each of these Chambers.

Greece

I. GENERAL

Justice in Greece is one of the three operations of the state, and is, according to the power discrimination principle, independent from the legislative and the executive powers.

It is administered by courts, which consist of ordinary judges, enjoying functional and personal independence. Judges are direct organs of the state, that is their power emanates only from the Constitution and from the laws compatible with it, and in no case are they obliged to comply with provisions of law which are not consistent with the Constitution.

The courts are divided in the three basic categories as outlined below.

A. Administrative Courts

The Administrative Courts' judge disputes between the state as a power and the citizens as administered individuals (in other words, Administrative Courts are those dealing with the solution of administrative disputes, namely disputes arising between the administration bodies and the administered citizens).

1. Ordinary Administrative Courts

The Ordinary Administrative Courts are the following: the Administrative Courts of First Instance and the Administrative Courts of Appeal.

The Administrative Courts of First Instance

These judge in first instance as one-membered or three-membered courts, according to the amount of the dispute, tax cases, cases of the insured of several insurance funds, as well as disputes of an administrative nature between private individuals on the one hand and the public and municipalities or communities on the other hand.

The three-membered Courts of First Instance

These courts also judge cases upon an appeal against judgments of the one-membered Courts of First Instance.

Administrative courts of appeal

These courts judge cases upon appeals against judgments of the three-membered Administrative Courts of First Instance. They also judge in the first instance petitions for the cancellation of acts of the administrative authorities concerning the service status of employees (dismissals, omissions of appointments, promotions, and so on)

Within the framework of operation of the Ordinary Administrative Courts is the institution of the General State Commissioner, whose competence is the administrative supervision of the above-mentioned administrative courts and the exercise of legal remedies against their judgments.

2. Council of State

The Supreme Administrative Court exercises its duties in plenary session and in divisions. The plenary session consists of the President, at least ten privy councillors, two associate judges and the court clerk.

There are six divisions: A, B, C, D, E and F.

The first four divisions (A, B, C and D) exercise the judicial competences of the Council, hold public meetings in open court and consist of their President (Vice-President of the Council of State), two privy councillors, two associate judges and the court clerk (five-membered composition). Each of the above-mentioned divisions also holds meetings in seven-membered composition by the addition of two more privy councillors only in the event of trying cases which are introduced in seven-membered composition by its President or are referred to it by the five-membered composition. The E Division, which is competent for the processing of decrees and the exercise of disciplinary power, is composed of its President (Vice-President of the Council of State), at least one privy councillor, one associate judge, who in the execution of his duties has a decisive vote, and the court clerk.

The F Division is competent for cassations of decisions referring to cases of the Public Revenues Collection Code and compensations arising from administrative disputes; its composition is similar to the composition of the first four divisions.

The main competences of the Council of State are determined by Article 95, paragraph 1, of the Constitution and are exercised as especially provided by the law. The administration has the obligation to comply with the rescinding decisions of the Council of State and the violation of this obligation creates a responsibility for any culpable body, according to the law.

The main competences of the Council of State are the following:

– cancellation of enforceable acts of the administrative authorities for abuse of power or infringement of the law;

– cassation of the final decisions of the Lower Administrative Courts for excess of power or infringement of the law;

– hearing of submitted administrative substantial disputes, according to the Constitution and the laws;

– processing of all decrees having a regulatory character. During the processing of the regulative decrees the Council investigates whether they are consistent with the Constitution and the laws. It also investigates the correct wording and several other issues of minor significance.

A regulative decree, which has not been processed by the Council of State, is declared by the courts illegal and void.

The first three competences are judicial, while the fourth competence is administrative and is assigned to the Council as an advisery body of the central administration. However, the Council retains its judicial character even in the exercise of this administrative competence.

3. The Exchequer and Audit Department

The Exchequer and Audit Department, which is a Supreme Court with a double-natured character, has judicial and administrative competences. It retains its judicial character even during the exercise of its administrative competences. The composition of the Department is similar to the composition of the Council of State. The Department exercises its competences in a plenary session, three divisions and echelons. Its main competences are the following:

– the audit of the state expense;
– the preparation of a report to the Parliament on the annual accounts and the balance sheet of the state;
– the expert opinion on the laws about pensions or recognition of public service for the grant of a pension right;
– the audit of the accounts of the public accountable;
– the hearing of legal remedies in disputes about award of pensions and audit of accounts in general;
– the hearing of cases referring to the responsibility of public civil or military employees for damages which they caused to the state intentionally or through carelessness.

The decisions of the Exchequer and Audit Department are not subject to the control of the Council of State.

B. The Civil Courts

The Civil Courts are competent for all disputes of private law and cases of non-contentious jurisdiction assigned to them by the law.

1. Magistrates' Court

This is a one-membered court and operates in almost all cities and towns of the country. In total 310 magistrates' courts are operating. The Magistrates' Court is composed of one justice of the peace and the court clerk.

The Magistrates' Courts try in principle money disputes which do not exceed 1 000 000 Greek Drachmas in value.

They also try cases of safety measures for the protection of possession or occupancy, some agricultural disputes and other disputes of a minor significance (for example tenancy disputes).

2. One-membered Court of First Instance

This is composed of the President of the judges of the First Instance Court or a judge of the First Instance Court, and the court clerk. It tries in first instance and is competent mainly for the following cases: all disputes appraisable in money, the value of which exceeds 1 000 000 Greek Drachmas, but does not exceed 5 000 000 Greek Drachmas, disputes concerning compensation from car accidents, labour disputes, support and alimony cases, tenancy disputes.

3. Multi-membered Court of First Instance

It is composed of the President of the judges of the First Instance Court, two judges (two judges of the First Instance Court or one judge of the First Instance Court and one associate judge) and the court clerk. The multi-membered Court of First Instance is the First Instance Court with a general competence, namely it tries in principle in first instance all the private law disputes which are not explicitly classified in the competence of the one-membered Court of First Instance or the Magistrates' Court.

It also tries serious cases of non-contentious jurisdiction (such as adoptions, judicial restraint). It also tries in second instance the appeals against judgments of the Magistrates' Court.

4. Court of Appeal

It is composed basically of three judges and the court clerk and in exceptional cases of five judges and the court clerk. The Court of Appeal, as a civil court, tries all the appeals against the judgments of the multi-membered and the one-membered Courts of First Instance. It also has an exceptional competence in some cases such as for example in the disputes from public work contracts, which are brought directly before the Court of Appeal.

*5. Supreme Civil Court (*Arios Pagos*)*

The Supreme Court (*Arios Pagos*) is the supreme civil (revocatory) court and examines upon a cassation whether the Lower Civil Courts correctly applied the law by their judgments. The Supreme Court tries in divisions and in a plenary session. Each of the divisions is composed of one of the Vice-Presidents as presiding judge and four judges of the Supreme Court, and the plenary session from the President or his legal substitute and the judges of the Supreme Court and the district attorney of the Supreme Court.

C. Criminal Courts

Criminal Courts are courts trying criminal cases, and are the following:

- police courts
- one-membered misdemeanour courts
- three-membered misdemeanour courts
- three-membered courts of appeal
- five-membered courts of appeal
- mixed jury first instance courts
- mixed jury courts of appeal
- juvenile courts
- the Supreme Criminal Court.

By virtue of special laws, criminal jurisdiction is exercised by the Court Martial, the Naval Court, the Military Aviation Court, as special courts.

Civilians cannot be brought under the jurisdiction of the above courts.

1. Police Courts

These are one-membered criminal courts and try offences, namely violations against which the law provides punishment of detention or a fine. Police courts are composed of Justices of the Peace, who in this case are renamed judges of the Police Court. Each magistrates' court is a Police Court as well, when it tries criminal cases. Mainly in the big cities there are special Police Courts as well, which try only criminal cases.

In the composition of the Police Courts, the public prosecutor participates as well. His competences are similar to those of the district attorney. The duties of the public prosecutor are mainly discharged by police officers.

2. One-membered Misdemeanour Court

This is composed of one judge of the Misdemeanour Court, the district attorney and the court clerk. The district attorney may be replaced by the deputy district attorney.

The President of the judges of the First Instance Court may try a case as the only judge of the Misdemeanour Court. The One-membered Misdemeanour Court tries basically the misdemeanours against which the law threatens the punishment of imprisonment for up to one year or a fine and the appeals against the judgments of the Police Courts.

3.Three-membered Misdemeanour Court

This court is composed of three ordinary judges, including the President, the district attorney and the court clerk.

In case of inability the replacement of only one judge is permitted by an associate judge of the First Instance Court, by a judge of the Police Court or by a Justice of the Peace.

The Three-membered Misdemeanour Court tries all the misdemeanours which are not brought under the competence of the One-membered Misdemeanour Court and the appeals against the judgments of these latter courts.

4. Three-membered Court of Appeal

This is composed of three judges of the Appeal Court including the President, the district attorney and the court clerk. It tries appeals against judgments of the Three-membered Misdemeanour Courts and as a Court of First Instance some felonies, namely criminal acts, for which a punishment of incarceration for 5 to 20 years or a life imprisonment is threatened, which have a mainly financial and proprietary content, such as drug trafficking, and so on.

5. Five-membered Court of Appeal for Felonies

This court is composed of the President of the judges of the Appeal Court or his substitute as the presiding judge and four judges of the Appeal Court, the district attorney and the court clerk. It tries appeals against judgments of the Three-membered Court of Appeal which have been issued on criminal acts to a felony degree as set out above.

6. Mixed jury (First Instance Court)

This court is composed of the President of the judges of the First Instance Court as presiding judge, two judges of the First Instance Court and four jurymen, who are determined by a draw, the district attorney and the court clerk at the seat of each Court of First Instance. It tries in first instance the most serious felonies, especially crimes against life, serious injuries caused intentionally, rapes, and so on.

7. Mixed Jury Appeal Court

This is composed of the President of the Court of Appeal as presiding judge, two judges of the Appeal Court and four jurymen, the district attorney and the court clerk at the seat of each Court of Appeal. It tries in second instance the appeals against the decisions of the Mixed Jury First Instance Court.

8. Juvenile Courts

These courts try crimes which have been committed by minors, from the age of twelve to seventeen.

The Juvenile Courts are divided as follows:

The One-membered Misdemeanour Juvenile Court

This is composed of one judge of the First Instance Court in each First Instance Court appointed together with one substitute for two years by virtue of a decision of the Supreme Judicial Council.

Three-membered Misdemeanour Juvenile Court

It is composed of a juvenile judge (judge of the First Instance Court), who presides over the court, two judges of the Misdemeanour Court, who are appointed by the President of the judges of the First Instance Court, the district attorney and the court clerk. It tries the most serious crimes committed by juveniles.

Three-membered Juvenile Appeal Court

It is composed of three judges of the Appeal Court, the district attorney and the court clerk, is presided over by the juvenile judge of the Appeal Court, and tries the appeals against the decisions of the One-membered and the Three-membered Juvenile Courts.

The hearings of the Juvenile Courts are held in camera.

*9. Supreme Criminal Court (*Arios Pagos*)*

The Supreme Court which is the Supreme Civil Court, is in parallel the Supreme Criminal Court. It tries the notices of appeal against judgments and the ordinances. Each criminal division of the Supreme Court is composed of one Vice-President or his legal substitute, four judges of the Supreme Court, the district attorney and the clerk.

As a criminal court, in the case in question, the court does not examine the merits of the case, but judges whether the provisions of the laws were correctly applied by the lower courts.

10. District Attorney's Office

In each court, apart from the Police Courts, there is a District Attorney's Office, organised as an independent judicial authority, whose competence is mainly participation in the criminal procedure. The basic mission of the District Attorney's Office is the start of proceedings, the supervision of the interrogation, and the exercise of legal remedies.

The origin and the organisation of the institution have as their model that of France.

11. Court Martial, Naval Court, Military Aviation Court

These constitute special criminal courts within whose competence, without exception, all the crimes committed by the military of the army, navy and air force respectively are classified.

D. Supreme Special Court

The Supreme Special Court, which has the structure of a constitutional court, in that most of the disputes coming under its jurisdiction are of a constitutional nature, is above all the other courts. This is composed of the President of the Council of State, the President of the Supreme Court (*Arios Pagos*), the President of the Exchequer and Audit Department, as well as four privy councillors of the state and four judges of the Supreme Court (*Arios Pagos*), who are appointed by a draw every two years.

The court is presided over by the senior of the Presidents of the Council of State or the Supreme Court. When it exercises its competence for the removal of the conflicts and the litigation regarding the substantial constitutionality or the meaning of provisions of a formal law, two ordinary law professors from law schools of Greek universities also participate in its composition.

Its competences, which are determined restrictively by Article 100 of the Constitution, are the following:

i. the hearing of the objections against the validity of general elections;

ii. the control of the validity and the results of a referendum, which is held according to Article 44, paragraph 2, of the Constitution;

iii. the judgment of incompatibilities or the downfall of Members of Parliament;

iv. removal of conflict between the courts and the administrative authorities or between the Council of State and the Ordinary Administrative Courts on the one hand and the Civil and Criminal Courts on the other hand, or, finally, between the Exchequer and Audit Department and the other courts;

v. removal of disputes about substantial anti-constitutionality or the meaning of provisions of a formal law if contrary decisions of the Council of State, the Supreme Court or the Exchequer and Audit Department were issued on them; and

vi. removal of the contention about the characterisation of rules of international law as generally admitted.

E. Special Court on Mistrial Actions

This court is provided by Article 99 of the Constitution and tries actions for miscarriage of justice against judges. It is composed of the President of the Council of State as its presiding judge, and one privy councillor of the Council of State, one judge of the Supreme Court, one councillor of the Exchequer and Audit Department, two ordinary professors of law at law schools of Greek universities and members of the Supreme Disciplinary Council of Lawyers, whose members are appointed by draw.

F. Special Ministers' Responsibility Court

This court is provided by Article 86 of the Constitution. The court is presided over by the President of the Supreme Court (*Arios Pagos*) and is composed of twelve judges, who are drawn by the Chairman of the Parliament in a public session of all judges of the Supreme Court and the President of the Appeal Court, who have been appointed before the charge.

It is competent to try criminal acts committed by ministers and deputy ministers during the discharge of their duties. It presupposes their committal by the Parliament.

II. Statistical data[1]

A. Administrative Courts

1. Ordinary administrative courts
   a. Administrative courts of first instance 30
   Presidents of first instance courts, judges of first instance courts and associate judges 426
   b. Administrative courts of appeal 9
   Presidents and judges of courts of appeal 195
   c. General Commissariat of State Judges 4
2. Council of State
   Judges 148
3. Exchequer and Audit Department
   Judges 161

B. Civil and Criminal Courts

1. Magistrates' courts 310
   Police courts 41
   Justices of the peace and police court judges 661
2. *a* Courts of first instance 63
   Presidents of first instance courts, judges of first instance courts and associate judges 1 090
   b. District attorney's offices of first instance courts 63
   District attorneys of first instance courts, deputy District attorneys and associate judges 375
3. *a.* Courts of appeal 13
   Presidents and judges of appeal courts 409
   b. District attorney's offices of appeal courts 13
   District attorneys and deputy district attorneys of appeal courts 121
4. *a.* Supreme Court (*Arios Pagos*)
   President, Vice-Presidents and judges of the Supreme Court 59
   b. District attorney's office of the Supreme Court
   District attorney and deputy district attorneys 13

III. Constitutional status of justice in Greece

A. Principle of separation of powers and independence of justice

The principle of separation of powers is today the most fundamental rule of constitutional order in all democratic states. This fundamental principle

1. Athens, February 1998.

which was declared for the first time by Aristoteles in his *Politika* (*Politics*) and took its final form as a doctrine by Montesquieu, who formulated it in a complete and substantial manner in his work *The Spirit of Laws* is enacted in all the Greek Constitutions, from the Constitution of Epidavros in the year 1827, during the Greek War of Independence of 1821, up to the present Constitution of 1975, which establishes it in its Article 26, where it is explicitly provided that: "The legislative function is exercised by the Parliament and the President of the Republic. The executive function is exercised by the President of Republic and the government. The judicial function is exercised by the courts. Their decisions are executed in the name of the Greek People".

From Article 26 of the Constitution it follows that all the state powers, which, according to its Article 1, paragraph 1, emanate from the people (principle of popular sovereignty), are exercised by particular organs of the legislative, the executive and the judicial functions, to which the work of lawmaking, administration and dispensation of justice are distributed respectively. In this way the structure of the state is formed and state organs have a clear distribution of competences determined by strict rules. This means, on the one hand, that the organ of one function is prohibited from developing state activity in a section belonging to the jurisdiction of another function (separation of powers), and on the other hand that a mutual control of functions is established, as regards the limits of their activity (balance of functions). In this meaning the principle of discrimination of powers appears not only as a means of distribution, but at the same time as a means of restriction of state power so that the freedom of individuals may be protected and the concentration of powers be prevented and the balance of the state organs becomes possible with as a further result the limitation of the abuse of its powers. The division of powers is relative since the Constitution itself allows crossings of functions and determines relations of co-operation among organs especially between legislative and executive powers (such as Article 26, paragraph 1). However, beyond this relation originating from the Constitution, within the framework of the regulated balance of the distinct organs, even the general importance of discrimination of powers is today relative as regards the legislative and the executive powers within the framework of the Parliamentary system, since the will of those functions is fused within the unity of the political party which governs. However, this development gives rise to a threat to freedom if the discrimination of powers is not absolute as regards the third function of the state, namely the judicial function. Consequently, the existence of an independent judicial function constitutes the only substantial guarantee for the personal freedom of citizens.

B. Constitutional guarantees of independence of justice

1. General remarks

As mentioned above, in states such as Greece, where the parliamentary system of government prevails, the discrimination between legislative and executive functions in the exercise of the state power and in the realisation of state purposes is not so strict due to the interaction of these functions. On the contrary, the discrimination between the judicial and the other two functions is strict, given that the main mission of the judicial function, namely the administration of justice, is particular in that it excludes any duplication with the other functions, especially in the form of co-operation. Consequently, the perception that the discrimination of functions constitutes a guarantee of freedom for citizens refers mainly to the existence of an independent judicial function.

The Constitution now in force declares explicitly the independence of justice in the provision of Article 87, paragraph 1, where it is provided that: "Justice is administered by courts formed from ordinary judges, enjoying functional and personal independence". Judicial independence is the freedom of judges during the administration of justice. In its broad sense, it means that the judges in the exercise of their office are independent from the other organs of the state, from the litigants but also from other pressure or interest groups (press, trade unions and so on), while in its narrow sense, it is the independence of judges *vis-à-vis* the carriers of public power of the other functions (legislative and executive). At this point, we must stress that judicial independence constitutes a precondition for the exercise of the right to legal protection secured by Article 20, paragraph 1, of the Constitution. According to this provision, every citizen is granted the possibility to resort to the courts in order to set out his (her) views in order to claim his (her) rights and protect his (her) interests. However, it is necessary that these courts be formed of independent judges. Without this precondition, there is no legal protection, since otherwise citizens would be in danger of being unfairly dealt with and losing their rights. As set out above, the Constitution secures the independence of judges in this narrow sense. This independence is divided into the functional and the personal.

2. The functional independence of judges

Meaning and content

Functional independence means that judges administer justice only according to the laws and their conscience without being subject to orders or following instructions or suggestions of other state bodies or hierarchically superior courts. Judicial independence is explicitly secured by the above-mentioned provision of paragraph 1 of Article 87 of the Constitution, while the meaning of functional independence of judges is defined in paragraph 2 of the same article, where it is provided that "judges in the exercise of their duties are subject only to the Constitution and the laws and in no case are obliged to comply with provisions which have been put in violation of the Constitution". From this provision it results clearly that any intervention of the organs of legislative and executive powers in the administration of justice is prohibited, even in the form of sending instructions or circulars, which in no case bind the judges, who are bound only by the Constitution and the law. Executive power through the Minister for Justice is competent only for the administrative management of justice (organisation of justice, infrastructure, financial issues), while, especially the Minister for Justice exercises, according to Article 19 of the Law 1756/1988 (Code of Courts By-Laws and status of judges), as replaced by Article 6 of the Law 1868/1989, a supervision but only on the administrative management of justice and not on the judges. Further, judges are not bound either by orders, instructions or suggestions of their superior judicial authorities or the hierarchically superior courts in relation to a particular case, and the supervision exercised occasionally by the superior or top-ranking judges consists only in the supervision and the issue of general instructions for the good operation of the court services and the district attorney's offices (Article 19, paragraph 2, of the Law 1756/1988 as it is valid today). It must be noted that according to an explicit provision of Article 19, paragraph 2, of the Law 1756/1988 as it is in force today, any instruction, recommendation or suggestion to a judge about a substantial or procedural issue in a particular case or category of cases is inadmissible and constitutes a disciplinary offence. It must also be noted that the term "judges" in the provision of Article 87, paragraph 2, of the Constitution includes all the judges, consequently the district attorneys too, while laws in the meaning of the aforesaid provision are the substantial and not only the typical laws, so that judges are bound not only by any written law provision but also by the customs, since they are also recognised as a source of law.

Special arrangements strengthening the functional independence of judges

The organs and the inspection of judges may affect the independence of judicial judgment in a particular case and, in general, the judge's independence. For this reason, Article 87, paragraph 3, of the Constitution provides that the inspection of ordinary judges is carried out by judges of a higher rank and, exceptionally, by the district attorney and the deputy district attorneys of the Supreme Court (*Arios Pagos*). Besides, whereas the administration could, by the method of transference of judges from one branch to another (such as from the Exchequer and Audit Department to the Council of State) change the composition of a court according to its desires and, in that way, affect the independence of judges, the Constitution in Article 88, paragraph 6, explicitly prohibits the transference of judges. Exceptionally, it allows the transference of ordinary judges for the fulfilment of up to two (according to a recent law) posts of deputy district attorneys of the Supreme Court (*Arios Pagos*) as well as the transference between associate judges of first instance courts and district attorney's offices after a request of the transferred judges. Finally, the strengthening of the functional independence of judges is also protected by the provision of Article 4 of the recent Law 1868/1989, by which the institution of the head in the major courts was abrogated and the heads in the administration of those courts were replaced by collective bodies, which are elected by the judges themselves.

The control of constitutionality of laws

The functional independence of judges is also protected by Article 93, paragraph 4 of the Constitution, according to which the courts are obliged not to apply a law whose content is contrary to the Constitution.

By the aforementioned provision, the discrimination between legislative and judicial functions is realised in a decisive manner and the long-standing practice, which imposed on the courts the control of the constitutionality of laws, refusing to apply the anti-constitutional laws, is validated, a practice known in Greece as of the end of the past century. The rationale of this provision is the view prevailing in Greece that "an anti-constitutional law is not a law".

There is a similar provision in the Constitution of 3 June 1927, in the form of the interpretative declaration under Article 5, where it was provided that "the true meaning of the provision is that the courts are obliged not to apply a law whose content is contrary to the Constitution". Despite the fact that a relevant provision was not included in the Constitutions of 1844, 1864, 1911 and 1952, the obligation of holding such control was generally acceptable, which resulted in the creation, in that way, of one of the few cases of a supplementary constitutional custom.

However, beyond the existence of that custom, the necessity of the provision of Article 94, paragraph 4, was imposed by the existence of Article 87, paragraph 2. In this way, it is certified that the judges are obliged to be loyal only to the Constitution as its keepers and guarantors and to no other authority or body.

As regards the necessity of Article 93, paragraph 4, and the magnitude of its importance, it is noted that without this article and on the basis of the effective parliamentary practice, which makes legislative power submissive to executive power, concentration of all the powers would be in the hands of executive power. By the application of Article 93, paragraph 4, the above danger is prevented, since no one legislative arrangement is applied by the courts unless its constitutionality is controlled.

Finally, it must be noted that the control of constitutionality of laws does not constitute an intervention of the judicial function in the legislative one. All the more so, it does not give an ascendancy of the judicial function over the legislative one. On the contrary, as set out above, the control of constitutionality of laws is a factor of state balance because it makes the courts independent from the legislative function so that they may secure the regular operation of law and order since they do not cancel the law in the particular case. So, according to all the above, the relations of the judicial function to the legislative and the executive ones are governed by the principle of submission of judges to the laws.

As is concluded from the above-mentioned provision of Article 93, paragraph 4, the Greek Constitution follows the general system of control of constitutionality of laws, since all the courts of all instances and jurisdictions are equally competent to proceed to the control of constitutionality of a law, on the basis of which they have to try a case. Concentrated control is provided only exceptionally in Article 100 of the Constitution and only in the event that contrary decisions have been made by two supreme courts regarding the substantial constitutionality of a provision of a formal law.

The control of the substantial and not the typical constitutionality of a law by the courts is made incidentally during the examination of the case under judgment and the court examines the constitutionality, which may also be raised by an objection of the litigants, as a prejudicial matter. If from the control it would result that any of these provisions is anti-constitutional, then the court does not apply that provision in the particular case, but, as has already been pointed out, without having the right to cancel it.

Especially as regards the exceptional concentrated control held by the Supreme Special Court which is provided by Article 100 of the Constitution, this court which is composed of three Presidents of the Supreme Courts (*Arios Pagos,* the Council of State and the Exchequer and Audit Department), four judges of the Supreme Court and four privy councillors of the state, has among other competences (hearing of objections against the validity of the general elections, control of the validity of a referendum, removal of conflict between courts and administrative authorities, and so on) also the competence to remove the contest about the substantial anti-constitutionality of the provisions of a formal law, if contrary decisions were made about them by the Supreme Court, the Council of State or the Exchequer and Audit Department and since there is a case to declare these provisions as anti-constitutional.

A provision of the law which is declared anti-constitutional is invalid as of the date of publication of the relevant decision or of the time appointed by the decision of the court, according to Article 100, paragraph 4.

Finally, control exercised by the Council of State when, according to Article 95, paragraph 1.*a* of the Constitution, it looks into petitions for the abrogation of the enforceable acts of administrative authorities for abuse of power or violation of a law is indirect and incidental, since, when it controls the validity of the acts of administration, it controls also the constitutionality of the law on the basis of which the said administrative act was issued and, if it judges that the administrative act is based on an anti-Constitutional law, it cancels it.

The principle of the natural judge and the functional independence of judges

Article 8 of the Constitution establishes the principle of the legal or natural judge. The legal judge is the judicial organ, which, on the basis of the effective organisational, procedural or other laws, is in advance generally determined as competent, due to the merits, place or other data, for a certain category or categories of cases. The above-mentioned article of the Constitution prohibits the classification in retrospect of a person in a different court from that provided by the aforementioned rules, because, only in this way, are the impartiality of the judge but also the safety of the individual secured. Besides, according to prevailing opinion, the Constitution does not secure only the determination in advance of the court of competent jurisdiction by a general and abstract law but also the determination of the particular judges who form the court in each case. Article 8 constitutes a fundamental base of judicial organisation of the country and a substantial element of judicial independence. In this meaning, it constitutes a precondition of Article 87, which on the other hand supplements and concretises Article 8, which would be substantially useless, if the judges would not be obliged to be independent appliers of the law. Thus, the judges of a court, which is composed in advance especially to try one or more particular cases, are not functionally independent.

An application of the principle of the natural judge is the introduction by Law 1868/1989 of the system of composition of the Criminal Courts by draw in big cities.

3. Personal independence of judges

Meaning of personal independence of judges

Personal independence consists in securing the official status of the judges *vis-à-vis* the legislative and executive functions. Personal independence is intended to secure the functional independence which is in danger not only when the judge is given instructions and orders but also when he is in danger of suffering, an adverse official treatment because of his decisions.

Content of personal independence

The personal independence of judges is secured by the Constitution with particular provisions concerning: appointment, lifelong permanency, official changes, the exercise of disciplinary power, works incompatible with judicial office, and preferential pay treatment of judges.

– The appointment of judges

The Constitution explicitly provides in Article 88, paragraph 1, that judges are appointed by a Presidential decree determining the qualifications and procedure of their selection. The judicial body is staffed with professional judges who are selected by special examinations. The National School of Judges has been operating for three years and success in examinations constitutes entrance to this school, as well. Furthermore, the provision of Article 88, paragraph 3, allows the enactment by a law of an educational and probational period for judges before their appointment, which usually lasts up to three years. During this period they may exercise the duties of an ordinary judge.

– The lifelong permanency of judges

A fundamental guarantee of personal independence of judges is their lifelong permanency which is secured by Article 88, paragraph 1. This provision extends lifelong permanency to district attorneys, deputy district attorneys, the justices of the peace and the judges of the Police Courts, for whom the previous Constitutions did not recognise lifelong permanency but only permanency. In this manner the judges are not only permanent but they remain in service even if their position is abolished. The institution of lifelong permanency protects the judges and contributes decisively in the unimpeded administration of justice, because, "any judge being afraid of his position does not administer justice any more".

Judges retire from service obligatorily only when they reach the age limit, which is determined by Article 88 of the Constitution (the age of 67 for the top-ranking judges and 65 for others). The dismissal of judges is allowed, according to Article 88, paragraph 4, of the Constitution only in case of a penal conviction for the perpetration of serious disciplinary offences, or disease, or disability, or service inadequacy which are certified as provided by the law and always after a court decision made according to constitutional principles of publicity of trial and the reasoning of the decision.

– Official changes of judges

According to the Constitution, official changes of judges are effected by special official councils formed exclusively of judges. In particular, Article 90, paragraph 1, provides that promotions, assignments, transfers, detachments and transferences are effected by Presidential decree which is issued after a decision of the Supreme Judicial Council, which is composed of the President and members of the respective Supreme Court, who are appointed by draw. Exceptionally, in the Supreme Judicial Council of Civil and Criminal Justice, the district attorney of the Supreme Court (*Arios Pagos*) participates as well and in the respective council of the Exchequer and Audit Department, the General Commissioner of the State. According to paragraph 2 of the same article, the composition of the Supreme Judicial Council is increased when judging promotion in the posts of privy councillors of the state, judges of the Supreme Court, deputy district attorneys of *Arios Pagos,* Presidents of the Appeal Courts, district attorneys of the Appeal Courts and councillors of the Exchequer and Audit Department. From the above provisions it is concluded that Article 90 of the Constitution establishes the administrative self-existence of justice, since all the decisions concerning the judgments and, in general, the official status and promotion of judges are taken by the judges themselves, namely without any intervention of the bodies of the legislative and the executive powers and undoubtedly contributes to the consolidation of the personal independence of judges.

The Minister for Justice is simply granted the right to resort to the plenary session of the respective Supreme Court in case of his disagreement with the judgment of the respective Supreme Judicial Council. The same right and under circumstances provided by the law is also granted to the judge who was omitted. Finally, it must be noted that the provisions of paragraphs 4 and 6 of Article 90 secure the validity of the decisions of the Supreme Judicial Court, since the first one provides that the decisions of the plenary session on the matter which has been referred to it as well as the decisions of the Supreme Judicial Court with which the Minister for Justice disagreed, are compulsory for him, while the second one provides that the decisions or the acts which are provided by the provisions of the aforesaid article and the Presidential decrees, issued in execution of the decisions of the supreme judicial council, are not appealed before the Council of State.

– The exercise of disciplinary power on judges

The irresponsibility of any public official is completely incompatible with democracy and the state of justice. So, it follows that judges, as other public servants as well, have a triple responsibility: criminal, civil and disciplinary. Criminal responsibility of judges is governed by the common criminal law. Their civil responsibility for culpable acts or omissions during the discharge of their duties comes under the competence of the Special Court established by Article 99 of the Constitution for the hearing of actions for miscarriage of justice, which is formed from top-ranking judges and professors of law, while disciplinary power on judges is exercised by councils or by the Supreme Disciplinary Council, as the case may be. More especially, for the judges up to the rank of Judge of the Supreme Court or the deputy district attorney of the Supreme Court and the respective ranks of other jurisdictions, disciplinary power is exercised by councils which are staffed by ordinary judges appointed by draw (Article 91, paragraph 3). Disciplinary power on judges from the rank of Judge of the Supreme Court or deputy district attorney of the Supreme Court (*Arios Pagos*) and ranks higher than that is exercised by the Supreme Disciplinary Council (Article 91, paragraph 1). The Supreme Disciplinary Council is formed of the President of the Council of State, as its presiding judge, of two Vice-Presidents or privy councillors of state, two Vice-Presidents or judges of the Supreme Court, two Vice-Presidents or councillors of the Exchequer and Audit Department and two ordinary professors of law schools of the country as members. The members of the above Council are appointed by draw and must have a previous service of at least three years in the post in which they serve. When an action of a member of a Supreme Court, district attorney or commissioner is judged, the members of the respective court are excluded. When it is about prosecution against members of the Council of State, the President of the Supreme Court presides. The disciplinary action in the first case is brought by top-ranking judges who are appointed especially by the law, and the Minister for Justice, who has an equal right, while in the second case only by the Minister for Justice.

– *Works incompatible with judicial office*

The Constitution now in force provides which work is incompatible with the judge's office, prohibiting them from exercising any profession or any other salaried service (Article 89, paragraph 1). Exceptionally, it allows the judges to become members of the Academy, professors or deputy professors of higher schools, to participate in special administrative courts and in councils or committees except the board of directors of corporations or commercial companies (Article 89, paragraph 2), while it also allows the assignment of administrative duties to judges (Article 89, paragraph 3). Finally, the provision of Article 89, paragraph 4, of the Constitution explicitly prohibits the judges from participation in government.

– *The special pay treatment of judges*

The provision of Article 88, paragraph 2, ("the pay of judges is proportional to their office") establishes the special pay treatment of judges as a consolidation and guarantee of their independence, which, as the quality of their work as well, is without fail influenced by the amount of their pay and, in general, their financial situation.

– *Provisions for deviation*

As has already been set out in detail above, promotions and so on of judges are effected by a supreme judicial council. An exception to this rule is introduced by Article 90, paragraph 5, of the Constitution. So, according to this provision, the promotions in the posts of the President and the Vice-Presidents of the Council of State, the Supreme Court and the Exchequer and Audit Department as well as the promotion in the post of the district attorney of the Supreme Court, are effected by a Presidential decree after a proposal of the Council of Ministers by a selection among the members of the respective court (and among the deputy district attorneys in case of promotion in the post of the district attorney of the Supreme Court as provided by the law. The exception may, theoretically, open a passage to interventions on the part of the executive power, if we take into account that the Presidents of the Supreme Courts as well as the district attorney of the Supreme Court and the General Commissioner of the State in the Exchequer and Audit Department participate obligatorily, namely without draw, in the composition of the respective judicial council. This provision has become the object of many deliberations and its advisability is questioned, although it is consistent with the principle of popular sovereignty established by Article 1 of the Constitution.

According to Article 91, paragraph 3 section *b,* of the Constitution, the Minister for Justice has, as set out above, the right to bring a disciplinary action against judges. This possibility could potentially be used as a means of pressure and intervention in judicial independence. But this possibility is very limited since, in any case, councils consisting of ordinary judges decide on the disciplinary action.

Hungary

I. Legal rules on judicial organisation and the appointment of judges

Constitutional rules on the organisation and operation of the courts are laid down in the Constitution, Act LXVI on the organisation and administration of the courts, Act LXVII on the status and remuneration of judges and Act LXVIII on the legal status of lawyers and court officials. These acts were promulgated by Parliament on 8 July 1997. The composition and powers of the courts are governed by the Code of Criminal Procedure and the Code of Civil Procedure.

Professional judges are appointed by the President of the Republic on the proposal of the National Judiciary Council. In the county courts there are commissions known as "judges' councils" which are elected by the judges themselves at six-year intervals. The role of judges' councils in the appointment procedure is to give a preliminary opinion on a candidate's professional suitability, but this opinion is neither binding nor a right of veto. Before being appointed, candidates must undergo testing of their analytical ability and intellectual capacity as well as psychological testing. Novice judges are appointed for a three-year term, after which they can request a life appointment. Court Presidents are appointed for six years. The President of the Supreme Court is elected by the Parliament for six years on the proposal of the President of the Republic, and can be re-elected. There is no recruitment by competitive examination.

II. The Constitutional Court

Within the strict meaning of constitutional law and civil procedure, the Constitutional Court is not a judicial body but a body which reviews the constitutionality of laws and provisions of international agreements.

III. Court hierarchy and composition

The hierarchy and territorial jurisdiction of the courts correspond to the administrative divisions of the country. Besides the capital, Hungary is divided into counties, cities and municipalities. The capital is itself divided into districts.

Following this division, jurisdiction is exercised by courts of first instance (local courts and labour courts), county courts and the Supreme Court. The Constitution and legislation on the organisation of the judicial system also make provision for courts of appeal, but these are not yet operational.

A. Courts of first instance

Under the terms of the law, the local courts are courts of first instance. They are composed of a President, one or two Vice-Presidents and judges. They are divided into chambers, which may sit with one or three judges (in the latter case a professional judge and two lay judges). Most cases are in fact heard by only one judge. Consequently, these courts of first instance are not always presided over by a bench.

Generally speaking, the powers of local courts extend to all civil and criminal cases. Appeals against local decisions are heard in the county courts.

B. Labour courts

There is a labour court in the capital and in each county. The jurisdiction of these courts is limited to disputes over employment contracts, which naturally include training contracts. They are composed of professional judges under a President and are divided into chambers, each of which comprises a presiding professional judge and two lay judges. The labour courts rule in the first instance. Appeals against their decisions are heard in the county courts.

C. County courts

These courts exist in each county and exercise mixed jurisdiction. They rule in the first instance on cases coming under the Code of Criminal Procedure and the Code of Civil Procedure. These include civil and commercial cases where the sum at issue exceeds ten million forints, and administrative cases. County court jurisdiction extends to the most serious of crimes, and they can hand down heavy penalties. In addition, however, they hear appeals concerning labour court rulings and local court decisions in civil and criminal cases, and have authority for the commercial register. Certain counties also have criminal courts which are responsible for military cases and presided over by senior military officers. There is no Hungarian military court.

Each county court is composed of a President, a Vice-President, chamber Presidents, chief sectional judges, professional judges and lay judges. They are divided into civil, criminal and administrative chambers (with powers to rule in the first or second instance), which are sub-divided into non-autonomous criminal, commercial and civil/administrative sections. Each section is overseen by a chamber President known as the "sectional head". The sections do not look at individual cases but review the decisions of the courts of first instance, give their opinion on the interpretation of the law and monitor the appointment of county court judges. The President of each county court also has authority over the local courts in that county.

Appeals against county court decisions are heard in the Hungarian Supreme Court.

D. Courts of appeal

As part of reforms to legislation on judicial organisation, it is planned to set up five regional courts of appeal. They were due to start functioning on 1 January 1999, but the government has postponed this to a later date.

E. The Hungarian Supreme Court

As the senior court in the judicial hierarchy, the Supreme Court gives the final ruling in cases referred from the County Courts and monitors the lawfulness of final decisions handed down by lower courts. It provides guidelines on case-law, in which respect its decisions are binding on all Hungarian courts.

The Supreme Court is composed exclusively of professional judges: the President, the Vice-Presidents, sectional heads, chamber Presidents and ordinary judges. The Court's sections have powers equivalent to those of the county courts. Its chambers are generally composed of three judges.

IV. Administration of the courts

One of the most important provisions of the legislation on judicial organisation is the categorical revocation of the Justice Minister's right to monitor the courts and the setting up instead of the National Judiciary Council, which is charged with their organisation and administration.

There are 15 members of the National Judiciary Council. They are chosen from very different backgrounds in order to optimise the Council's dealings with government offices and allow it considerable professional and political independence. The President of the Supreme Court also presides over the Council, and there are nine judges. One seat is reserved for the Chief Public Prosecutor attached to the Supreme Court, one for the Minister for Justice and one for the Chair of the Hungarian Bar. The final two members must be members of Parliament. With the exception of those holding political office, who sit for the term of their elected post, members are appointed for a period of six years and can be reappointed.

The Council has an office whose task is to supervise the administration of the courts.

V. The Office of the Public Prosecutor

The basic difference from the French system is that the Office of the Public Prosecutor is composed not of law officers but of civil servants. The office is organised in the same way as the courts as regards areas of jurisdiction. Local and county prosecutors are answerable to the Chief Prosecutor.

The Chief Prosecutor organises and is responsible for the public prosecution service. (S)he is elected by the Parliament, on the proposal of the President of the Republic, for a six-year term, and is fully accountable to the Parliament. The Office of the Public Prosecutor is independent of the Ministry of Justice and is answerable only to the law. Public prosecutors may not be members of political parties and may not engage in political activities.

Public prosecutors are appointed by the Chief Prosecutor for an indefinite term. In the case of senior posts (Deputy Chief Prosecutor of the Republic, chief and deputy chief county prosecutors and heads of local prosecution services), before making an appointment the Chief Prosecutor must request the view of the consultative councils. Other public prosecutors can be appointed without need for such an opinion.

Under the terms of the Constitution, the Office of the Public Prosecutor must act to uphold the law, of which it is guarantor. It protects the rights of citizens and the organisation of the state.

Public prosecutors are answerable to the Chief Prosecutor. Authority at the respective levels is held by the Chief Prosecutor, the chief county prosecutors and the heads of local prosecution services.

The Hungarian judicial system

National level Appeal on points of law Appeal on merit	Supreme Court Civil/commercial chambers Criminal chambers Administrative chambers	Constitutional Court
County level Appeal First instance	Country courts Civil/administrative chambers Criminal chambers Commercial chambers	
Local level First instance	Court of First Instance Civil chambers Criminal chambers	Labour courts

Iceland

I. General

According to Article 1 of the Constitution, Iceland is a republic with a parliamentary government. Article 2 provides for a division of the functions of the state into three branches, that is, legislative, administrative and judicial, and that judges exercise judicial powers. Furthermore, it follows from Article 59 of the Constitution that the organisation of the judiciary can only be established by statute law, and therefore this cannot be done by means of directives from holders of administrative or executive authority.

As a general principle there are two judicial instances in Iceland. These are the District Courts, which are courts of the lower instance, and the Supreme Court, which is a court of appeals of the higher instance. Subject to certain conditions the decisions of the District Courts can be referred to the Supreme Court by appeal. The limitation relates mainly to the monetary value of the claim made.

But single and final judicial instances also exist with courts of special jurisdiction. Judgments of the Court of Impeachment, which according to Article 14 of the Constitution is to pass judgment if Parliament impeaches a Cabinet Minister on account of an action taken in office, or judgments of the Labour Court, which resolves disputes relating to labour agreements and labour law violations, cannot be referred to a higher instance.

Recently the number of courts of special jurisdiction has been markedly reduced, and most such courts now belong to history. This is the case with the Maritime and Commercial Disputes Court, the Criminal Court of Drugs Abuse Cases, the Ecclesiastical Court, and the appeal instance of that court. The general courts, that is, the District Courts, now have jurisdiction in cases previously coming under the jurisdiction of the special courts.

Iceland does not have any separate administrative or constitutional courts, and Article 60 of the Constitution specifies that the judiciary is empowered to settle all disputes regarding the competence of administrative authorities. Furthermore, the rule that the courts are empowered to determine whether statute law conforms to the Constitution is firmly established by custom.

Until 1989, judicial and administrative powers were to a certain extent intertwined in Iceland. The same officials functioned in both fields, rendered judgments and discharged various duties as agents of the administrative branch of government. Thus the sheriffs or magistrates were in charge of criminal investigation as commissioners of police, and also adjudicated criminal cases. The reasons behind this arrangement were mostly due to the conditions of former times, namely sparse population and difficult communications in the geographical and climatic conditions prevailing in Iceland. The judicial system was thoroughly reorganised by amendments taking effect 1 July 1992. Judicial powers were then removed from the sheriffs and magistrates, and committed to the various District Courts (even though Icelanders may still use the title of magistrate when speaking or writing English, this does not imply a judicial function). The maintenance of real estate and mortgage records, and enforcement proceedings, which until then had come under the definition of judicial acts, were, on the other hand, committed to the magistrates. Only disputes of law arising in the course of such proceedings can be referred to the courts.

The District Courts are eight in number. Their jurisdiction is limited to certain geographical areas, after which they are named. The jurisdiction of the Supreme Court, to which the judgments of the District Courts can be referred, is not geographically limited. Similarly, the Labour Court has jurisdiction anywhere in Iceland.

The Minister for Justice appoints District Court judges after having obtained the opinion of a particular committee, which considers the qualifications of applicants for such office. On the other hand the President of Iceland commissions Supreme Court judges according to the nomination of the Minister for Justice, after having obtained the opinion of the Supreme Court relating to the applicants. The commission or appointment of a judge is not limited in time, and a judge can only be removed from office by judgment, as provided for by Article 61 of the Constitution.

Icelandic District Court judges are 38 in number, and their number with the respective District Court varies. In all there are nine Supreme Court judges.

Each case is usually handled by one District Court judge. A judge can, if he deems that expert knowledge is needed for the resolution of a case, appoint two such experts to serve with him on the bench. A case of high general importance or of a very extensive scope may be adjudicated by three District Court judges, or two judges and one expert. Most cases in the Supreme Court are adjudicated by three judges, but adjudication by five judges is also frequent. In cases of very high importance the President of the Supreme Court may decide on adjudication by seven judges. When a case is committed to five or seven judges, they shall generally be those who have served longest with the court. A case of or summary appeal where the interests at stake are not considered great, and where argumentation takes place in writing, can also be adjudicated by one judge. However, this possibility has not been used so far.

Assistants with legal training are among the staff of the courts, both the District Courts and the Supreme Court. They are not charged with judicial functions, but assist the various individual judges in various ways, for example in organising their work, examining the case files, checking juridical literature, and in communicating with the parties to an action or their representatives.

The general courts of both instances handle both private cases and criminal cases. Private cases are those where the parties themselves have decided to commence litigation, have the power to make dispositions concerning the subject matter of the action, and can decide on their own what requests they make in court and what facts they invoke in their support. Criminal cases are cases of legal action brought by holders of public authority where requests are made for criminal sanctions to be ordered.

The courts are empowered to adjudicate any matter subject to law, unless exempted from their jurisdiction by statute or custom, or by the nature of the matter. It is not possible, however, to refer to the courts a contrived dispute or otherwise to ask of them questions of law not unrelated to a material dispute. In certain exceptional cases an action may be brought for recognition of a right, if the plaintiff has a legally protected interest in having the existence or substance of such a right confirmed.

The principal rule of Icelandic procedural law is oral argumentation of a case in court. A judge may nevertheless decide on the presentation of a case in writing if he considers that there is a risk of the matter not being adequately clarified by oral presentation. It is also possible to receive a case for adjudication without argumentation if the parties agree on that procedure. Cases of summary appeal are also usually presented in writing to the Supreme Court. These are, for example interlocutory appeals, that is, appeals against decisions of the District Courts that are rendered on various procedural matters while litigation is in progress.

A court will pass judgment on both issues of fact and issues of law. Resolutions of issues of fact are not committed to juries under Icelandic procedural law.

The judges act independently and are personally responsible. When resolving a case they are, according to Article 61 of the Constitution, obliged to proceed only according to law. A judicial act cannot be revised except on appeal to a superior court.

In a court of many judges, the majority of judges decides the outcome of a case. Dissenting opinions are printed with the majority opinions.

II. Further information on the various courts

The following observations are made in order to clarify further the diagrammatic overview presented later on in the chapter of the courts of Iceland.

A. Ordinary courts

1. The District Courts

It should be noted that Icelandic judicial resolutions fall into two categories. They are either judgments, involving a final resolution of a dispute (subject to ordinary appeal as the case may be), or decisions (which in English may be referred to in various contexts as decisions, rulings, orders or decrees). The latter either provide for urgent measures or specify how the court itself intends to proceed. Many such decisions can be summarily appealed against. Practically all resolutions of the Supreme Court are judgments in the above sense.

The District Courts are the primary and lower judicial instance. They are eight in number. Their jurisdiction is limited to certain areas, from which they derive their names. The judges of the District Courts are 38 in number, but the number of judges at each District Court varies.

The District Courts are empowered to adjudicate any matter subject to law, unless exempted from their jurisdiction by statute or custom, or by the nature of the matter. They resolve both issues of fact and issues of law.

Usually a case is handled by one District Court judge, who is a lawyer and appointed to office without limitation in time. A judge can, if he deems that expert knowledge is needed for the resolution of a case, appoint two such experts to serve with him on the bench. A case of high general importance or of a very extensive scope may be adjudicated by three District Court judges, or two judges and one expert.

The following decisions of the District Courts may be referred to the Supreme Court by summary appeal:

– Interlocutory decisions on various procedural matters in the lower instance, such as a judge's withdrawal (disqualification, and so on), and matters concerning discovery, survey, assessment or appraisal, submission of documents, deferments, and so on.

– Decisions resolving disputes of law arising in the course of enforcement proceedings conducted by magistrates.

– Decisions enabling various measures to be taken in the context of criminal investigation (remand, and so on).

– Decisions on legal competence taken under the Legal Competence and Majority Act.

– A summary appeal against a decision of a District Court shall be lodged within two weeks, counted from its date or from when the party in question obtained knowledge of it. Summary appeal cases are usually presented in writing before the Supreme Court, but oral argumentation can be allowed. The Supreme Court renders a judgment on the matter as soon as possible, so as not to delay further the procedure in the lower instance.

Judgments of the District Courts may be referred to the Supreme Court by appeal:

– Appeal may take place for annulment of a District Court judgment and a remand of the case for renewed, lawful adjudication; for dismissal from the District Court, for a change of the District Court's conclusion, or for a judgment sustaining the District Court's conclusion.

– Appeal against a District Court judgment shall take place within three months from the date when it is rendered.

– Appeal can not take place against a judgment where the monetary amount at stake is below a certain minimum. In exceptional cases the Supeme Court can allow appeal even if the interests at stake do not reach this minimum, provided the outcome is deemed to be of general significance, the case has a relationship to important interests, or the evidence available indicates that the outcome may be changed by the Supreme Court.

2. The Supreme Court

The Supreme Court is the higher judicial instance, the only appeal court in Iceland, and its jurisdiction is not geographically limited. The court has its offices in the capital, Reykjavík. Appeal to the Supreme Court can be lodged against District Court resolutions (judgments and decisions; cf. II.A.1 above), and interlocutory decisions of the Labour Court (cf. II.B.2 below).

Generally the Supreme Court considers both issues of fact and issues of law. The court will, however, not reconsider the evidential value of witnesses' statements in criminal cases. The Supreme Court can either sustain a judgment of a District Court or change its conclusion. It may also invalidate a District Court's procedure in whole or in part and remand the case to the District Court, or dismiss a case from the District Court or from the Supreme Court.

The judges of the Supreme Court are nine in number. They are all lawyers, and permanently commissioned. Most cases are adjudicated by three judges, but adjudication by five judges is frequent. Cases of exceptional importance may also be adjudicated by seven judges. When a case is adjudicated by five or seven judges these shall generally be those who have the longest experience as supreme court judges. A summary appeal case presented in writing, where the interests at stake are not deemed significant, may also be adjudicated by one judge, who also directs the handling of the case prior to adjudication.

Resolutions of the Supreme Court are final, and cannot be referred to a higher instance.

B. Special courts

1. The Court of Impeachment

The Court of Impeachment is the only judicial instance in the cases within its jurisdiction, which is not geographically limited. The court shall generally assemble in Reykjavík, but can however assemble elsewhere in Iceland. The Court of Impeachment shall, in accordance with Article 14 of the Constitution, render judgment in legal actions brought by Parliament against Ministers of the executive government on account of actions taken by them in official capacity.

The Court of Impeachment shall be composed of 15 judges. These shall be the five judges of the Supreme Court with the longest experience in office, the Chief Judge of the District Court of Reykjavík, a professor of constitutional law of the University of Iceland, and eight judges selected by Parliament. At each session of the court the judges shall be at least ten in number, and include at least four of the six legally trained judges first mentioned. The President of the Supreme Court shall be the presiding judge of the Court of Impeachment.

The Court of Impeachment has never assembled since it was first established by an act of law in 1905.

Judgments of the Court of Impeachment are not subject to appeal.

2. The Labour Court

The Labour Court is a court of one instance, and has jurisdiction anywhere in Iceland. Its offices are in Reykjavík. Its role is to adjudicate disputes concerning alleged violations of the Act on Labour Unions and Labour Disputes, disputes concerning strikes and lockouts, and interpretation of labour law. In addition to this the court may render judgments on disputes which the social partners may agree to bring before it, subject to the approval of the majority of the court.

The judges of the Labour Court are five in number, appointed for a term of three years. The Supreme Court shall appoint the President of the Court and one additional judge. The Minister for Social Affairs shall also appoint one judge out of a group of three nominated by the Supreme Court. Finally, two judges shall be appointed by the social partners. Of the five judges, only the two appointed by the Supreme Court must have legal training.

Judgments of the Labour Court are final. Resolutions concerning the formal aspects of a case, including questions of jurisdiction, are however subject to interlocutory appeal to the Supreme Court.

III. Statistical data

The following information is available on the number of cases brought before the courts of Iceland since 1996.

The District Courts resolved a total of 9 408 private cases. Of these, 1 243 were orally argued, and in 8 165 cases judgments were rendered by default. Criminal cases in the District Courts numbered a total of 2 142. Of the total number of cases, both private and criminal, approximately 66% were resolved in Reykjavík.

Appeal to the Supreme Court took place in a total of 299 cases. Of these, 217 were private cases, and 72 were criminal cases. Summary appeals to the Supreme Court numbered 176, of which 117 concerned private cases, and 59 criminal cases. The Supreme Court rendered a total of 335 judgments, 260 in private cases, and 76 in criminal cases. The court also adjudicated a total of 168 summary appeals. Of these, 117 concerned private cases, and 51 criminal cases. Default judgments were rendered by the Supreme Court in a total of 36 cases.

The Icelandic judicial system

<table>
<tr><td>Courts of Second Instance and other higher courts</td><td>Hæstiréttur
(The Supreme Court of Iceland)</td><td rowspan="2">Félagsdómur
(Labour Court: Questions of procedure can be appealed to the Supreme Court)</td><td rowspan="2">Landsdómur
(The High Court of State)</td></tr>
<tr><td>Courts of First Instance</td><td>Héradsdómur
(District Courts)</td></tr>
<tr><td></td><td>Ordinary jurisdiction</td><td colspan="2">Special jurisdiction</td></tr>
</table>

IRELAND

I. INTRODUCTION[1]

The existing courts system which had evolved under the previous regime was taken over on the foundation of the state. The Constitution of the Irish Free State, which came into effect in 1922, provided for the setting up of new courts and a judiciary committee was established in 1923 to advise on the establishment and jurisdiction of the new courts. As a result of the recommendations of that committee a new system of courts was established in 1924. In 1937 the Constitution of Ireland replaced the earlier Constitution and the courts existing at present are those established under the provisions of the Constitution of Ireland. These courts are similar to the courts established in 1924.

The Constitution of Ireland provides that justice shall be administered in public in courts established by law by judges appointed by the President on the advice of the government; that these courts shall consist of courts of first instance and a court of final appeal (to be known as the Supreme Court); that the Courts of First Instance shall include a high court with full original jurisdiction and courts with local and limited jurisdiction (these courts are represented by the Circuit Court and the District Court). The judges of all courts are, under the Constitution, completely independent in the exercise of their judicial functions. A judge may not be removed from office except for stated misbehaviour or incapacity and then only following resolutions passed by both Houses of the *Oireachtas* (Parliament).

In regard to the trial of offences the Constitution provides that no person shall be tried on any criminal charge save in due course of law; that minor offences may be tried by courts of summary jurisdiction; that special courts may be established by law in cases where it may be determined in accordance with such law that the ordinary courts are inadequate to secure the effective administration of justice and the preservation of public peace and order; that military tribunals may be established to deal with offences against military law and also to deal with a state of war or armed rebellion; and that save in regard to minor offences or offences tried by special courts or military tribunals no person shall be tried on any criminal charge without a jury.

The courts established under the Constitution of Ireland are as follows:

II. *AN CHÚIRT DÚICHE* (THE DISTRICT COURT)

As of 1 May 1998 the District Court consists of the President of the District Court and 47 judges. The 1995 Courts and Court Officers Act provides for an increase in the maximum number of judges who may be appointed to the District Court to 51 including the President of that court. For the purpose of

1. This is information on the Irish judicial system. It is not intended to be a legally binding document nor is it an interpretation of legislation. Enquiries to: Courts Division, Department of Justice, Equality and Law Reform, 72-76 St. Stephen's Green, Dublin 2 Ireland. Tel. (+ 353) 1 602 8202; Fax.(+353) 1 661 5461; e-mail: courtsinfo@justice.ie; URL: http://www.irlgov.ie/justice/.

the District Court, the country is divided into 23 districts to each of which one judge is permanently assigned, except in the case of the Dublin Metropolitan District and Cork where the volume of business requires the permanent assignment of a number of judges. The President of the District Court, who is assigned to the Dublin Metropolitan District, is charged with the duty of ensuring the prompt and efficient discharge of the business of the District Court throughout the country and has special duties in relation to the despatch of business arising in the Dublin Metropolitan District. There is provision for 38 judges, excluding the President, to be permanently assigned to districts and for 12 "moveable" judges who may be temporarily assigned to any district to deputise for a permanently assigned judge during periods of absence due to sickness or annual leave or to assist in the disposal of business.

The criminal jurisdiction of the District Court falls under the following headings:

– *Minor offences* tryable in a summary way before the District Court. This makes up the great bulk of the work of the District Court, and these offences are exclusively statutory in origin;

– *Indictable offences* specified in the appropriate legislation which are tryable summarily on the basis that in the view of the judge, the facts alleged constitute a minor offence, that the accused, on being informed of his/her right to be tried by a jury, does not object to being tried summarily, and that, in the case of certain offences, the Director of Public Prosecutions has consented to a summary trial;

– *Indictable offences* (other than certain offences including rape, aggravated sexual assault, murder, treason and piracy) where the accused, when before the District Court, pleads guilty and the judge is satisfied that he understands the charge. With the consent of the Director of Public Prosecutions the judge may deal with the cases summarily. Otherwise, the accused is sent forward to the Circuit Court for sentence. When before the Circuit Court he may withdraw his/her plea and alter it to "not guilty" in which case trial takes place;

– *Indictable offences* not tryable summarily. In such case, there is a preliminary examination by the judge. The accused is served with a statement of the charge and of the evidence intended to be adduced, with a list of witnesses and exhibits. Evidence may be taken on deposition if either side so requires. The judge considers the material before him/her and any submissions on behalf of prosecution or accused. If he/she thinks there is a sufficient case, he/she sends the accused forward to the Circuit Court or Central Criminal Court for trial. Otherwise, he/she discharges him/her.

The civil jurisdiction of the District Court may be summarised as follows:

– in contract generally where the claim does not exceed 5000 Irish Pounds and in actions founded on hire-purchase and credit-sale agreements where the hire-purchase price of the goods or, as the case may be, the amount of the claim does not exceed 5000 Irish Pounds;

– in tort, with certain exceptions, where the claim does not exceed 5000 Irish Pounds.

– in ejectment for non-payment of rent or overholding where the annual rent does not exceed such sum as amounts, or might amount, to 5 000 Irish Pounds per annum;

– in actions for wrongful detention of goods where the value of the goods claimed does not exceed 5 000 Irish Pounds.

In addition, the District Court has a number of other jurisdictions, such as the power to make maintenance, barring, custody, access and affiliation orders, jurisdiction in relation to the enforcement generally of the judgments for debt of any court (including power to examine debtors as to their means and to order payment of the debt by instalments and the power to commit the debtor to prison for default in payment) jurisdiction in relation to a large number of licensing provisions, for example the granting of certificates for intoxicating liquor licences, the granting of certificates for auctioneer's and the lottery licences, the granting of licences for public dancing and so on and jurisdiction in respect of applications for malicious damages where the amount claimed does not exceed 5 000 Irish Pounds.

The District Court sits at 248 venues (including Dublin) throughout the country. Sittings are usually at least once monthly, but are more frequent in populous areas. In Dublin a number of courts sit daily simultaneously. Sittings to deal with juvenile business are held separately from other sittings of the court.

Generally, the venue at which a case is heard depends:

– in criminal proceedings, on where the offence was committed or where the defendant resides or carries on business or was arrested,

– in civil cases, where the contract was made,

– in licensing cases, on where the licensed premises are situated.

III. *An Chúirt Chuarda* (the Circuit Court)

The country is divided into eight circuits for the purposes of the Circuit Court. As of 1 May 1998, the Circuit Court consists of the President of the Court and 25 ordinary judges. The Courts Act, 1996, provided for an increase in the maximum number of judges who may be appointed to the Circuit Court to 28, including the President of that Court. One circuit judge is assigned to each circuit except in the case of the Dublin and Cork circuits to which, under the provisions of the Courts and Court Officers Act, 1995, 10 judges can be assigned to Dublin and three to Cork. The President of the Circuit Court, who is, *ex officio,* an additional judge of the High Court, is charged with the duty of ensuring an equitable distribution of the work of the Circuit Court amongst the several judges and the prompt despatch of business.

In criminal matters, the Circuit Court has the same jurisdiction as that vested in the Central Criminal Court in all indictable offences except murder, rape, aggravated sexual assault, treason, piracy and allied offences. The jurisdiction is excercisable by the judge of the circuit in which the offence has been committed or in which the accused person has been arrested or resides. He/she sits with a jury of twelve and generally a unanimous vote of the jury is necessary to determine a verdict. However, in accordance with section 25 of the Criminal Justice Act, 1984, a verdict need not be unanimous in a case where there are not fewer than eleven jurors if ten of them agree on the verdict. The judge is empowered to transfer a criminal trial from one part of his circuit to another. Also, on application by the Director of Public Prosecutions or the accused person, the relevant judge may, if satisfied that it would be manifestly unjust not to do so, transfer the trial from the Circuit Court sitting outside of the Dublin circuit to the Dublin Circuit Court.

The civil jurisdiction of the Circuit Court is a limited one unless all the parties to an action consent, in which event the jurisdiction is unlimited.

The limits of the court's jurisdiction are mainly:

– in actions in contract and tort where the claim does not exceed 30000 Irish Pounds;

– in probate matters and suits for the administration of estates, where the rateable valuation of the real estate does not exceed 200 Irish Pounds;

– in equity suits, where the rateable valuation of the land does not exceed 200 Irish Pounds;

– in ejectment actions or applications for new tenancies (fixing of rent and so on) where the rateable valuation of the property does not exceed 200 Irish Pounds;

– in actions founded on hire-purchase and credit-sale agreements, where the hire-purchase price of the goods or, as the case may be, the amount of the claim does not exceed 30000 Irish Pounds.

The Circuit Court has jurisdiction in family law proceedings, (including judicial separation, divorce, nullity and appeals from the District Court). Where the rateable valuation of the property exceeds 200 Irish Pounds, the parties may opt to transfer the case to the High Court.

The Circuit Court also has jurisdiction in all cases of application for new liquor on-licence (that is, licences for sale of liquor for consumption on the premises) and has appellate jurisdiction from decisions of arbitrators in disputes in relation to ground rents under the Landlord and Tenant Legislation. Civil cases in the Circuit Court are tried by a judge sitting without a jury.

The Circuit Court has exclusive jurisdiction in respect of applications under the former Workmen's Compensation Code, that is, in cases where the right to compensation arose prior to 1 May, 1967. It acts as an appeal court from the District Court in both civil and criminal matters. The appeal takes the form of a re-hearing and the decision of the Circuit Court is final and not appealable.

IV. *An Ard-Chúirt* (the High Court)

The Courts (No. 2) Act, 1997 increased the maximum number of ordinary judges which can be appointed to the High Court to 24. The President of the Circuit Court is, *ex officio,* an additional judge of the High Court.

Under the Constitution the High Court has full original jurisdiction in and power to determine all matters and questions, whether of law or fact, civil or criminal. The jurisdiction of the High Court shall extend to the question of the validity of any law having regard to the provisions of the Constitution (except a law which has already been referred to the Supreme Court by the President of Ireland) and no such question may be raised in any court other than the High Court or the Supreme Court.

Probate actions, matrimonial causes and matters, actions for libel, slander, seduction, false imprisonment and malicious imprisonment are also normally tried by a judge and jury. In all cases a majority vote of nine of the twelve jurors is sufficient to determine the verdict.

The High Court acts as an appeal court from the Circuit Court in civil matters. Apart from its appellate jurisdiction in circuit court civil appeals, the High Court also has power to review the decisions of all inferior tribunals by the issue of prerogative orders of *mandamus, prohibition* and *certiorari*. These orders relate not to the merits of the decision of the inferior tribunals but to the question of whether jurisdiction has been exceeded.

The High Court may give rulings on a question of law submitted by the District Court and may hear appeals in certain other circumstances provided by statute that is, in regard to decisions of the District Court on applications for bail.

Normally the High Court sits in Dublin to hear original actions. It also sits in Cork and Galway four times each year, Limerick three times each year, Waterford, Sligo and Dundalk twice each year, Kilkenny and Ennis once a year to hear original actions. The High Court on circuit hears appeals from the Circuit Court twice a year at the following venues outside Dublin: Carlow, Carrick-on-Shannon, Cavan, Castlebar, Clonmel, Cork, Dundalk, Ennis, Galway, Kilkenny, Letterkenny, Limerick, Longford, Monaghan, Mullingar, Naas, Nenagh, Portlaoise, Roscommon, Sligo, Tullamore, Tralee, Trim, Waterford, Wexford and Wicklow.

Matters coming before the High Court are normally heard and determined by one judge but the President of the High Court may direct that any cause or matter or any part thereof may be heard by two or more judges.

V. *An Phríomh-Chúirt Choiriúil* (the Central Criminal Court)

The High Court exercising its criminal jurisdiction is known as the Central Criminal Court. It consists of a judge or judges of the High Court nominated from time to time by the President of the High Court. The court sits at such time and in such places as the President of the High Court may direct and tries criminal cases which are outside the jurisdiction of the Circuit Court.

Normally trials are conducted by a single judge sitting with a jury of twelve, but the President of the High Court has power to direct two or more judges to sit together for the purpose of a particular trial. A majority (of 10) verdict of the jury is required.

VI. *An Chúirt Choiriúil Speisialta* (the Special Criminal Court)

The Offences against the State Act, 1939, provides in part V for the establishment of special criminal courts. A special criminal court sits with three judges but no jury. The rules of evidence that apply in proceedings before a

Special Criminal Court are the same as those applicable in trials in the Central Criminal Court. A Special Criminal Court is authorised by the 1939 Act to make rules governing its own practice and procedure. An appeal against conviction or sentence by a special criminal court may be taken to the Court of Criminal Appeal.

The government made a Proclamation on 26 May 1972 bringing part V of the Offences against the State Act, 1939, into operation and on 30 May 1972 an order was made establishing a special criminal court. The 1939 Act also provides that the government shall appoint serving judges to sit in the Special Criminal Court. Currently there is a panel of nine judges appointed to that court who are drawn from the High, Circuit and District Courts.

VII. *An Chúirt Achomhairc Choiriúil* (the Court of Criminal Appeal)

The Court of Criminal Appeal consists of the Chief Justice or an ordinary judge of the Supreme Court and either two ordinary judges of the High Court or the President of the High Court and one ordinary judge of the High Court. It deals with appeals by persons convicted on indictment in the circuit or Central Criminal Court where the appellant obtains a certificate from the trial judge that the case is a fit one for appeal or, in the case of such certificate being refused, where the Court of Criminal Appeal itself, on appeal from such refusal, grants leave to appeal. The appeal is heard and determined on a record of the proceedings at the trial and on a transcript thereof verified by the trial judge with power to the court to hear new or additional evidence or to refer any matter for report by the trial judge.

If the appeal is against the conviction and the sentence, the court may affirm or reverse the conviction in whole or in part, or order a new trial or vary the sentence. If the appeal is limited to either conviction or sentence, the court is confined to dealing with the matter which is the subject of the appeal, for example if the appeal is against conviction only, the court may not increase the sentence. The decision of the Court of Criminal Appeal is final unless the court or the Attorney-General or the Director of Public Prosecutions certifies that the decision involves a point of law of exceptional public importance and that it is desirable in the public interest that an appeal be taken to the Supreme Court.

VIII. *An Chúirt Uachtarach* (the Supreme Court)

As of 1 May 1998, the Supreme Court consists of the Chief Justice (who is *ex officio* an additional judge of the High Court) and seven ordinary judges. The Courts and Court Officers Act, 1995, increased the maximum number of ordinary judges which can be appointed to the Supreme Court to seven which enables the court to sit in more than one division at the same time. The President of the High Court is *ex officio* an additional judge of the Supreme Court. The Supreme Court has appellate jurisdiction from all decisions of the High Court.

The Supreme Court also has jurisdiction to hear an appeal from the Court of Criminal Appeal if the Court of Criminal Appeal or the Attorney-General certifies that the decision involves a point of law of exceptional public importance and that it is desirable in the public interest that an appeal should be taken to the Supreme Court. The court may also give a ruling on a question of law submitted to it by the Circuit Court.

The Supreme Court has power to decide whether a Bill (or any provision or provisions of it), which has been passed by both Houses of the *Oireachtas* and presented to the President of Ireland for his/her signature before being enacted into law, is repugnant to the Constitution, on the matter being referred to the court by the President.

If a question of the permanent incapacity of the President arises such question falls to be decided by the Supreme Court.

Appeals to or other matters cognisable by the Supreme Court are heard and determined by five judges unless the Chief Justice directs that any appeal or other matter (apart from matters relating to the Constitution) be heard and determined by three judges.

IX. The Attorney-General

The Constitution provides for an office of Attorney-General. The holder of this office is the adviser to the government in matters of law and legal opinion and exercises powers, functions and duties conferred by the Constitution and by law. Prior to the passing of the Prosecution of Offences Act in 1974, which established the Office of the Director of Public Prosecutions, all charges prosecuted upon indictment in any court were prosecuted at the suit of the Attorney-General.

X. The Director of Public prosecutions

The Office of the Director of Public Prosecutions was established consequent upon the passing of the Prosecution of Offences Act, 1974. Under the Act, the Director is empowered to perform all functions capable of being performed in relation to criminal matters and in relation to election petitions and referendum petitions which had hitherto been performed by the Attorney-General.

XI. The Small Claims Court

The Small Claims Procedure operates within the District Court structure and is designed to handle consumer claims speedily, cheaply and informally without involving a solicitor. The procedure was launched on a nationwide basis in December, 1993. To be eligible to use the procedure, the consumer must have bought the goods (or the service) to a value not exceeding 600 Irish Pounds for private use from someone selling them in the course of business. The procedure covers claims for bad workmanship and faulty goods as far as most everyday transactions for goods and services are concerned and covers minor damage to private property and the non-return of rent deposits. The procedure does not cover debts or personal injuries.

XII. Administrative tribunals

Outside the system of courts outlined above there are a number of administrative tribunals to decide questions arising out of the administration of legislation. The decisions of some of these tribunals are subject to statutory right of appeal to the courts, others are not.

XIII. The Courts Service

The Courts Service Act, 1998 provides for the establishment of an independent and permanent body with financial and management autonomy to manage the courts system. The Act provides for the establishment of a Courts Service Transitional Board to make preparations for the establishment of the Courts Service and, in this regard, it appointed a chief executive designate in January, 1999. The Transitional Board is, in conjunction with the Department of Justice, Equality and Law Reform, actively involved in making the necessary arrangements for the establishment of the Court Service and it is expected that this task will be completed later this year. In accordance with the provisions of the Act, the Minister for Justice, Equality and Law Reform will, by order, formally establish the Courts Service.

The structures which are now being put in place will, it is expected, allow the Courts Service to meet the demands placed on it in the new millennium and enable it to provide a first class service to judges, practitioners, court staff and most importantly, the users of the system.

ITALY

I. Political structure of the state

Article 1 of the Constitution, which entered into force on 1 January 1948, states that "Italy is a democratic republic founded on labour. Sovereignty belongs to the people, who exercise it in the manner and within the limits laid down by the Constitution".

Legislation is enacted by Parliament, which consists of the Chamber of Deputies and the Senate. Both Houses of Parliament are elected by direct universal suffrage for five years. Any person entitled to vote and aged over 25 is eligible for election to the Chamber of Deputies but must have reached 40 to be eligible for election to the Senate. Moreover, the latter is elected on a regional basis by voters who have reached the age of 25.

The Chamber of Deputies has more members than the Senate, which includes a category of life senators (consisting of former Presidents of the Republic and five citizens who have brought honour to their fatherland as a result of distinguished service in the social, scientific, artistic or literary fields).

The President of the Republic is head of state and represents national unity. He or she is elected by the full Parliament, that is, at a joint sitting of the two Houses. Three delegates from each region (except for the Aosta Valley, which has only one) also take part in the election. The President must be at least 50 years old.

The numerous functions of the President include promulgating laws passed by Parliament, announcing the holding of referenda, dissolving both Houses of Parliament (after consulting the Speaker of each House), commanding the armed forces, ratifying international treaties and presiding over the Legal Service Commission (*Consiglio Superiore della Magistratura*).

The government of the Republic consists of the President of the Council (that is the Prime Minister) and the Ministers, who together constitute the Council of Ministers (the Cabinet).

The Prime Minister is nominated by the President of the Republic, who, on the advice of the former, also appoints the Ministers.

The Prime Minister conducts, and is directly responsible for, the general policies of the government and for maintaining the unity of political and administrative policy by promoting and co-ordinating the work of the Ministers.

Territorially, the Republic is divided into regions, provinces and communes, which are self-governing entities with their own powers and functions. The regions are empowered to legislate on subjects specifically mentioned in the Constitution. They have financial autonomy and possess their own assets. The provinces and communes have administrative functions and are also areas of decentralised regional and state authority.

II. The Constitutional Court (*Corte costituzionale*)

The Constitutional Court consists of 15 judges, one-third of whom are appointed by the President of the Republic, one-third by both Houses of Parliament at a joint sitting and one-third by the judges of the ordinary and administrative Supreme Courts (that is, the Council of State and the Court of Audit).

Justices are elected for a term of nine years by the judges (including retired judges) of the Higher Courts, university law professors and lawyers who have practised law for twenty years.

The court adjudicates: a) disputes concerning the constitutionality of laws of the state and the regions and of statutory instruments with the force of law; b) disputes concerning jurisdiction arising between the state authorities, between the state and the regions and between the regions; c) accusations against the President of the Republic or Ministers (for high treason or violation of the Constitution), in conformity with the Constitution. In the latter case, in addition to the ordinary justices of the court the trial takes place before sixteen members chosen at the beginning of each legislative period at a joint sitting of Parliament from among citizens who meet the conditions of eligibility for the Senate.

Questions concerning the constitutionality of instruments with the force of law can be raised only by judges (in response to an objection or of their own motion) in the course of judicial proceedings. If the court declares a provision of a law or an instrument with the force of law unconstitutional, it becomes inoperative on the day following the publication of the decision.

III. The ordinary courts

The Italian judicial system assigns judicial functions to two different types of body: the Courts of General Jurisdiction and Special Courts.

General jurisdiction is exercised by judges appointed under and governed by the provisions on the administration of justice for both criminal and civil cases, but excluding matters falling within the jurisdiction of the Special Courts (such as the Courts Martial).

The Special Courts established under our system are as follows:

– The Administrative Courts, which have jurisdiction over disputes between the administrative authorities and individuals, viz the Regional Administrative Courts and the Council of State.

– The Court of Audit, which is responsible for examining public accounts.

– The Courts Martial, which have sole jurisdiction over breaches of military law committed by members of the armed forces.

– The Provincial Tax Commissions and the Regional Tax Commissions, which are responsible for dealing with tax matters.

Article 104 of the Constitution states that the judiciary is independent and not subject to any other authority. Its institutional independence is guaranteed by the Legal Service Commission (*Consiglio Superiore della Magistratura*), an autonomous body presided over by the President of the Republic and consisting of two *ex officio* members (the President and Chief Public Prosecutor of the Court of Cassation) and 30 members elected for a term of four years (20 by judges and prosecutors from among their own category and 10 by the two Houses of Parliament from among university law professors and lawyers who have practised for at least 15 years).

The powers of the Legal Service Commission cover recruitment, appointments and transfers, promotion and disciplinary measures relating to judges.

The latter may not be dismissed or suspended from office or transferred to other posts or functions except by decision of the Commission taken either with their consent or for such reasons, and subject to such guarantees for their defence, as are laid down in the Organisation of the Courts Act.

Judges are recruited by competitive examination. However, the Constitution also makes provision for honorary judges to be elected to carry out all the individual functions assigned to a judge.

A. Courts with general jurisdiction

The ordinary courts for civil, commercial and employment cases are as follows:

1. The justice of the peace (Giudice di pace)

The justice of the peace is an unpaid judge sitting alone. He or she hears disputes concerning movable property not exceeding 5 million lire in value and applications for compensation of up to 30 million lire for damage caused as a result of accidents involving motor vehicles or boats. He or she also hears, irrespective of the amount, disputes concerning boundaries and distances to be observed when planting trees or hedges, concerning the measurement and use of co-ownership services, and concerning noxious emissions.

Appeals against the decisions of the justices of the peace lie to the District Court (*tribunale*). An application for review may be made to the Court of Cassation against a decision *ex aequo et bono* and not subject to appeal.

2. The District Court (Tribunale)

The District Court is the Court of First Instance for all matters that do not come under the jurisdiction of the justice of the peace.

Following the recent reform which entered into force on 2 June 1999 and has, *inter alia,* abolished the Magistrates' Court (*pretore*), the District Court normally consists of a single judge except for cases expressly provided for by law, for which a bench of three judges is required.

When sitting as a bench, the court tries the following matters: cases requiring the intervention of the Public Prosecutor's Office (*pubblico ministero*), bankruptcy cases, disputes concerning the liability of judges, applications to set aside company decisions, disputes concerning the liability of administrative authorities, disputes concerning the supervision of companies, actions to declare wills void, or to reduce bequests where the disposable portion of an estate has been exceeded, cases assigned to the jurisdiction of special sections, and proceedings in chambers (for example, separations and divorces).

In labour cases, the functions previously assigned to the magistrate (*pretore*) are now exercised by a single judge of the District Court. Since 1999 public employment jurisdiction has been transferred from the Regional Administrative Court to the single District Court judge.

All decisions by the District Court in civil or labour cases are subject to appeal to the Court of Appeal. However, the District Court also hears appeals against the decisions of the justice of the peace; a further appeal on points of law then lies to the Court of Cassation.

*3. The Juvenile Court (*Tribunale per i minorenni*)*

This is a separate chamber of the District Court. The bench consists of a judge from the Court of Appeal, who presides, a District Court judge and two unpaid judges (a man and a woman) chosen from a group of experts in such matters as psychiatry, criminal anthropology, education and psychology.

In civil cases, it deals with the adoption of minors, the placement of children and the exercise of parental authority, deprivation of legal capacity and incapacity during the final year before reaching the age of majority, and the exercise of entrepreneurial activities.

A special chamber of the Court of Appeal hears appeals against decisions of the Juvenile Court. It consists of five members: a judge from the Court of Cassation, who presides, two judges from the Court of Appeal and two experts (a man and a woman). Appeals against its decisions lie to the Court of Cassation.

*4. The Court of Appeal (*Corte d'appello*)*

The Court of Appeal is a collegiate body with jurisdiction over a district. It sits as a bench of three judges who all have a right to vote and belong to the ordinary judiciary.

It hears appeals lodged against judgments delivered by the District Court, with the exception of decisions *ex aequo et bono.* Appeals lie to the Court of Cassation.

*5. The Court of Cassation (*Corte suprema di cassazione*)*

The Court of Cassation is the highest ordinary court and sits in Rome. It ensures the precise observance and uniform interpretation of the law, the unity of domestic substantive law and respect for the limits to the jurisdiction of the various courts. It settles disputes as to jurisdiction and fulfils all the other functions assigned to it by law.

It consists of three civil chambers and one chamber that deals with labour disputes, each always sitting as a bench of five judges who all have the right to vote.

It sits as a full court consisting of nine members with the right to vote to hear appeals concerning jurisdiction, a point of law that the individual chambers have already dealt with differently or a particularly important question of principle.

B. Criminal justice

Criminal justice is dispensed by the following bodies:

1. The District Court

The District Court is the Court of First Instance for all cases that do not come under the jurisdiction of the Assize Court.

Following the recent reform (entry into force on 2 June 1999), which abolished the Magistrates' Court (*pretore*), the District Court normally consists of a single judge except for cases expressly provided for by law, for which a bench of three judges is required.

When sitting as a bench, the court tries, among others, the following matters: offences specified in section 407 (2) (1) (A) of the Code of Criminal Procedure (collective murder, mafia-type criminal organisations, attempted murder, aggravated robbery with violence, aggravated extortion, unlawful detention of persons for the purpose of extortion, arms trafficking, and so on), violations of the rules of public administration committed by persons in public office, breaches of the peace, damage against the public interest (such as criminal associations and causing railway accidents), rape, incest, money laundering, usury, offences against the social structure, fraudulent bankruptcy, unlawful secret associations, and offences related to armaments and chemical weapons.

Appeals against judgments delivered by the District Court lie to the Court of Appeal.

Attached to each district court is an investigating judge (*Giudice per le Inchieste Preliminari*), a single judge who supervises the acts of the Public Prosecutor's Office at the preliminary stage of inquiries when these acts represent a restriction on the fundamental rights of the individual (for example provisional measures and telephone taps). He or she also has powers to supervise the action taken in a criminal case by the Public Prosecutor's Office and the duration of the inquiries. In his or her capacity as judge responsible for the preliminary hearing, he or she confirms the existence of the conditions required for the proceedings to take place and can draw up the judgment under the alternative procedures provided for, such as *patteggiamento* (voluntary appearance in court) or *giudazio abbreviato* (expedited proceedings).

*2. The Juvenile Court (*Tribunale per i minorenni*)*

This is a separate chamber of the District Court. The bench consists of a judge from the Court of Appeal, who presides, a district court judge and two unpaid judges (a man and a woman) chosen from a group of experts in such matters as psychiatry, criminal anthropology, education and psychology.

In criminal cases, it deals with all offences committed by juveniles under 18.

A special chamber of the Court of Appeal deals with appeals lodged against the decisions of the Juvenile Court. It consists of five members: a judge from the Court of Cassation, who presides, two judges from the Court of Appeal and two experts (a man and a woman).

Appeals against judgments delivered by this chamber of the Court of Appeal lie to the Court of Cassation.

*3. The Assize Court (*Corte d'assise*)*

This court consists of a judge from the Court of Appeal, who presides, a judge from the District Court and six lay jurors, the latter representing the direct participation of the people in the administration of justice in conformity with Article 102 of the Constitution. It deals at first instance with offences punishable by life imprisonment or a maximum sentence of at least 24 years (that is, the most serious crimes against the person, homicide and other offences that have caused the death of one or more persons), as well as offences against the state and other crimes specified in section 5 of the Code of Criminal Procedure.

Appeals against judgments of this court lie to the Assize Court of Appeal, which also consists of eight members (namely two judges, one from the Court of Cassation and one from the Court of Appeal and six jurors).

Appeals against judgments delivered by the Assize Court of Appeal lie to the Court of Cassation.

4. The Court of Appeal (Corte d'appello)

The Court of Appeal is a collegiate body with jurisdiction over a district. It sits as a bench of three judges who all have the right to vote and belong to the ordinary judiciary.

It hears appeals against judgments delivered by the District Court and by the investigating judge. Appeals lie to the Court of Cassation.

5. The Court of Cassation (Corte suprema di cassazione)

The Court of Cassation is the highest ordinary court and sits in Rome. It ensures the precise observance and uniform interpretation of the law, the unity of domestic substantive law and respect for the limits to the jurisdiction of the various courts.

It comprises six criminal chambers, each always sitting as a bench of five judges who all have the right to vote.

In criminal cases, an appeal to set aside a judgment is admissible both for a breach of the law and against measures restricting individual liberty.

It sits as a full court consisting of nine members with the right to vote to hear appeals concerning jurisdiction, a point of law that the individual chambers have already dealt with differently or a particularly important question of principle.

C. Administrative Courts and the Court of Audit

The Constitution provides that anyone may have recourse to the Ordinary or Administrative Courts against acts of the public administrative authorities in order to protect his or her rights and legitimate interests.

The jurisdiction of these courts is determined by the personal legal situation claimed by the individual. In general, the protection of personal rights comes under the jurisdiction of the Ordinary Courts, while a violation of a legitimate interest, that is, rights enshrined in law, comes under the jurisdiction of the Administrative Courts.

Administrative jurisdiction is exercised by the Regional Administrative Courts at first instance and by the Council of State on appeal.

1. The Regional Administrative Courts

These courts were not created until 1971, although the 1948 Constitution provided for them to be set up.

The Administrative Court, of which there is one in each main regional town, consists of three judges. Recruitment is by a public competitive examination reserved for specific professional categories (lawyers, ordinary court judges, notaries, senior civil servants and university teachers).

The Regional Administrative Courts generally rule on violations of legitimate interests as a result of unlawful administrative acts (lack of jurisdiction, *ultra vires,* breaches of the law). They also have a special power to consider the merits (which permits them also to assess the appropriateness of administrative acts) and exclusive jurisdiction (which allows them to decide questions relating to personal rights) in certain areas determined by law.

Appeals against the decisions of the Regional Administrative Courts lie to the Council of State.

*2. The Council of State (*Consiglio di Stato*)*

The Council of State is a complex institution consisting of several permanent bodies: the sections, the full court and the General Assembly.

The Council has six sections, three of which have consultative functions and three judicial, the latter always sitting as a bench of five judges with the right to vote.

The General Assembly, which consists of all the serving judges, has only consultative functions.

The full court, which has only judicial responsibilities, consists of the President and twelve judges (four from each judicial section). Its function consists in guiding the courts towards a particular judicial doctrine but its decisions are not binding on the other administrative courts.

The Council of State hears appeals against the judgments of the Regional Administrative Courts and has exclusive jurisdiction over matters formally assigned to it by law.

Appeals against the decisions of the Council of State lie to the Court of Cassation on questions of jurisdiction and to the Council itself for an action to have its own decisions set aside.

Half the Council of State judges are recruited from among the Regional Administrative Court judges, who must have served for at least four years in that capacity; one-quarter are recruited by competitive examination on the basis of their qualifications and one-quarter are appointed by the Cabinet from among university law professors, ordinary court judges, lawyers and senior civil servants.

For the Region of Sicily, the functions of the Council of State are exercised by the Council of Administrative Justice for the Sicilian Region. This has a mixed composition, being made up partly of judges from the Council of State and partly of unpaid judges appointed by the Sicilian regional government.

In 1982, the so-called Presidency Council was set up, a body that in principle carries out the same functions as the Legal Service Commission for ordinary court judges.

*3. The Court of Audit (*Corte dei Conti*)*

According to Article 103 of the Constitution, the Court of Audit has jurisdiction over matters relating to public accounts.

This jurisdiction covers civil liability for damage caused to the public administrative authorities by the servants of the state in the exercise of their functions, the financial liability of public and civil servants responsible for the accounts of the state, and civilian and military pensions.

Law No. 19 of 1994 set up regional chambers of the court, which exercise their jurisdiction at first instance (sitting as benches of three) in the aforementioned cases. Appeals against their decisions may be lodged with the central chambers of the court, which sit as benches of five judges. Appeals against the latter's decisions lie to the Court of Cassation on the following grounds: lack of jurisdiction, plea of nullity, objections raised by third parties, and applications for a decision by default to be set aside.

The full court, consisting of seven judges, deals with disputes as to jurisdiction and questions of principle (in the case of conflicting decisions) that have been referred to it.

The judges at the Court of Audit are recruited by a competitive public examination based on qualifications and reserved for specific professional categories (lawyers, ordinary court judges, notaries, senior civil servants and university teachers).

IV. The Public Prosecutor's Office (*Pubblico Ministero*)

The Public Prosecutor's Office is an organ of the state attached to the Court of Cassation, the Courts of Appeal, the Ordinary Courts and the Juvenile Courts. Its functions differ from those of the judicial bodies at which they are exercised and are carried out by prosecutors under the supervision of the Minister for Justice.

The Public Prosecutor's Office ensures that the laws are observed, that the administration of justice is swift and efficient and that the rights of the state, legal persons and those lacking legal capacity are protected. It also ensures that breaches of the law are punished and that security measures are applied (section 73 of the Organisation of the Courts Act).

In criminal cases, the principal functions of the Public Prosecutor's Office are to set in motion the prosecution of offenders (mandatory under Article 112 of the Constitution), to handle preliminary investigations, to supervise the police, to apply (to the investigating judge) for persons to be remanded in custody, to plead in court and to challenge or enforce the decisions of the judge.

The Public Prosecutor's Office may sometimes institute civil proceedings and must act in certain types of case specified by law, in cases that involve a public interest and in all disputes before the Court of Cassation.

In 1992, with a view to ensuring the more effective co-ordination of investigations into organised crime, district anti-mafia departments were set up at all the Public Prosecutor's Offices attached to the District Courts located in the main towns. These departments are staffed by specialists in this type of investigation.

A National Anti-Mafia Department has been set up at the Chief Public Prosecutor's Office attached to the Court of Cassation. Its task is to help co-ordinate inquiries carried out by the district departments.

V. Statistical data

A. Number of courts

Civil and criminal courts 164
Juvenile courts 29
Assize courts 93
Regional administrative courts 20

Regional chambers of the Court of Audit 20
Courts of appeal 26
Juvenile chambers of courts of appeal 29
Assize courts of appeal 28

The Court of Cassation and the Council of State have jurisdiction over the whole country.

B. Number of judges and prosecutors

1. Judges and prosecutors at the ordinary courts

President of the Court of Cassation 1
Chief Public Prosecutor attached to the Court of Cassation 1
Vice-President of the Court of Cassation 1
President of the High Court for Public Waterways 1
Presidents of the Sections and Advocates-General at the Court of Cassation, Presidents of, and Chief Public Proesecutor attached to, the Court of Appeal 112
Judges and prosecutors of the Court of Cassation 616
Judges and prosecutors of the Courts of Appeal and the District Courts 8227
Trainee judges and prosecutors. 150
Total. 9109

2. Judges and officers at the Administrative Courts and the Council of State

President of the Council of State. 1
Presidents of the Sections of the Council of State. 15
Presidents of the Regional Administrative Courts. 22
Judges at the Council of State 74
Judges at the Regional Administrative Courts, senior officers, officers 325
Total 431

3. Judges and officers at the Court of Audit

President of the Court of Audit. 1
Chief Public Prosecutor attached to the Court of Audit. 1
Presidents of the Chambers. 40
Judges, senior officers, officers 495
Total 630

LITHUANIA

I. Introduction[1]

The Constitution of the Republic of Lithuania (1992) provides that in the Republic of Lithuania justice is administered exclusively by courts. Pursuant to the Constitution, while administering justice judges and courts are independent and obey only the law.

The formation and competence of courts are defined in the Law on Courts of the Republic of Lithuania (1994).

The court system of the Republic of Lithuania consists of the Supreme Court of Lithuania (*Lietuvos Aukščausiasis Teismas*), the Court of Appeal of Lithuania (*Lietuvos apeliacinis teismas*), 5 county courts (*apygardų teismai*) and 54 district courts (*apylinkiu teismai*). These are the courts of general jurisdiction. On 1 May 1999, specialised administrative courts were established for the adjudication of administrative cases. A two-tier system of administrative courts consists of 5 county administrative courts (*apygardų administraciniai teismai*), the Superior Administrative Court (*Aukštesnysis administracinis teismas*) and the Administrative Cases Division of the Court of Appeal of Lithuania (*Lietuvos apeliacinio teismo administracinių bylų skyrius*).

As of May 1999, the number of judges in Lithuania was: in district courts: 344; county courts: 131; the Court of Appeal of Lithuania: 28; the Supreme Court of Lithuania: 26; administrative courts: 28; total: 557. In Lithuania, all judges are professional judges. There are neither lay judges nor is there trial by jury in Lithuania.

A. District courts

Lithuania is divided into 54 court districts. A district court consists of a chairperson, vice-chairpersons, other judges and an office of the clerk of the court. Vice-chairpersons are appointed in district courts with at least six judges. In April 1999, specialisation of judges was introduced in district and county courts of Lithuania in cases involving under-age parties, including juvenile delinquents.

A district court is the first instance for:

- civil cases;
- criminal cases;
- cases involving violations of the administrative law;
- cases relative to the enforcement of judgments;
- passing of decisions (rulings) relative to the application of coercive measures established by laws; and
- in cases involving complaints against the actions of an investigator or a prosecutor.

B. County courts

A county court consists of the chairperson, division chairpersons and other judges. A county court contains the Civil Cases Division and the Criminal Cases Division.

1. Information dated 4 June 1999.

The county court is the first instance for civil cases where the amount in controversy exceeds 100 000 Litas, except for cases relative to the division of family property by spouses, which are heard in district courts. The county courts also hear civil cases involving intellectual property rights, company bankruptcy, when a foreign state is a party, and so on.

The county court is the first instance for criminal cases like high treason, espionage, attempted assasination of a state official or a representative of a foreign country, instigation of war, genocide, illegal transportation of persons, and so on.

The county court is the instance of appeal for the decisions, judgments and rulings of district courts.

C. The Court of Appeal of Lithuania

The Court of Appeal of Lithuania consists of the chairperson of the Court of Appeal, division chairpersons and other judges.

The Court of Appeal contains the Civil Cases Division, the Criminal Cases Division and the Administrative Cases Division.

The Court of Appeal is located in the capital of the Republic of Lithuania, Vilnius.

The Court of Appeal is the appellate instance for cases heard by county courts as the Courts of First Instance.

The Court of Appeal is the last instance for all administrative cases (cassation is not provided for administrative cases).

In addition, the Court of Appeal hears other cases which the laws of the Republic of Lithuania assign to the competence of the court.

D. The Supreme Court of Lithuania

The Supreme Court of Lithuania consists of the chairperson of the Supreme Court, chairpersons of divisions and other judges.

The Supreme Court contains the Civil Cases Division, the Criminal Cases Division and the Supreme Court Senate.

The Supreme Court is located in the capital of the Republic of Lithuania, Vilnius.

The Supreme Court is the only cassation instance for effective court decisions, judgments and rulings. Such cases are heard by the chamber of three or seven judges or by the plenary session of the Supreme Court.

The Supreme Court forms uniform judicial practice in applying laws. The court periodically publishes the bulletin *Judicial Practice* (*Teismų praktika*). The bulletin contains proposed and approved rulings by the chambers of judges or the plenary session of the Supreme Court. The courts, state and other institutions as well as other subjects while applying the same laws have to take into account the interpretations of the application of the laws provided in such rulings. In addition, the bulletin contains overviews of judicial practice in specific categories of cases which are approved by the Senate of the Supreme Court.

E. Administrative courts

In May 1999, a two-tier system of administrative courts started functioning in Lithuania. The system of administrative courts consists of five county administrative courts, a Superior Administrative Court (in Vilnius) and an Administrative Cases Division of the Lithuanian Court of Appeal.

The jurisdiction of administrative courts is equal to that of courts of general jurisdiction of the respective level. Administrative courts hear cases concerning the legality of legal acts adopted by state and municipal councils and their executive bodies, institutions, and their officers, as well as the legality and validity of actions carried out by certain officials, or their refusal to perform, or obvious procrastination in performing, actions within their competence. In addition, the administrative courts adjudicate disputes relating to the indemnification of loss incurred by state and municipal institutions and their officers, as well as tax disputes and conflicts arising from official relations between public officers serving in state and municipal institutions.

II. The Constitutional Court

The Constitution of the Republic of Lithuania (1992) provides for the establishment of the Constitutional Court. The Constitutional Court was established in 1994.

The Constitutional Court is not a part of the Lithuanian judicial system. Its status and the procedure for the execution of its powers are defined in the Law on the Constitutional Court of the Republic of Lithuania (1993).

The Constitutional Court consists of nine judges appointed for an unrenewable term of nine years. Every three years, one-third of the Constitutional Court is reconstituted.

In fulfilling their duties, judges of the Constitutional Court act independently of any other state institution, person or organisation, and observe only the Constitution of the Republic of Lithuania.

The Constitutional Court decides whether the laws and other legal acts adopted by the Seimas (the Parliament) are in conformity with the Constitution and whether the legal acts adopted by the President and the government do not violate the Constitution or laws. In addition, the court presents conclusions concerning the violation of election laws during Presidential elections or elections to the Seimas, whether the health of the President of the Republic is not limiting his or her capacity to continue in office, the conformity of international agreements of the Republic of Lithuania with the Constitution, and the compliance with the Constitution of concrete actions of the members of the Seimas or other state officers against whom impeachment proceedings have been instituted.

While hearing a case in any of the Lithuanian courts, where there are grounds to believe that the law or the legal act applicable in the case contradicts the Constitution, a judge must suspend the proceedings and appeal to the Constitutional Court to decide whether the law or the legal act in question complies with the Constitution.

The decisions of the Constitutional Court on issues assigned to its jurisdiction by the Constitution are final and may not be appealed.

Judicial organisation of Lithuania

Supreme Court of Lithuania
Criminal Cases Division, Civil Cases Division

Court of Appeal of Lithuania
Criminal Cases Division, Civil Cases Division
and Administrative Cases Division

Administrative Cases Division of the Court of Appeal of Lithuania
5 courts

County administrative courts
5 courts

Superior Administrative Court

District courts
54 courts

LUXEMBOURG

IN the Grand Duchy of Luxembourg, the judicial system as such (the ordinary courts) is constructed on the traditional continental European model: it is divided into three levels of jurisdiction of which the lower two are distinguished mainly by the value of the claim, while the highest level is an exclusively appellate jurisdiction (although this partly applies to the middle level too). The entire system is controlled by a regulatory supreme court which from the purely organisational point of view is the same body that exercises appellate jurisdiction, though provision is made to safeguard the principle that no judge may sit on a case he or she has already heard at another level. There are certain exceptions to the general system as far as the courts martial, the labour tribunals and the social security tribunals are concerned.

There are two levels of administrative jurisdiction, one that functions as a court of appeal and one as a court of cassation. In certain circumstances, cases are also dealt with by an intermediate body known as the Court of Audit (*Chambre des comptes*).

Commencing at the top, this judicial system is divided into two types of jurisdiction, ordinary (judicial) and administrative. In principle, and unless otherwise provided by law, the former are competent to deal with all cases involving so-called "civil" rights, which is a complicated concept that includes, in particular, actions for damages or other actions against the state, even in its capacity as a sovereign authority. In this respect, the Luxembourg system differs from the French, to take one example.

In addition, the ordinary courts have exclusive jurisdiction in criminal matters, which need to be distinguished from disciplinary cases.

An important characteristic of the Luxembourg system is the existence of a single supreme body, the Supreme Court of Justice (*Cour Supérieur de la Justice*), which functions both as a court of cassation and a court of appeal. As the former, it checks whether the law has been correctly applied and the proper procedures have been followed in the case not only of the court's own appellate judgments (delivered by a different bench) but also of the Higher Social Insurance Board (*Conseil Supérieur des Assurances Sociales*). Applications to set aside judgments may be based only on a breach of the law, which is an area that has been fairly strictly defined in the decisions of the Luxembourg courts.

The Supreme Court of Justice sitting as a court of cassation hears appeals against the decisions of the High Military Court (*Haute Cour Militaire*), which, though a separate court, is a kind of offshoot of the Supreme Court.

The Supreme Court of Justice sits as a bench of three judges (*conseillers*) when it functions as a court of appeal (except for the criminal bench, which consists of five judges) and five judges when it functions as a court of cassation. A member of the court sitting as a single judge hears appeals against the decisions of the Juvenile Court (*Juge de la jeunesse*).

The County Court (*tribunal d'arrondissement*) is the ordinary court for civil and commercial matters and tries cases that do not expressly fall within the jurisdiction of another court. All its chambers sit as benches of three judges.

In criminal cases, the County Court has separate chambers for trying either minor offences (*délits* – tried by *chambres correctionnels*) or more serious crimes (crimes – tried by *chambres criminelles*).

The division dealing with commercial cases is called the Commercial Court (*tribunal de commerce*). It sits without the assistance of lay assessors.

The County Court acts as a court of appeal from the judgments delivered by the magistrates (*justices de paix*).

The preliminary investigation of criminal offences is the responsibility of the investigating judge (*juge d'instruction*). The judge's chamber (*Chambre du conseil*) of the County Court, which sits in private, is responsible for preliminary investigations at first instance. The Juvenile Court has a single judge. The President of the County Court sits as a single judge (known as juge des référés) to hear summary applications for provisional orders in urgent cases.

The Court Martial (*Conseil de Guerre*) – one for the whole country – is the Court of First Instance in military cases. The superior courts are the Military Court of Appeal (*Cour d'Appel Militaire*) and the High Military Court (*Haute Cour Militaire*).

At the lowest level of the judicial system in the strict sense of the term are the Magistrates' Courts (*justices de paix*), which consist of a single judge and have jurisdiction over civil and commercial claims up to a value of 30 000 Belgian Francs in cases not subject to appeal and of 400 000 Belgian Francs in cases subject to appeal. In criminal cases, where they are called police courts (*tribunaux de police*), they are in principle competent to deal with petty offences (*contraventions*). Apart from their general jurisdiction, the magistrates are competent to try many special cases and play a key role in non-contentious proceedings.

In the area of employment law, the labour tribunals (*tribunaux de travail*) have exclusive jurisdiction as a matter of public policy over disputes relating to contracts of employment and apprenticeship. Their judgments are subject to appeal.

Where social insurance matters are concerned, it should be noted that there are two appellate authorities, the Social Insurance Arbitration Board (*Conseil arbitral des assurances sociales*) and the Higher Social Insurance Board (*Conseil supérieur des assurancess sociales*).

Administrative jurisdiction is exercised by the Administrative Tribunal (*tribunal administratif*) and the Administrative Court (*cour administrative*). These courts have jurisdiction over appeals to set aside decisions for lack of jurisdiction, action *ultra vires* or the misapplication of powers, violations of the law or protective enactments and, in the cases provided for by law, appeals on the merits (known as "appeals with full jurisdiction" [*recours de pleine juridiction*]).

Disputes about jurisdiction between the ordinary and the administrative courts are dealt with by the Supreme Court of Justice.

Since 1 October 1997, Luxembourg has had a Constitutional Court, which rules on the conformity of laws with the Constitution. Before passing judgment, any court can ask it for a preliminary ruling on the constitutionality of laws, with the exception of laws relating to the approval of treaties.

The judicial system of Luxembourg

Constitutional Court (5 judges)

Supreme Court of Justice sitting as Court of Cassation (5 judges)

Administrative Court (3 judges)
Higher Social Insurance Board (3 judges, 2 lay assessors)
Juvenile Court of Appeal (single judge)
Supreme Court of Justice sitting as Court of Appeal in civil, commercial and minor criminal cases (3 judges)
Administrative Tribunal (3 judges)
Court of Audit
Social Insurance Arbitration Board (1 President (lawyer) 2 lay assessors)
Juvenile Court (single judge)
County Court (civil, commercial and criminal cases) (3 judges)
Administrative authorities
Magistrates' Courts (civil, commercial and petty criminal cases) (single judge)
Labour Tribunal (1 justice of the peace, 1 chief assessor and 1 assessor)

Malta

I. General

The Constitution of Malta provides for the establishment of superior and inferior courts; this is also the organisational structure traditionally known to Maltese law. The Chief Justice and a number of other judges (at present fourteen) sit in the Superior Courts; magistrates sit in the Inferior Courts.

A. Independence of the judiciary

Provision is made in the Constitution for safeguarding the independence of the judiciary. Moreover, by virtue of an Act of Parliament enacted in 1987, the European Convention on Human Rights, including the provisions guaranteeing the right to a fair trial by an independent and impartial tribunal, was incorporated in the municipal law of Malta, and access to the European Court of Human Rights is allowed.

B. Commission for the Administration of Justice

The Constitution also provides for the setting up of a Commission for the Administration of Justice. The Commission consists of the President of the Republic, who is the Chairman, the Chief Justice, the Attorney-General, two judges of the Superior Courts, two magistrates of the Inferior Courts, one member elected by the Prime Minister, one member elected by the Leader of the Opposition and the President of the Chamber of Advocates. The functions of the Commission, as defined in the Constitution, are the following:

– to supervise the workings of all the superior and inferior courts and to make such recommendations to the minister responsible for justice as to the remedies which appear to it conductive to a more efficient functioning of such courts;

– to advise the minister responsible for justice on any matter relating to the organisation of the administration of justice;

– when so requested by the Prime Minister, to advise on the appointment of judges and magistrates;

– to draw up a code or codes of ethics regulating the conduct of members of the judiciary;

– on the advice of the Committee for Advocates and Legal Procurators to draw up a code or codes of ethics regulating the professional conduct of members of those professions:

– to draw the attention of any judge or magistrate on any matter, in any court in which he sits, which may not be conducive to an efficient and proper functioning of such court, and to draw the attention of any judge or magistrate to any conduct which could effect the trust conferred by their appointment, or to any failure on his part to abide by any code or codes of ethics relating to him;

– to exercise, in accordance with any law, discipline over advocates and legal procurators practising their profession; and

– such other function as may be assigned to it by law.

II. Judicial organisation

The organisation and functions of the courts are regulated by the Constitution, by the Code of Organisation and Civil Procedure, and by the

Criminal Code. Other special laws set up special tribunals with limited jurisdiction.

III. The Superior Courts

A. The Constitutional Court

At the apex of the judicial organisation of Malta there is the Constitutional Court, established by Article 95 of the Constitution. The Constitutional Court is composed of three judges, one of whom is usually the Chief Justice, who is also the President of that court.

The Constitutional Court has jurisdiction to hear and determine the following:

– any question whether any person has been validly elected as a member of the House of Representatives, whether any member of the House has vacated his seat or is required to cease to perform his functions as a member, or whether any person has been validly elected as Speaker of the House or has vacated the office of Speaker;

– any reference made to it in accordance with section 56 of this Constitution on voting in parliamentary elections, and any matter referred to it in accordance with any law relating to the election of members of the House of Representatives;

– appeals from decisions of the Civil Court, First Hall, on questions whether there has been violation of any of the provisions of the Constitution guaranteeing fundamental rights and freedoms of the individual or whether there has been a violation of any of the provisions of the European Convention on Human Rights;

– appeals from decisions of any court of original jurisdiction in Malta as to the interpretation of the Constitution other than those provisions relating to fundamental rights and freedoms of the individual;

– appeals from decisions of any court of original jurisdiction in Malta on questions as to the validity of laws other than on the grounds of incompatibility with the provisions of the Constitution guaranteeing fundamental rights and freedoms of the individual or with the provisions of the European Convention on Human Rights;

– any question decided by a court of original jurisdiction in Malta together with any of the questions referred to above on which an appeal has been made to the Constitutional Court.

It will be observed that, except in cases concerning the composition of the House of Representatives and concerning parliamentary elections, where it has original jurisdiction, the Constitutional Court is mostly a court of appellate jurisdiction.

B. The Court of Appeal

The Court of Appeal composed of three judges hears appeals from decisions of the Civil Court, First Hall, except where such appeals are reserved to the Constitutional Court.[1] It also hears appeals from decisions of the Inferior

1. See below.

Courts in civil and commercial matters, in which case it is composed of one judge only. In addition, the Court of Appeal hears appeals, usually on points of law only, from various special tribunals.

C. The Court of Criminal Appeal

The Court of Criminal Appeal is composed of three judges for the hearing of appeals from the decisions of the Criminal Court,[1] and of a single judge for the hearing of appeals from decisions of the Court of Magistrates sitting as a court of criminal judicature.[1]

A convicted person may appeal against his conviction in all cases whatsoever, and against the sentence passed on his conviction in all cases where the sentence is not one fixed by law. An appeal cannot result in a sentence of greater severity (*reformatio in peius*). The accused may also appeal against a verdict of insanity returned by the jury. In certain cases, the court may also order a new trial.

The right of appeal of the prosecution is, on the other hand, very limited.

D. The Civil Court, First Hall

The First Hall of the Civil Court is a court of general jurisdiction in civil and commercial matters where the matter at issue does not exceed *ratione valoris* the jurisdiction of the Inferior Courts. It takes cognisance of all cases which are not, by a special law, reserved to another court or tribunal. In addition to hearing civil and commercial cases, the Civil Court, First Hall, has original jurisdiction to hear cases concerning the validity of laws on the ground of alleged incompatibility with the provisions of the Constitution of Malta, and cases concerning alleged violations of fundamental rights protected under the Constitution and the European Convention on Human Rights. It also has power to review administrative acts.

This court is composed of a single judge.

E. The Civil Court, Second Hall

The Second Hall of the Civil Court is a court of voluntary (non-contentious) jurisdiction in matters of a civil nature, such as tutorship of minors, adoption, interdiction and incapacitation of persons of unsound mind, opening of successions and confirmation of testamentary executors.

The authorisation of the Second Hall of the Civil Court is also required before a spouse can institute an action for personal separation before the First Hall of the Civil Court, which is a court of contentious jurisdiction. In such cases, the Second Hall has also a limited contentious jurisdiction, having power to decide provisionally on questions of custody of children and maintenance *pendente lite*.

F. The Criminal Court

The Criminal Court, composed of one judge, sits with a jury of nine to try, on indictment, criminal cases exceeding the jurisdiction of the Court of Magistrates sitting as a court of criminal judicature. The Criminal Court is

1. See below.

the only court sitting with a jury in Malta. In the matter of the number of votes required for a legal verdict (six out of nine), the Maltese jury system steers a middle course between the English unanimity rule and the Scottish bare majority rule.[1]

IV. The Inferior Courts

The Court of Magistrates (Malta) and the Court of Magistrates (Gozo) make up the Inferior Courts. The magistrates sitting in these courts are, like the judges, all professional, there being no lay judges or magistrates in the Maltese judicial system.

A. The Court of Magistrates (Malta)

The Court of Magistrates for the Island of Malta, composed always of a single magistrate, exercises both civil and criminal jurisdiction. In civil matters this court has only an inferior jurisdiction of first instance, in general limited to claims (including those of a commercial nature) not exceeding 1 000 Maltese Lire. In criminal matters, this court has a twofold jurisdiction, namely as a court of criminal judicature for the trial of offences falling within its jurisdiction and as a court of enquiry in respect of offences falling within the jurisdiction of the Criminal Court.

In the exercise of its function as a court of criminal judicature, this court is competent to try all offences punishable with up to six months imprisonment. In the exercise of its function as a court of criminal enquiry it conducts the preliminary enquiry in respect of indictable offences and transmits the relative record to the Attorney-General. If the court commits for trial, it will be up to the Attorney-General to decide, on the basis of the record of the enquiry, whether there are sufficient grounds for the preferment of an indictment.

If there is no objection on the part of the persons concerned, the Attorney-General may send for trial by the Court of Magistrates sitting as a court of criminal judicature persons charged with a crime punishable with imprisonment for a term exceeding six months but not exceeding ten years.

B. The Court of Magistrates (Gozo)

The Court of Magistrates (Gozo) also exercises both civil and criminal jurisdiction. As a court of first instance in civil matters, the court, composed of one magistrate, has a twofold jurisdiction, namely:

– an inferior jurisdiction, comparable to that exercised by its counterpart in the Island of Malta, in respect of claims against persons ordinarily resident in Gozo or Comino,[2] and

– a superior jurisdiction, both civil and commercial, in respect of causes which in Malta are cognisable by the First Hall of the Civil Court. Within the

1. On the Maltese jury system in general, see J.J. Cremona "The Jury System in Malta" in *American Journal of Comparative Law,* Vol. 13 No. 4, Autumn 1964, pp. 570-583.
2. Gozo and Comino are the smaller islands of the Maltese Archipelago.

limits of its territorial jurisdiction, this court has also the powers of a court of voluntary jurisdiction.

Magistrates of both the Inferior Courts also hold inquests *in loco* in regard to the subject matter of offences when their perpetrators may still be unknown, and inquests in cases of sudden, violent and unexplained deaths and deaths of persons while in prison or under custody.

V. Special courts and tribunals

A. The Small Claims Tribunal

The Act of Parliament setting up the Small Claims Tribunal provides for the appointment of an adjudicator who decides small claims not exceeding 100 Maltese Lire in value on principles of equity and law. Proceedings are summary and informal. The adjudicator may be a lawyer with at least one year of practice or a Legal Procurator with three years of practice. Sittings of this tribunal are held in Malta and Gozo.

B. Commissioners of Justice

A small number of infringements of the law such as minor traffic offences (for example parking in a non-parking area, and so on), illegal disposal of litter, non-compliance with the Education Act, have been depenalised and are heard by Commissioners of Justice. The Commissioners are selected from among persons holding a law degree and are given a three-year appointment.

C. The Juvenile Court

The Juvenile Court Act (Chapter 287) provides for the constitution of a juvenile court to hear charges against, or proceedings relating to, persons under the age of sixteen. In these matters, the Juvenile Court has the same jurisdiction as the Court of Magistrates.

D. Other special courts and tribunals

In addition to the courts exercising ordinary civil and criminal jurisdiction, and the special tribunals mentioned above, there are various other courts and tribunals with special limited functions, such as the Industrial Tribunal (whose function is ultimately to settle trade disputes), the Land Arbitration Board (exercising functions, such as assessment of compensation, in connection with compulsory acquisition of land), the Court of Revision of Notarial Acts (exercising supervision over all notaries, the Notarial Archives and the Public Registry), the Rent Regulation Board and the Rural Leases Control Board (exercising functions under the laws regulating urban and rural leases) and the Board of Special Commissioners of Income Tax (hearing appeals from income tax assessments).

From the decisions of these tribunals there is as a rule a right of appeal to the Court of Appeal, usually on a point of law only but in some cases (notably decisions of the rent tribunals allowing or disallowing the resumption of possession of premises by the lessor on the termination of the lease) also generally. These tribunals are usually presided over by a judge or by a magistrate.

VI. The Ecclesiastical Courts

The Ecclesiastical Courts, whose jurisdiction is limited by the Ecclesiastical Courts (Constitution and Jurisdiction) Law (Chapter 3) to "merely spiritual causes and in regard to members of the Roman Catholic Church only", deal in particular with cases concerning the validity of marriages celebrated according to the Canon Law. In terms of the Marriage Act (Chapter 255), the ordinary courts do not have jurisdiction with regard to the annulment of Catholic marriages celebrated after 15 May 1995. Such jurisdiction is vested in the Ecclesiastical Courts.

MOLDOVA

I. Introduction

According to Article 1 of the Constitution, which entered into force on 27 August 1994, Moldova is a republic.

Article 6 of the Constitution provides for the separation of powers between the legislature, the executive and the judiciary.

Legislative power is exercised by the Parliament, which is the state's sole legislative authority. It consists of 101 members and is elected by universal suffrage in equal, direct, secret and free elections. The electoral term is four years.

The President of the Republic of Moldova is the head of state and is elected for a term of four years. A person may hold the office of President for no more than two consecutive terms.

The President of the Republic of Moldova, after consulting the parliamentary majority, nominates a candidate for the office of Prime Minister and appoints the government following a vote of confidence passed by the Parliament.

The government conducts the domestic and foreign policy of the state and is responsible for general public administration.

Justice is administered by the Supreme Court of Justice, the Court of Appeal, the Regional Courts and the District Courts.

Certain types of case may be dealt with by specialised courts, such as the Commercial Court and military tribunals.

According to the law, judges shall be independent and impartial and may not be removed from office. They are appointed by the President of the Republic of Moldova on the recommendation of the Judicial Service Commission. On being recruited by competitive examination, they are appointed in the first instance for a period of five years, after which they are given tenure until they reach the age limit for retirement.

The President and judges of the Supreme Court of Justice are appointed by Parliament on the recommendation of the Judicial Service Commission.

II. The Supreme Court of Justice

The Supreme Court of Justice is the highest judicial authority and ensures the correct and uniform application of the laws by all the courts and resolves disputes that arise when the laws are applied. It guarantees the fulfilment by the state of its responsibilities towards its citizens and vice versa.

The Supreme Court of Justice consists of the President, two Vice-Presidents, who are at the same time the Presidents of the civil and criminal chambers, and 12 members who make up the chambers and sit as members of the Plenary Court.

The Supreme Court of Justice has seven legal assistants and is divided into the following administrative sections: case-law and judicial statistics, legal records and data processing, financial administration and the secretariat.

Attached to the Supreme Court of Justice is the Consultative Council, which consists of legal scholars and practitioners.

The administration of the Supreme Court of Justice is the responsibility of its President and Vice-Presidents.

Depending on their nature, cases before the Supreme Court of Justice are dealt with by the civil or the criminal chamber, the enlarged court or a bench established by the full court.

The responsibilities of the Supreme Court of Justice are as follows:

a. It functions as an appellate court with respect to decisions of the Court of Appeal and other decisions whose examination falls within its jurisdiction.

b. It rules on appeals in the interests of the law and applications to set aside judicial decisions, as provided for by law.

c. It exercises original jurisdiction as provided for by law.

d. Seeks rulings from the Constitutional Court, either of its own motion or at the request of the lower courts, on the constitutionality of judicial acts.

e. It ensures the standardisation of judicial practice, analyses judicial statistics and provides, of its own motion and without obligation on the part of the judges, explanations concerning problems of legal practice in so far as they do not involve an interpretation of the laws.

f. It affords judges methodological assistance with regard to the application of the law.

g. It exercises, within the limits of its jurisdiction, the responsibilities deriving from the international treaties to which Moldova is a party.

The President, Vice-Presidents and judges of the Supreme Court of Justice are appointed by Parliament on the recommendation of the Judicial Service Commission.

The members of the Supreme Court of Justice are required to retire at the age of 65.

In order to be appointed a member of the Supreme Court of Justice, a judge must fulfil the conditions laid down by law with respect to his or her status and have at least fifteen years' service.

III. The Court of Appeal

The Court of Appeal consists of:

– a criminal chamber,
– a civil chamber, and
– a commercial chamber.

If necessary, other chambers can be set up, as circumstances demand.

The administration of the chambers is the responsibility of the Vice-Presidents of the Court of Appeal.

The President, Vice-Presidents and members of the Court of Appeal are appointed by the President of the Republic of Moldova on the recommendation of the Judicial Service Commission.

The responsibilities of the Court of Appeal are as follows:

a. It exercises original jurisdiction in cases defined by law and hears limited and special forms of appeal.

b. It rules on ordinary appeals against decisions delivered at first instance by the Regional Courts and by the Specialised Courts;

c. It rules, within the limits of its jurisdiction, on cases subject to special forms of appeal.

d. It ensures the standardisation of judicial practice.

e. It resolves conflicts of jurisdiction between Regional Courts.
f. It carries out other functions in conformity with the law.

IV. The Regional Courts

Each Regional Court exercises its jurisdiction within a judicial region comprising several District Courts.

The President, Vice-Presidents and judges of the courts are appointed by the President of the Republic of Moldova on the recommendation of the Judicial Service Commission.

The responsibilities of the Regional Courts are as follows:

– they exercise original jurisdiction in cases defined by law;

– they hear ordinary and limited appeals against decisions delivered at first instance by the District Courts;

– they hear limited appeals against decisions which, according to the law, are not subject to ordinary appeal;

– they hear special appeals assigned to their jurisdiction by the law;

– they deal with conflicts of jurisdiction between District Courts in their region;

– they ensure the standardisation of judicial practice.

V. District Courts

The Courts of First Instance are located in the districts and city districts.

The President, Vice-Presidents and members of the Courts of First Instance are appointed by the President of the Republic of Moldova on the recommendation of the Judicial Service Commission.

The District Courts examine all cases and applications not assigned by law to the jurisdiction of other courts.

VI. Specialised courts

A. Military Courts

The Military Courts are a constituent part of the judicial system and administer justice in the armed forces in the manner laid down by law.

The President, Vice-Presidents and members of the Military Courts are appointed by the President of the Republic of Moldova on the recommendation of the Judicial Service Commission.

The system of military justice consists of the Military Courts, the relevant chambers of the Court of Appeal and the Supreme Court of Justice.

The Military Courts deal with offences committed:

– by ordinary soldiers, commissioned and non-commissioned officers of the National Army, the paramilitary police of the Ministry of the Interior and the Ministry of National Security, the soldiers, commissioned and non-commissioned officers of the Department of Civil Defence;

– by prison officers;

– by persons specified by the law currently in force;

– by conscripts.

Apart from criminal cases, the Military Courts also deal with civil matters that arise in the military units and involve the payment of compensation to natural or legal persons for damage caused by a military offence.

B. Commercial Courts

The Commercial Courts, which are a constituent part of the judicial system of the Republic of Moldova, administer justice by resolving disputes arising in commercial relations between natural and legal persons.

The President, Vice-Presidents and members of the Commercial Courts are appointed by the President of the Republic of Moldova on the recommendation of the Judicial Service Commission.

The system of commercial courts consists of:

– the District Commercial Courts,

– the National Commercial Court, and

– the Supreme Court of Justice sitting as a commercial court in conformity with the law.

The National Commercial Court has two appellate benches, one for ordinary and one for limited forms of appeal.

The District Commercial Court hears cases and applications at first instance assigned to its jurisdiction by the law.

The responsibilities of the National Commercial Court are as follows:

– it exercises original jurisdiction in cases defined by law;

– it hears ordinary appeals against decisions delivered at first instance by the District Commercial Courts;

– it hears limited appeals against decisions given at first instance by the District Commercial Courts that have become final in law and against the decisions of the appellate bench;

– it ensures the standardisation of judicial practice;

– it carries out other functions assigned to it by the law.

The first appellate bench of the National Commercial Court hears ordinary appeals against final decisions delivered at first instance by the District Commercial Courts and appeals against its own decisions.

The second appellate bench of the National Commercial Court supervises the judicial work of the District Commercial Courts and the first appellate bench.

VII. The Judicial Service Commission

The Judicial Service Commission is a self-governing judicial body. It consists of eleven members: the Minister for Justice, the President of the Supreme Court of Justice, the President of the Court of Appeal, the President of the National Commercial Court, the Chief Public Prosecutor, three judges elected by secret ballot by the chambers of the Supreme Court of Justice and three elected by Parliament from among university law professors.

At present, each member of the Judicial Service Commission holds the position of President in rotation since the manner of electing him or her is not regulated by law (the existing provisions relating to the appointment to this office have been declared unconstitutional).

The responsibilities of the Judicial Service Commission are as follows:

– it makes proposals to the President of the Republic of Moldova or to Parliament concerning the appointment, transfer, promotion or dismissal of a judge or President or Vice-President of a court;

– it arranges a judge's transfer to a court of the same level of jurisdiction, as well as his or her suspension from office in the cases laid down by law;

– it takes the oath from judges;

– it deals with the problem of the resignation of a judge;

– it ensures the inviolability of judges;

– it approves the programme of training for the office of judge;

– it ratifies the decisions of the disciplinary boards and the panels responsible for examining qualifications;

– it examines objections to the decisions of the disciplinary boards and panels;

– it submits proposals to Parliament concerning the number of courts, their location and their geographical jurisdiction, as well as the number of judges at the District Courts, the Regional Courts, the Court of Appeal and the Supreme Court of Justice;

– it submits to Parliament for approval the level of funding necessary for the proper functioning of the courts;

– it requests from the courts, the Ministry of Justice and other institutions and organisations the information and documents necessary for the exercise of its responsibilities.

VIII. The Constitutional Court

The Constitutional Court is the only authority in the Republic of Moldova with jurisdiction over constitutional matters. It is composed of six judges, two of whom are appointed by the Parliament, two by the President of the Republic and two by the Judicial Service Commission.

The President of the Constitutional Court is elected by secret ballot from among its own members.

The Constitutional Court's responsibilities are as follows:

– it examines the constitutionality of laws, regulations and decisions of the Parliament, decrees of the President of the Republic of Moldova, decisions made and provisions enacted by the government and international treaties to which Moldova is a party;

– it interprets the Constitution;

– it advises on proposals for revision of the Constitution;

– it confirms the results of national referenda;

– it confirms the results of parliamentary and Presidential elections;

– it confirms the circumstances justifying the dissolution of Parliament and the suspension from office of the President or acting President of the Republic of Moldova;

– it deals with exceptional cases concerning the non-constitutionality of legal measures referred to it by the Supreme Court of Justice;

– it deals with problems relating to the constitutionality of political parties.

IX. The Public Prosecutor's Office (*Prokuratura*)

The Chief Public Prosecutor and public prosecutors subordinate to him or her are responsible for supervising the correct and uniform application of the laws by the public administrative authorities, natural and legal persons and their associations; for protecting the legal order and the rights and freedoms of citizens and for contributing to the proper dispensation of justice.

The public prosecution service includes the central and regional prosecution services and specialised prosecuting authorities.

Junior prosecutors are appointed by the Chief Public Prosecutor.

The Chief Public Prosecutor's deputies are appointed by Parliament on the Chief Public Prosecutor's recommendation.

X. Ordinary remedies

A. Ordinary appeal

1. Civil cases

Appeals against decisions delivered at first instance by the District Courts lie to the Regional Courts. Appeals against decisions delivered at first instance by the Specialised Courts (military and commercial) and the Regional Courts lie to the Court of Appeal.

2. Criminal cases

Appeals may be lodged against all criminal judgments except:

- judgments of the District Courts concerning offences for which the law provides for a non-custodial sentence;
- judgments of the Military Courts concerning offences for which the law provides for a non-custodial sentence;
- judgments of the Court of Appeal and the Supreme Court of Justice.

B. Limited appeal

1. Civil cases

A limited form of appeal is available against:

- decisions of the Supreme Court of Justice at first instance; and
- decisions delivered at first instance.

A limited appeal may not be lodged against a decision in respect of which the parties or participants in the proceedings have not entered an ordinary appeal or have withdrawn it.

2. Criminal cases

A limited appeal may be lodged against:

- judgments of the District Courts concerning offences for which the law provides for a non-custodial sentence;
- judgments of the Court of Appeal;
- judgments of the Supreme Court of Justice.

A limited appeal may not be lodged against a judgment in respect of which an ordinary appeal has not been entered or has been withdrawn.

XI. Special remedies

1. Civil cases

Action (by a party) to set aside a judgment

An action to set aside a final decision may be brought when it has not been possible to challenge it by means of an ordinary remedy because

– the case has been examined in the absence of a party or of another participant in the proceedings who has been summoned to appear in conformity with the law;

– the decision has been reached in violation of the rules relating to jurisdiction.

Application (by the state) to set aside a judgment

The Chief Public Prosecutor and his assistants may, at the request of the parties, make an application to the Supreme Court of Justice to set aside any final decision.

2. Criminal cases

Action to set aside a judgment

An action may be brought to set aside a judgment in criminal proceedings when:

– the procedure to bring the party before the court was not in conformity with the law;

– the party proves that the period in which the case was dealt with by the Appellate Court prevented the party from appearing before it and informing it of the difficulty;

– two final decisions have been delivered against a person for the same offence.

Application to set aside a judgment

The Chief Public Prosecutor and his assistants may, either on their own initiative or at the request of the parties, make an application to the Supreme Court of Justice to set aside any final decision.

See overleaf for chart showing judicial organisation in the Republic of Moldova

Judicial organisation in the Republic of Moldova

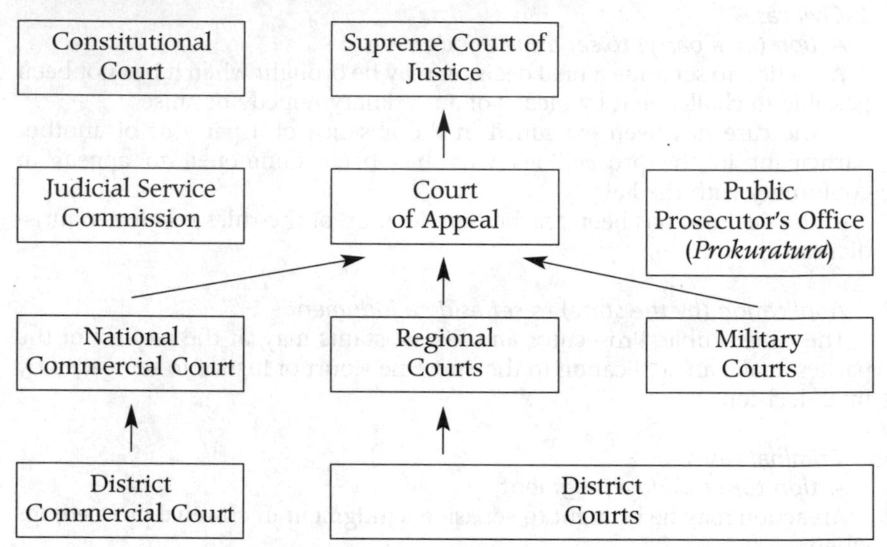

NETHERLANDS

I. INTRODUCTION

According to Article 112 of the Netherlands Constitution, all litigation relating to civil rights and claims fall within the jurisdiction of the ordinary courts. Jurisdiction in disputes not arising under civil law may be assigned by law either to the ordinary courts or to the administrative courts. The method of dealing with such cases and the consequences of decisions shall be regulated by law.

According to Article 113 of the Constitution, the offences described by the criminal law shall also be brought before the ordinary courts. Custodial sentences may be imposed only by the ordinary courts.

Article 116 of the Constitution stipulates that ordinary jurisdiction shall only be exercised by judges appointed by law and that the functioning, composition and jurisdiction of the ordinary courts shall be determined by law. In application of Article 116, paragraph 3 of the Constitution, the law may provide for persons who are not members of the judiciary to participate in the trial of certain cases.

From these provisions, it is obvious that ordinary courts are competent to deal with all civil cases. The term "civil" includes commercial cases as well. Dutch law does not differentiate between civil and commercial cases and does not provide for commercial courts.

As Article 120 of the Constitution provides that laws cannot be violated, judges may not decide whether laws are in contradiction with the Constitution. For this reason, constitutional courts have never existed and do not exist in the Netherlands.

Dutch law does not provide for special courts to deal with disputes between employers and employees, on the basis of labour law. These disputes are considered to be civil law questions and thus subject to ordinary jurisdiction.

Expropriations are also dealt with by ordinary courts.

As regards fiscal matters, which normally fall under administrative law, some of them are dealt with by ordinary courts, though examined by special chambers. Another part of fiscal disputes, in particular those concerning customs and tax laws, is dealt with by the *Tarief-commisie* (Customs and Excise Tribunal). However, on the basis of the Law of 1971 on the Customs and Excise Tribunal, from 1975 onwards tax law disputes have been dealt with by ordinary courts.

Disputes arising from rural properties are dealt with by special organs. In the first instance, these disputes are dealt with by a special canton tribunal composed of one judge and two lay judges. The appeal instance is concentrated at the Court of Appeal of Arnhem, which deals with these cases through its special chamber composed of three court advisers and two lay judges. Lay judges of canton courts and of the Court of Appeal of Arnhem do not belong to ordinary jurisdictions (see Article 116 of the above-mentioned constitution).

Disputes concerning the budget of companies, investigations concerning the direction and management of limited companies, of co-operatives, of various types of banks are also dealt with by ordinary courts, although the exclusive competence in this field belongs to the companies' chamber of the

Court of Appeal of Amsterdam. The companies' chamber is composed of three members of the Court of Appeal and two lay judges (who do not belong to judicial authorities – see Article 116 of the Constitution). These judgments may be subject to appeal at the Supreme Court.

Actions against the state or any other public authority, that is, not only those actions concerning a contract or a title, but also those following an illegal act of the state and any other public authority, are normally considered civil law matters and are therefore dealt with by ordinary courts. However, if some of these actions are of an administrative character, there is a law which provides for a special procedure before an administrative authority; the ordinary courts may also deal with these cases.

Cases involving disputes between civil servants and the bodies for which they work are heard at first instance by (the administrative section of) the Regional Courts (*Arrondissementsrechtbanken*). Appeals are heard by the Administrative Court of Appeal for matters involving the civil service and the social security (*Centrale Raad van Baroep*).

Similarly, cases arising from social security legislation are heard at first instance by (the administrative section of) the Regional Courts. As in the cases specified in the previous paragraph, appeals are heard by the Administrative Court of Appeal for civil service and social security matters (*Centrale Raad van Beroep*).

All criminal cases are dealt with by ordinary courts. Economic crimes are dealt with by economic chambers specifically set up by the courts and, in the case of an appeal, by economic chambers specifically set up by the Court of Appeal. Criminal military jurisdiction belongs to the military judicial authority (war council and higher military court). Dutch law provides neither for jury courts nor for courts of assizes. Punishable behaviour is divided into two categories: crimes and contravention. Dutch law does distinguish between crimes and *délits*.

Ordinary jurisdiction is carried out by judges who must have a university degree in law. The only exceptions allowed are:

– for lay judges who sit in chambers dealing with rural properties and in the companies' chamber (see above);

– for the members of the fiscal chamber of the Court of Appeal (under the condition that certain exams were passed before March 1972);

– as a transitional measure, for temporary judges of the cantons.

Members of ordinary courts are appointed for life – but with an age limit of 70. This rule also applies to judges and temporary judges of the Courts of Appeal and of Regional Courts, as well as to the judges of the cantons. Temporary canton judges, as well as lay judges who sit in the companies' chamber of the Court of Appeal of Amsterdam, in the chambers dealing with rural properties of the Court of Appeal of Arnhem and in the Canton Courts are appointed for five years, with the possibility of extending this appointment.

For the appointment of the counsellors to the Cassation Court, the following procedure applies:

The Supreme Court sends a list with six names to the Lower House of the States General (that is the House of Representatives). The latter then submits to the Crown a list of three names of which the Crown chooses one. By virtue of a constitutional convention now established for more than a century, the Crown always appoints the person placed first on the list submitted by the Lower House.

The synoptic chart (see below) by its very nature only allows a simplified presentation of the Netherlands judicial system. This note provides certain explanations but is itself, perforce, very summary. For instance, it does not deal with the following matters:

– conflicts of jurisdiction;

– questions relating to pending actions;

– the jurisdiction of the Criminal Courts to deal with claims by injured persons – this jurisdiction is very limited and the procedure therefore of scant significance;

– extraordinary remedies (applications to a court to review its own decisions, re-hearings and third party intervention, such remedies being rarely exercised);

– the transfer of proceedings by a court which considers that it has no jurisdiction to a court considered competent to hear the proceedings;

– extension of time limits;

– the possibility in civil cases, with the agreement of the other party, to submit a plea of nullity to the Supreme Court against a judgment subject to appeal.

II. The courts

A. Ordinary courts

There are four types of ordinary court:
District Courts (*Kantongerechten*);
Regional Courts (*Arrondissementsrechtbanken*);
Courts of Appeal (*Gerechtshoven*);
Supreme Court (*Hoge Raad*).

*1. District Courts (*Kantongerechten*)*

Jurisdiction

The principal cases in which the District Courts exercise jurisdiction in civil matters are:

– purely "personal" claims where the claim does not exceed 2 500 Dutch Guilders (not subject to appeal) or 5 000 Dutch Guilders (subject to appeal);

– disputes relating to employment contracts, collective labour agreements, agency contracts and hire-purchase contracts;

– rural tenancy matters in which the court sits and decides in the form of a Rural Tenancies Section, constituted by a district judge and two lay assessors (see above);

– with some exceptions, matters relating to the letting of premises for residential or professional occupancy.

In addition the district judges have jurisdiction in a large number of non-contentious proceedings.

On the criminal side the District Courts deal with most petty offences (and one crime).

Composition
A single judge except in rural tenancy cases (see above).

Remedies
In civil matters appeal may be lodged against decisions of the District Court if the amount involved exceeds 2 500 Dutch Guilders. The appeal goes to the Regional Court or, in rural tenancy cases, to the Arnhem Court of Appeal.

If a civil judgment of a District Court is not appealable it may be possible – but in very few cases – to submit a plea of nullity to the Supreme Court.

An application may be made to set aside any civil judgment by default, that is, the losing party may apply to the court by which the judgment was given. In criminal cases application to set aside a judgment by default can be made only if the judgment was given at first instance and no appeal is lodged.

In criminal cases the judgments of the District Court are subject to appeal by the accused except in the following cases:

– if no sentence or measure has been imposed;

– if the only punishment imposed is a fine not exceeding 50 Dutch Guilders or a reprimand.

The prosecution may appeal unless:

– no sentence or measure has been sought: or

– no sentence or measure has been sought other than the two mentioned above.

Appeal is lodged to the Regional Court.

2. Regional Courts (Arrondissementsrechtbanken*)*

Jurisdiction
In civil matters the Regional Courts have original jurisdiction in all cases in which jurisdiction is not expressly conferred on another court by law.

In criminal matters they have original jurisdiction over all crimes (except one) and a few petty offences.

Apart from this they have a jurisdiction in civil and criminal matters to hear appeals against those judgments of District Courts which are subject to appeal.

The District Courts are also competent, as courts of first instance, to hear administrative cases assigned to them by the law.

Composition
As a general rule, the Regional Courts sit and decide as a bench of three. There are, however, a large number of exceptions to this rule where the jurisdiction of the Regional Court is exercised by a single judge.

The main exceptions are:

– summary proceedings, in which matters requiring urgent attention are decided by the President of the Regional Court. Summary procedure is used very frequently in the Netherlands;

– cases involving children in which jurisdiction is exercised by the children's judge;

– a large number of simple criminal cases dealt with by a single judge known as a "police magistrate". Simple economic offences are, however, dealt with by a special police magistrate;

– those civil cases which are referred to a single judge;

– in order to establish the facts and decide administrative cases, the District Courts sit and adjudicate, in accordance with the proposal made by the presiding judge, either as single judges or as benches of three judges. Administrative cases are investigated and decided by a single judge, except as provided for by law.

Remedies

In civil matters, with some exception, appeal lies to the Court of Appeal against judgments at first instance.

The most important exception to this rule refers to expropriation matters in which the Regional Court's decision is final.

In criminal cases, with one minor exception, there is always an appeal. Appeals are heard by the Court of Appeal.

Judgments of the Regional Court, whether civil or criminal, given at second instance – that is, either on appeal or where a judgment at first instance is not applicable – are subject to a plea of nullity.

As regards application to set aside see under "District Courts" above.

3. Courts of Appeal (Gerechtshover)

Jurisdiction

The Courts of Appeal have jurisdiction to hear appeals against the civil and criminal judgments of the Regional Courts. The Arnhem Court of Appeal hears appeals from the judgments of the rural tenancies sections of the District Courts. The Amsterdam Court of Appeal has exclusive jurisdiction in matters relating to business accounts and the right of investigation.

In addition, in fiscal matters, the Courts of Appeal hear appeals against decisions by inspectors of income tax.

Composition

The Courts of Appeal sit and decide as a bench of three. In tax matters chambers consisting of a single judge can be constituted.

The rural tenancies division of the Arnhem Court of Appeal and the commercial division of the Amsterdam Court of Appeal hear and decide cases with a bench of three judges and two lay assessors.

Remedies

Decisions of the Courts of Appeal in civil, criminal and tax matters are subject to a plea of nullity.

As regards applications to set aside judgments, see under "District Courts" above.

The plaintiff and the administrative authority may (in the majority of cases) appeal to the Administrative Division of the Council of State (*Afdeling Bestuursrechtspraak van de Raad van State*) against a judgment on an administrative matter unless the appeal must be lodged with the

Administrative Court of Appeal for matters involving the civil service and social security.

*4. Supreme Court (*Hoge Raad*)*

Jurisdiction

Except in a few rare cases where the Supreme Court has original or appellate jurisdiction, its jurisdiction is limited to hearing applications in nullity. The Supreme Court may quash judgments subject to a plea of nullity on two grounds:

– violation of procedural formalities where such violation expressly entails nullity or where nullity follows from the nature of the formality violated;

– violation of the law, other than the law of foreign states.

The Supreme Court is thus exclusively concerned with questions of law. As regards the facts, the Supreme Court is bound by the findings of the judgment attached. But, contrary to the system of cassation in some other countries, the Supreme Court, if it finds that the plea of nullity is well-founded, may, if the case is suitable, give judgment itself. Otherwise, if the Supreme Court quashes the judgment, it must refer the case – according to rules specified by law – either back to the court which gave the judgment or to another court.

Apart from a plea of nullity by a party, there also exists nullity "in the interests of the law". In this case the Procurator General attached to the Supreme Court applies for the annulment of a judgment against which an ordinary remedy does not lie or is no longer available. The court decides in the same manner as in ordinary cases, but its decision does not affect the rights of the parties.

Formerly the Supreme Court could set judgments aside only if a written rule of Netherlands law had been violated. Since 1963 the jurisdiction of the Supreme Court has been extended to unwritten law which is of particular importance as regards public and private international law, both of which are deliberately decided not to extend the Supreme Court's jurisdiction to questions of foreign law.

It should finally be mentioned that, under an arrangement between the Netherlands and the Netherlands Antilles, the Supreme Court hears applications in nullity from decisions of the courts of the Netherlands Antilles.

There is, however, no such arrangement with regard to Surinam.

Application cannot be made to set aside default judgments of the Supreme Court except in some cases of minor importance.

Composition

The Supreme Court sits and decides as a bench of five.

Remedies

There is of course no remedy against the judgments of the Supreme Court as it is the highest court in the land.

B. Administrative jurisdiction

There are many different bodies that exercise administrative jurisdiction. Only the most important are shown below.

– Administrative sections of the Regional Courts (see above), which have replaced the former social security tribunals (*Raden van Beroep*) and civil service tribunals (*Ambtenarengerechten*);
– Administrative Court of Appeal for civil service and social security matters (*Centrale Raad van Beroep*);
– Industrial tribunal (*College van Beroep voor het bedrijfsleven*);
– Administrative Division of the Council of State (*Afdeling Bestuursrechtspraak van de Raad van State*);
– Customs and Excise Tribunal (*Tariefcommissie*);
– Study Grants Tribunal(*College van Beroep Studiefinancering*).

1. Administrative sections of the Regional Courts

Jurisdiction

The Regional Courts have original jurisdiction for administrative cases assigned to them by the law.

Composition

In order to investigate and decide administrative cases, the District Courts sit and adjudicate as single judges or as benches of three, in accordance with the proposal made by the presiding judge.

Procedure

Proceedings in administrative cases are held before a single judge, except as provided for by law.

Remedies

The plaintiff and the administrative authority may (in the majority of cases) appeal to the Administrative Division of the Council of State (*Afdeling Bestuursrechtspraak van de Raad van State*) against a judgment on an administrative matter. Appeals against judgments involving civil servants and social security matters lie to the Administrative Court of Appeal for civil service and social security matters (*Centrale Raad van Beroep*).

2. Administrative Court of Appeal (for civil service and social security matters)

Jurisdiction

The plaintiff and the administrative authority may appeal to the Administrative Court of Appeal against a judgment delivered by the administrative section of the Regional Court in civil service and social security matters.

Moreover, the Administrative Court of Appeal has sole jurisdiction over cases involving pensions and equivalent benefits.

Composition

Cases before the Administrative Court of Appeal are heard and decided, in accordance with the proposal made by the presiding judge, either by a single judge or a bench of three members, one of whom presides.

Procedure
As a general rule, cases are heard by a bench. If appropriate, a case may be referred to a single judge. If the latter is of the opinion that it cannot be heard by a single judge, he or she will refer it to the bench. Appeals are limited to cases that have also been adjudicated at first instance by a single judge.

Remedies
There is a very limited possibility of applying to the Supreme Court (*Hoge Raad*) to have a decision set aside.

*3. Industrial Tribunal (*College van Beroep voor het bedrijfsleven*)*
Jurisdiction
This court has sole jurisdiction to hear appeals against the decisions or acts (other than acts governed by private law) of the public authorities with powers in certain sectors of economic life (for example, a decision or act of the Social and Economic Council (*Sociaal Economische Raad*)), of an organ belonging to an interprofessional association governed by public law, a (principal) professional association or an organ of a group with common interests specified in section 110 of the Law on Company Organisation (*Wet op de Bedrijfsorganisatie*).

In addition, the court is competent to hear disputes assigned to it for judgment by a law, for example the Law on the Transport of Persons (*Wet Personenvervoer*), the Law on the Supervision of Credit Institutions (*Wet Toezicht Kredietwezen*), the Law on the Establishment of New Businesses (*Vestigingswet Bedrijven*), the Law on the Hotel and Catering Trade and the Sale of Alcoholic Drinks (*Drank- en Horecawet*), the Law on Agriculture (*Landbouwwet*) and the Law on Games of Chance (*Wet op de Kansspelen*).

Composition
The court sits and adjudicates, in accordance with the proposal made by the presiding judge, as a single judge or as a bench of three, one of whom presides.

Procedure
As a general rule, cases are heard by a bench. If appropriate, a case may be referred to a single judge. If the latter is of the opinion that it cannot be heard by a single judge, he or she will refer it to the bench.

Remedies
There is a very limited possibility of applying to the Supreme Court (*Hoge Raad*) to have a decision set aside.

4. Administrative Division of the Council of State
Jurisdiction
This division has sole jurisdiction to hear specific cases. It rules, for example, on decisions taken by virtue of the Law on Land-Use Planning (*Wet op de Ruimtelijke Ordening*), the Law on the Protection of the Environment (*Wet Milieubeheer*), the Law on Land Clearance (*Ontgrondingenwet*), the Law on

Rural Development (*Landinrichtingswet*) and the Law on Retirement Homes (*Wet op de Bejaardenoorden*).

It is also competent to hear appeals against the decisions of the administrative sections of the Regional Court, with the exception of appeals brought before the Administrative Court of Appeal for civil service and social security matters.

Composition

The section sits and adjudicates, in accordance with the proposal made by the presiding judge, as a single judge or as a bench of three, one of whom presides.

Procedure

Cases brought before the Administrative Division are heard by a bench. If appropriate, a case may be referred to a single judge. Appeals are limited to cases that have also been adjudicated at first instance by a single judge. If the latter is of the opinion that the matter cannot be heard by a single judge, he or she will refer it to the bench. This is possible whatever the case.

Remedies

There is no appeal against the Administrative Division's decisions.

5. Customs and Excise Tribunal

Jurisdiction

The Customs and Excise Tribunal is currently still responsible for proceedings relating to customs, excise and import duties.

Remedies

There is no appeal against the decisions of the Customs and Excise Tribunal.

6. Study Grants Appeal Tribunal

Jurisdiction

Appeals against the decisions taken by virtue of the Law on Study Grants (*Wet op de Studiefinancering*) may be lodged with the Study Grants Appeal Tribunal.

Remedies

There is no appeal against the decisions of this tribunal.

III. The Public Prosecutor's Department

The Public Prosecutor's Department operates on three levels:

a. the Supreme Court;

b. the Courts of Appeal, and

c. the Regional and District Courts.

At levels *b* and *c* the Public Prosecutor's Department deals almost exclusively with criminal matters and prosecutes persons suspected of having committed an offence. At these levels an officer of the department has the right to be present at all civil hearings of the court to which he is attached and can ask to be heard in a number of cases, but in practice this right is rarely exercised.

At level *a* the department is not required to conduct prosecutions, but must be heard in every criminal or civil case (not tax cases) on which it presents a conclusion, that is, a legal opinion. The Supreme Court is not bound by this opinion; but owing to the high standing of the members of the Public Prosecutor's Department attached to the Supreme Court, such conclusions always have considerable influence.

Officers of the Public Prosecutor's Department at levels *b* and *c* are subordinate to the Minister for Justice. Their organisation is as follows:

Minister for Justice

Procurator General attached to the Courts of Appeal	Advocates General attached to the Courts of Appeal
Principal Public Prosecutor attached to the Regional Court	Public Prosecutors and Deputy Public Prosecutors Traffic Commissioners (*Verkeersschouten*)

Since the entry into force of the amendments to the Administration of Justice Act in October 1972, Traffic Commissioners may be appointed in the regional offices of the Public Prosecutor's Department. They have the same powers as Principal Public Prosecutors with respect to offences against the Road Traffic Act and the Motorists' Liability (Compulsory Insurance) Act. All members of the Public Prosecutor's Department except the Traffic Commissioners must hold a law degree.

The Procurator General attached to the Supreme Court has certain other duties, for example:

i. to prosecute ministers, members of the states general and some high officials for offences committed in office. There has hitherto been no case of such prosecution;

ii. to initiate the proceedings for the dismissal or suspension of members of the judiciary appointed for life.

In order to guarantee his independence, the Procurator General attached to the Supreme Court is appointed for life (with an age limit of 70).

Other members of the Public Prosecutor's Department are subject to ordinary civil service regulations and must retire at 65. In the exceptional case of the Advocates General attached to the Supreme Court the age limit is 70.

Although, as mentioned above, members of the Public Prosecutor's Department at level *b* and *c* are subordinate to the Minister for Justice, the latter rarely interferes with prosecutions. The question whether a prosecution should or should not be brought is almost always left to the department itself. (It should be mentioned that the Netherlands follows the so-called principle of "relative" prosecution apart from exceptional procedure; the department is not obliged to prosecute all punishable offences which come to its knowledge. In practice, proceedings relating to a considerable percentage of less serious offences are closed without prosecution or settled by composition.)

IV. Statistical data

A. Number of courts in each category

There are:
61 district courts
19 regional courts
5 courts of appeal
1 Supreme Court
and
1 administrative court for civil service and social security matters
1 Industrial Tribunal
1 Study Grants Tribunal
1 Customs and Excise Tribunal

B. Number of judges (October 1997)

There are around:
80 members of the Supreme Court
238 members of appeals courts
978 members of regional courts
168 members of district courts
74 members (jurists) of the administrative court for civil service and social security matters
15 members (jurists) of the Industrial Tribunal
24 members (jurists) of the Study Grants Tribunal
5 members (jurists) of the Customs and Excise Tribunal.

C. Number of cases heard before the various courts and number of judgments given.

Criminal cases	1970	1975	1980	1985	1990	1995
Cases heard by						
Supreme Court	400	416	1 007	1 566	1 988	2 487
Courts of appeal	2 999	3 904	6 673	-		-
Regional courts	57 785	-	-	-		-
District courts	263 613	-	-	-		-
Final judgments given by						
Supreme Court	417	374	953	1 178	1 830	2 546
Courts of appeal	2 550	3 487	5 939	7 404	8 453	7 740
Regional courts	55 411	64 608	89 476	90 774	95 164	102 331
District courts	256 371					

Contentious civil proceedings	**1970**	**1975**	**1980**	**1985**	**1990**	**1995**
Cases heard by						
Supreme court	107	147	171	287	282	351
Courts of appeal	1571	1911	2710	4027	5091	5200
Regional courts	36423	45532	57708	58726	60889	35800
District courts	69426	88948	101027	138935	167100	226500
Final judgments given by						
Supreme court	86	105	129	287	282	351
Courts of appeal	1064	1231	1514	2368	3205	3300
Regional courts	37259	44373	51421	59527	56398	25200
District courts	62192	79841	89090	128401	152000	215700
Tax cases						
Cases heard by						
Supreme court	172	315	638	781	659	841
Court of appeal	5562	9625	20846	23361	24545	18620
Final judgments given by						
Supreme court	162	289	650	635	670	722
Court of appeal	1522	2457	4590	9967	10471	10929
Administrative cases						
Cases heard by						
Administrative court of appeal						
social security	2096	3271	3674	5611	4933	8671
civil service	221	307	448	698	1018	879
Regional courts						
social security	16761	24583	31688	31646	33242	43592
civil service	944	1 223	2062	5511	7270	4368
Industrial Tribunal	292	500	294	4746	4140	1705
Final judgments given by						
Administrative court of appeal						
social security	1330	2229	2128	2564	3067	1555
civil service	155	208	300	497	696	585
Regional courts						
social security	19137	23397	30997	33194	29080	25693
civil service	523	770	1146	2884	3759	3313
Industrial Tribunal	124	125	196	1316	1554	1040

NORWAY

I. Introduction

The Norwegian legal system is essentially based on time-honoured national custom. However, it is also closely related to the judicial systems of other Nordic countries, which have largely the same traditions with regard to legal history and legal policy. When the union between Norway and Denmark was dissolved in 1814, the Norwegian Constitution was adopted, establishing fundamental principles concerning the organisation of national government and the legal system. Inspired by European political thinking of the day and the constitutions of countries such as Britain, France and the United States, the authors of the Constitution laid down principles concerning the sovereignty of the people, the separation of powers between the King (the government), the Storting (the Norwegian National Assembly) and the courts, and individual rights. These tenets have formed the basis for the further development of Norwegian legal tradition.

The system of court procedure is codified. The most important acts of legislation are the Courts of Justice Act of 13 August 1915, the Civil Procedure Act of the same date and the Criminal Procedure Act of 22 May 1981, which replaced the corresponding Criminal Procedure Act of 1887. The Act of 1981 is largely based on the Act of 1887, but has now been amended by the Act of 11 June 1993. Court procedure in civil and in criminal cases differs in some respects, but the Courts of Justice Act applies to both types of cases.

The Act of 22 June 1962 established the institution of the Norwegian Parliamentary Ombudsman for Public Administration. It is the duty of the Ombudsman to see that the public administration does not commit an injustice against any citizen. However, the competence of the Ombudsman does not extend to control of the Courts of Justice.

II. The status of the Courts of Justice

The Norwegian Constitution of 17 May 1814 (*Grunnloven*) is based, *inter alia,* on the principle that the powers of the state shall be divided between a legislative, an executive and a judicial authority, mutually independent of each other. Since the introduction of the principle of parliamentary government in 1884, it can no longer be maintained that the executive power is independent of the legislative. However, the Courts of Justice have fully preserved their independence of the other authorities.

Disputes concerning the validity of decisions made by administrative bodies are dealt with by the Ordinary Courts of Law. The courts may try the issue of whether the administrative body concerned is in fact empowered by law to make a decision of the kind in question and whether it has dealt with the case in the way prescribed by law. However, the purely discretionary aspect of the decision cannot, as a rule, be tried by the court. Nevertheless, the court may set aside a decision which appears to be the result of the abuse of power, or if the discretionary finding appears to be arbitrary. In recent years the Courts of Justice seem to be showing a growing tendency to try the purely discretionary aspect of decisions made by the administrative bodies. This is probably connected with the extended jurisdiction of administrative bodies in many fields.

Although no specific provision to this effect has been laid down by the Constitution, or by formal law, it is a firmly established principle, based on constitutional customary law, that the Courts of Justice have the power to examine the validity of a statute in relation to the Constitution and set aside the statute if it is found to conflict therewith. The courts are bound by statutory law and by the Constitution, but in the event of a conflict between them, the Constitution must take precedence as the highest source of law.

When the Storting is not in session, the King has certain powers to issue provisional decrees (*provisoriske anordninger*). The decrees are valid for a limited period of time, but otherwise they generally have the same effect as a formal Act passed by the Storting. In practice, however, the courts have exercised great caution in setting aside statutes and provisional decrees which are alleged to be at variance with the Constitution.

Under Norwegian constitutional law a special court, the Court of Impeachment (*Riksretten*), adjudicates cases brought by the *Odelsting* (a separate chamber of the Storting) against members of the government, the Storting and the Supreme Court for any criminal acts that they may have committed in their official capacity. This court is normally composed of five judges of the Supreme Court and ten members of the *Lagting* (the other chamber of the Storting). Since 1814, impeachment proceedings have been instituted eight times against members of the government, but never against members of the Storting or judges of the Supreme Court. No case has been brought before the Court of Impeachment since 1926-27.

III. Court procedure in civil cases

The three ordinary instances in civil cases are, the District or the City Court, the Court of Appeal and the Supreme Court. In certain cases, an agency of mediation, the conciliation board, may also deliver judgment. Furthermore, a special committee of the Supreme Court – the Interlocutory Appeals Committee – makes a number of decisions acting as a court.

A. The conciliation board (*Forliksrådet*)

In general, a person wishing to institute legal proceedings against another person cannot bring the case before a court until conciliation proceedings have been held to try to reach a settlement between the parties.

Mediation is carried out by a conciliation board, which consists of three members who are elected by the municipal council for a term of four years. Both sexes shall be represented on the conciliation board. Normally, there is a conciliation board in each municipality, but the municipality may be divided up into several conciliation districts. At present there are around 450 conciliation boards in Norway. Practising lawyers and certain senior officials may not be elected as conciliators.

Some cases have been excluded from mediation by a conciliation board, such as matrimonial cases, lineage cases and cases against the state or a municipality. In certain categories of cases other than those mentioned above, a conciliation board may mediate if the plaintiff so desires, but mediation is not mandatory. In cases where conciliation proceedings are mandatory, the court before which the case is subsequently brought must on its own initiative verify that such proceedings have taken place, and if not, summarily dismiss the case, even if neither of the parties so requests.

If the parties meet and the conciliation board succeeds in getting them to agree to a compromise, a settlement is reached. This settlement has the same effect as a final judgment. If the parties do not reach an agreement, the case is generally referred to a court of law.

In all cases, however, the conciliation board may deliver judgment if both parties attend the meeting and one of them requests a judgment and the other consents or accepts the claim of the opposite party. If only one of the parties so requests, the conciliation board may pronounce judgment in cases concerning assets, if the defendant fails to submit a defence, or accepts the plaintiff's claim in his reply, if the plaintiff attends the meeting and the defendant fails to attend, or if both parties attend the meeting and one of them requests a judgment. In practice, judgments by default play a major role in the conciliation board. They are delivered on the basis of the plaintiff's presentation of the circumstances of the case unless it conflicts with known facts.

Judgments of the conciliation board may be appealed to the District or the City Court, where the case will be dealt with according to the same rules that apply to cases ordinarily brought before the court in question at first instance.

B. The District Court and the City Court (*herredsretten og byretten*)

The District Court and the City Court are simply different names for the same type of court, depending on whether its jurisdiction covers a rural district or a city district.

During the main hearing, the court is generally convened with only one professional judge, but each of the parties may request that the court be convened with two lay judges (*meddommere*), in addition to the professional judge. When the court finds it advisable, it may also summon lay judges on its own initiative, in certain judicial districts from special panels of lay judges which include experts. If necessary, the court may also appoint expert lay judges from outside the panels. The professional judge acts as President of the court (*rettens formann*), but when deciding the case each vote in the court has equal weight, so that the two lay judges may outvote the professional judge. The lay judges take part in trying the facts and applying the law in the case, as well as in deciding any procedural questions that might arise during the main hearing.

Most district and city courts also have deputy judges (*dommerfullmektiger*). A deputy judge may perform a judge's functions on his behalf, although he may not conduct a main hearing or deliver judgment except when specially authorised to do so or in the unforeseen absence of the judge.

During the main hearing, the plaintiff's legal representative is the first to address the court, followed by the legal representative of the defendant. Each party then makes his personal statement, after which the witnesses are examined, first the plaintiff's and then the defendant's. Finally, each of the legal representatives may speak twice.

In 1996, a trial system called judicial mediation (*rettsmegling*), was introduced on a trial basis for use in civil cases which are brought before the courts. Under judicial mediation, the judge or another person may be appointed to attempt to mediate in the case. This is a considerable extension of the court's traditional activities as regards mediation. Judicial mediation is tried out in one court of appeal and five district and city courts.

An appeal against a judgment pronounced by a district or a city court is generally brought before the Court of Appeal. However, with the consent of the Interlocutory Appeals Committee of the Supreme Court (see below), a judgment may be appealed directly to the Supreme Court when the decision has a significance beyond the case in question or the case has been adjudicated by expert lay judges. This may also be done when it is very important for special reasons on account of the circumstances of one of the parties or to obtain a swift decision in the case.

C. The Court of Appeal (*lagmannsretten*)

There are six courts of appeal (situated in Oslo, Hamar, Skien, Bergen, Trondheim and Tromsø). Each of the courts is headed by a senior judge President (*førstelagmann*) and has at least one judge President (*lagmann*) and several appellate court judges (*lagdommere*).

A district or a city court judgment may only be brought before the Court of Appeal if the monetary value involved is 20000 Norwegian Kröner or more. However, the senior judge President may consent to other cases also being brought before the Court of Appeal, but this is done in very few cases. Cases concerning matters which by their nature involve no monetary value, such as cases relating to the dissolution of a marriage, lineage or the right to personal names, etc., may always be brought before the Court of Appeal.

The Court of Appeal consists of three professional judges, but each of the parties may request that lay judges be summoned. Four lay judges are normally summoned in such cases, but the parties may agree to request only two. The court may also summon two lay judges on its own initiative. There shall be an equal number of lay judges of either sex. They adjudicate on an equal footing with the professional judges in the Court of Appeal in the same way as in the Lower Courts.

The main hearing in the Court of Appeal is conducted in the same way as in the District and the City Court, with witnesses and other evidence being presented directly to the Court of Judgment. The court reviews every aspect of the former decision, as regards both the facts and the application of law in the case.

Judgments delivered by the Court of Appeal may be appealed to the Supreme Court.

D. The Supreme Court (*Høyesterett*) and the Interlocutory Appeals Committee of the Supreme Court (*Høyesteretts kjæremålsutvalg*)

Judgments of the Court of Appeal may be appealed to the Supreme Court, provided that the monetary value involved is 100000 Norwegian Kröner or more. For a lower value, the appellant must have the consent of the Interlocutory Appeals Committee of the Supreme Court, which consists of three supreme court judges. However, cases concerning matters of no monetary value may always be brought before the Supreme Court.

Contrary to the Court of Appeal, all evidence in the Supreme Court is submitted indirectly. However, experts may be examined directly before the Supreme Court, and an inquiry may be conducted by the Supreme Court when this does not necessitate a local inspection. Because evidence is submitted indirectly in the Supreme Court, the court is generally cautious about setting aside the Lower Court's assessment of evidence.

E. Special legal procedures

In some cases, the issue is not so much finding a solution to a legal dispute as assessing the extent of damage or the financial loss sustained as a result of such damage. In expropriation cases (*ekspropriasjonssaker*) and a number of other types of cases specified by statute, it has therefore been decided that the compensation or loss is to be determined by means of a special legal procedure called official assessment (*skjønn*). The Court of Assessment consists of a professional judge – usually from the District or the City Court – and four lay judges (assessors). The review decision is final as far as the discretionary aspect of the decision is concerned. The decision may, however, be appealed to the Court of Appeal on the basis of procedural error or misapplication of law. In certain cases, assessment proceedings in rural districts are conducted by a subordinate state official who is not a lawyer (*lensmann or district sheriff*). A review of the assessment in such cases may be sought from a District or a City Court. Current legislation is under revision and a new act relating to official assessment procedure is now being drafted.

District and City Courts are also courts of enforcement (*namsrett*). They also function as probate and bankruptcy courts (*skifterett*) in connection with the distribution of the estates of deceased persons, marital community estates and estates in bankruptcy and with public debt settlement proceedings. In general, a District or a City Court judge is also a notary public, and keeps registers of real property in which established legal rights must be entered in order to gain wider legal protection against a third party. A central register of legally protected encumbrances on movable property (*løsøreregisteret*) is maintained for the entire country outside the courts.

In addition to the Ordinary Courts, there are a number of special courts which deal, for instance, with certain issues pertaining to land (land consolidation court – *jordskifteretten*) and with collective wage disputes in business and industry (industrial disputes court – *arbeidsretten*).

There is nothing to prevent the parties to a legal dispute from agreeing that the dispute is to be decided by arbitration (*voldgift*), provided that they are free to dispose of the object of the dispute. Cases such as the dissolution of a marriage are thus excluded.

IV. Legal procedure in criminal cases

The Ordinary Courts of justice – the Supreme Court, the Court of Appeal and the District and the City Courts – also try criminal cases. After a major reform implemented in 1995, all criminal cases now start in a district or a city court. The gravest offences, such as homicide, sexual assault and serious drug offences used to be tried directly before a jury in the Court of Appeal, and appeal possibilities were limited. Now, the issue of guilt can be appealed to the Court of Appeal in all cases.

A. The District Court and the City Court (*herredsretten og byretten*)

In order to bring a case before the court, usually at the place where the criminal act was committed, the prosecuting authority prefers an indictment (*tiltalebeslutning*). The indictment is served on the person indicted, and if it has not already been done, the prosecuting authority ensures that the court appoints a defence counsel (*forsvarer*) at the public expense for the person indicted as soon as possible whenever he is entitled to such counsel.

During the hearing of individual cases, the District or the City Court consists of one professional judge and two lay judges. In special cases, the court may be reinforced with two extra professional judges and three lay judges. The lay judges adjudicate on an equal footing with the professional judge in every respect, and take part in deciding both the question of guilt and the sentencing.

Court proceedings take place orally, and the proceedings and pronouncement of judgment and sentence are usually open to the public. The judgment is based solely on the evidence submitted during the trial.

Under certain circumstances, a case may be tried and adjudicated by a District or a City Court functioning as a court of examination and summary jurisdiction (*forhørsretten*). The court is then constituted without lay judges. This applies only to cases involving a criminal act punishable by imprisonment for no more than ten years, and in which the person charged makes an unreserved confession in court which is corroborated by other evidence in the case. It is also required that both the prosecuting authority and the person charged request a judgment in the Court of Examination and Summary Jurisdiction, and that the court does not find such proceedings inadvisable.

Judgments of the District or the City Court, including judgments of courts of examination and summary jurisdiction, may be appealed to the Court of Appeal.

B. The Court of Appeal (*lagmannsretten*)

The appeal may be based on a procedural issue, the application of law, the sentencing or the assessment of evidence in connection with the question of guilt. The time limit for appeal is 14 days.

In the Court of Appeal, the appeal is first subjected to a summary hearing by three judges. They may dismiss the appeal summarily if it is lodged too late or if the notice of appeal does not meet the statutory requirements. They must also decide whether to refer the case to an appeal hearing or whether to refuse to allow the appeal to proceed.

In certain cases, the appeal may be decided without an appeal hearing. This applies, for instance, when the court unanimously finds it obvious that the judgment should be set aside.

In cases where the appeal is referred to an appeal hearing, as a rule no lay judges are summoned, and the case is decided by three professional judges after the usual oral proceedings. However, in appeal hearings that deal with the assessment of evidence regarding the question of guilt, or with sentencing for felonies punishable by law with imprisonment for more than six years, the Court of Appeal is constituted with four lay judges in addition to the three professional judges. Moreover, when the assessment of evidence in connection with the question of guilt is contested and the appeal concerns a sentence for a felony which is punishable by law with imprisonment for more than six years, the Court of Appeal is constituted with a jury (*lagretten*). In such cases, the Court of Appeal is constituted with three professional judges and a jury of ten members who decide the question of guilt. Only in exceptional cases do the professional judges overrule the verdict of the jury.

When the Court of Appeal does not try the issue of the assessment of evidence in connection with the question of guilt, it is, as a rule, bound by the grounds of appeal stated in the appeal (*begrenset anke*). In cases where the issue of the assessment of evidence in connection with the question of guilt is to be tried, the appeal hearing ends with the delivery of an entirely new judgment (*fullstendig anke*).

In all other respects, the main hearing in the Court of Appeal is conducted according to approximately the same rules as in other appeal cases, apart from the changes that follow from the use of a jury.

Judgments of the Court of Appeal may be appealed to the Supreme Court.

C. The Supreme Court (*Høyesterett*) and the Interlocutory Appeals Committee of the Supreme Court (*Høyesteretts kjæremålsutvalg*)

Appeals to the Supreme Court may not be based on errors in the assessment of evidence in connection with the question of guilt. In cases that have been adjudicated with a jury in the Court of Appeal, an appeal concerning the application of law may only be based on errors recorded in the summing up.

The preliminary proceedings are conducted by the Interlocutory Appeals Committee of the Supreme Court, which is composed of three judges. In criminal cases, appeals to the Supreme Court may not proceed without the consent of the Interlocutory Appeals Committee, and consent is only given when the appeal concerns issues that have significance beyond the case in question, or when it is particularly important for other reasons to have the case tried before the Supreme Court. Even though the decision to refuse consent must be unanimous, this means that only a very few criminal cases are tried at third instance. Appeals may be decided by the Interlocutory Appeals Committee in the same way as they may be decided in the preliminary proceedings in the Court of Appeal.

Appeals that are referred to the Supreme Court are dealt with by a division of five judges and in accordance with rules that largely correspond to those that apply to civil cases. The proceedings are always oral, with the appellant addressing the court first. Evidence is submitted by reading the case documents aloud first.

V. The prosecuting authority

Legal procedure in criminal cases takes the form of adversarial proceedings. On one side, there is the public prosecuting authority and on the other the person charged and his defence counsel, if any. The prosecuting authority, headed by the Director General of Public Prosecutions (*riksadvokaten*), is directly subordinate to the King (the government) and is independent of the Ministry of Justice. In addition, there are ten offices of the public prosecuting authority located in different parts of the country, each of which is headed by a chief public prosecutor (*førstestatsadvokat*) and staffed by several public prosecutors (*statsadvokater*).

In most Norwegian municipalities there is a mediation board (*konfliktråd*). This arrangement was introduced in 1991 as an alternative to traditional criminal proceedings. The prosecuting authority may decide that a minor case is to be transferred to the mediation board, if appropriate. Both the aggrieved party and the person charged must consent to the case being transferred to the mediation board. The agreement must be approved by the mediator. The prosecuting authority may only reopen criminal proceedings if the person charged commits a serious breach of the agreement.

If the prosecuting authority finds that a case should be decided by means of a fine or confiscation, or both, it may issue a writ giving the person charged an option to that effect instead of instituting a prosecution (*forelegg*). If the person charged agrees to pay the fine, the writ has the same effect as a judgment. Otherwise, the case is brought before a court and the writ serves as an indictment.

VI. Statistical data

A. Number of courts

The Norwegian judicial system consists of the Supreme Court, 6 courts of appeal and 93 district or city courts. At present there are around 450 conciliation boards.

B. Number of conciliation cases and court cases

In 1996, the conciliation boards dealt with 101 507 civil cases. A settlement was reached in 3 555 cases. Judgment was delivered in 73 801 cases (the vast majority being judgments by default). 5 308 cases were referred to the courts. A total of 12 531 civil cases were brought before the District or the City Court in 1996. Judgment was delivered in 6 040 cases. In the same period 1 745 appeals were lodged with the Courts of Appeal, whereas judgment was delivered in 953 cases. A total of 1 142 appeals were lodged with the Supreme Court (777 of these being ruled on by the Interlocutory Appeals Committee of the Supreme Court). Judgment was delivered in 71 cases.

In 1996, 12 637 criminal cases were brought before the District or the City Courts. In addition, the District or the City Court acted as court of examination and summary jurisdiction in 29 144 penal cases. A total of 2 674 criminal cases were brought before the Courts of Appeal, of which 1024 were tried in a new main hearing. The total number of appeals lodged with the Supreme Court was 579 (541 of these being ruled on by the Interlocutory Appeals Committee of the Supreme Court). Judgment was delivered in 95 cases.

C. Number of judges

At present, the Supreme Court consists of 19 permanent judges, including the Chief Justice (*Justitiarius*). The Supreme Court currently has two divisions, each staffed by five judges. In the Court of Appeal there are 113 judges. In the District or City Courts there are 300 judges and 145 deputy judges.

POLAND

I. The constitution of the Republic of Poland[1]

In 1997 the new Constitution of the Republic of Poland came into effect. Its provisions are of great importance in terms of issues of law and the administration of justice. The constitutional standards are or will be further developed and implemented in the provisions of other legislative acts. These standards are either a continuation of the previous ones or a modification of them, sometimes very significant.

The issues regulated in the chapter on civil and political freedoms and rights include the following:

– legal protection of life;

– prohibition of torture and cruel, inhuman or degrading treatment;

– personal immunity and freedom (including rules in regard to recourse to the courts, the requirement to notify a member of the family or another person indicated by one deprived of his liberty, the obligation to communicate reasons for the arrest, deadlines, the humanitarian treatment of an imprisoned person, compensation for unlawful imprisonment);

– principles of criminal liability (*nullum crimen sine lege,* etc.);

– the right to defence;

– the presumption of innocence;

– rules concerning statutes of limitation;

– the right to fair and open trial, without undue delay, by an independent court of proper jurisdiction;

– protection of the privacy of communication and inviolability of one's home;

– prohibition of extradition of a Polish national and other rules of extradition, as well as the right of asylum;

– prohibition of statutory restriction of recourse to court based on a claimed violation of freedoms or rights;

– the right to have judgments and decisions issued in the first instance reviewed;

– the complaint challenging constitutionality of individual decision – that may be lodged by everyone.

The chapter on the sources of Polish law specifies a catalogue of them and the principles of the system of sources of law. In Poland those are the Constitution, national legislation, ratified international agreements, sub-statutory acts and acts of local law. This chapter gives the principle of direct application of the provisions of a ratified international agreement after its promulgation in the *Official Journal.*

The chapter on courts and tribunals includes the following items and institutions:

– a catalogue of authorities exercising the administration of justice in Poland (these are the Supreme Court, common courts, administrative courts and military courts);

– the principle of at least two instances of court proceedings;

– the principle of jurisdiction of common courts;

1. Text prepared by the Institute of Justice in Warsaw.

– the independence, irremovability and immunity of judges;
– the principle of judicial oversight by the Supreme Court over the decisions of the courts;
– the High Administrative Court;
– the National Council of the Judiciary.

II. The Constitutional Tribunal, the Tribunal of State and the High Administrative Court

A. The Constitutional Tribunal

The Constitutional Tribunal judges the constitutionality of national legislation and international agreements, the compliance of national legislation with ratified international agreements whose ratification required the prior approval by the Parliament, the compliance of legal regulations issued by central state authorities with the Constitution, ratified international agreements and legislative acts, and the constitutionality of the objectives or activities of political parties; it also acts on a constitutional complaint. The Constitutional Tribunal settles disputes as to delimitation of powers between the central constitutional authorities of the state. Its judgments are universally binding and final.

Inter alia, the following persons may refer a case to be considered by the Constitutional Tribunal: the President of the Republic of Poland, the Speaker of the Sejm (lower house of the Polish Parliament), the Speaker of the Senate (upper house of the Polish Parliament), the Prime Minister, 50 deputies to the Sejm, 30 senators, the Chief Justice of the Supreme Court, the President of the High Administrative Court, the Attorney-General, the President of the Supreme Audit and Inspection Board, the Ombudsman, and also individuals filing a constitutional complaint.

Any court may refer to the Constitutional Tribunal a question about the compliance of a regulatory act with the Constitution, a ratified international agreement or national legislation, in connection with pending proceedings (a preliminary ruling procedure).

The Constitutional Tribunal consists of twelve members, all of them elected by the Sejm for nine years from among persons distinguished by their legal knowledge. Re-election is not allowed. The President and Vice-President of the Constitutional Tribunal are appointed by the President of the Republic from among the judges of the Tribunal – candidates put forward by the General Assembly of Judges of the Constitutional Tribunal. The Constitutional Tribunal judges are independent, enjoy immunity and are barred from entering politics.

B. The Tribunal of State

The Tribunal of State decides on the accountability of persons who occupy (or occupied) the highest posts in the state for violating the constitutional provisions or those of other legislative acts. The following persons may be brought before the Tribunal of State: the President of the Republic of Poland, the Prime Minister and Ministers, the President of the National Bank of Poland, the President of the Supreme Audit and Inspection Board, the

Commander-in-Chief, heads of central offices, acting ministers or heads of central authorities, members of the National Broadcasting Board, and – to a very limited extent – deputies to the Sejm and senators.

The Tribunal of State is elected by the Sejm from among deputies to the Sejm and senators for the period equal to the Sejm's term. The Tribunal of State consists of its President, two Vice-Presidents and sixteen members. The Chief Justice of the Supreme Court is *ex officio* the President of the Tribunal of State. At least half of the members of the Tribunal should have the qualifications required for the post of judge.

The members of the Tribunal are independent. In the first instance the adjudging panel consists of the presiding judge and four members, and in the second instance of the presiding judge and six members, with those members who adjudged in the first instance being disqualified.

Proceedings on constitutional accountability include indictment, proceedings before the (parliamentary) Constitutional Accountability Committee, proceedings before the Tribunal itself and enforcement proceedings.

The right to bring a person to justice in a constitutional accountability case is vested in the Sejm, and in respect of the President of the Republic of Poland in the National Assembly (the Sejm and the Senate acting as a single body).

The provisions of the Code of Criminal Procedure are applied to the proceedings before the Tribunal to the extent to which the Law on the Tribunal does not provide otherwise.

In addition to criminal liability (pursuant to the provisions of criminal law), the Tribunal may impose the penalty of loss of the right to vote and to hold elected office. It may ban a person from occupying posts of special responsibility and performing functions in state authorities and community organisations, and decide forfeiture of orders and awards. A declaration of culpable constitutional accountability results in the loss of the occupied post in connection with which such a decision was issued.

C. The High Administrative Court

The High Administrative Court is a judicial body. The court acts in Warsaw and in branches outside Warsaw established for one or more provinces. The court adjudges on whether resolutions of local government bodies or regulatory acts of provincial authorities of the state administration comply with the law. The High Administrative Court also adjudges on complaints against administrative decisions, decisions issued in administrative proceedings which can be subject to a complaint or which close the proceedings, and appellable decisions as to the merit of the case; certain resolutions of authorities of municipalities and their associations; and acts of supervision over the local government authorities. The court also issues replies to questions as to the law submitted for its consideration by local government appellate bodies.

Judges of the High Administrative Court are appointed by the President of the Republic of Poland upon the motion of the National Council of the Judiciary. The President of the Republic also appoints – from among the High Administrative Court judges – the President and Vice-Presidents of the court. The candidatures are put forward by the General Assembly of Judges.

The President of an outside branch is appointed – from among the High Administrative Court judges – by the President of the court. This decision must be approved by the board of senior officials of the court. The judges of the High Administrative Court are independent. Supervision over its adjudication activities is exercised by the Supreme Court.

Within the High Administrative Court functions the General Assembly of Judges, convened at least once a year by the President of the court.

The Judicature Reports Office lies within the structure of the High Administrative Court.

III. National Council of the Judiciary

The National Council of the Judiciary, having its seat in Warsaw, considers nominations for the posts of judges of the Supreme Court, the High Administrative Court, common courts and military courts, and submits to the President of the Republic motions for their appointment. It also considers and decides motions on moving a judge to another post, expresses its opinion on rules of professional conduct of judges, takes position on proposals to amend the law on the Common Courts, acquaints itself with draft regulatory acts concerning courts; gives its opinion on training programmes for trainees and the examination requirements for prospect judges.

The National Council of the Judiciary may apply to the Constitutional Tribunal as to the constitutionality of regulatory acts to the extent that they concern the independence of the judiciary.

The Council consists of the Chief Justice of the Supreme Court, the Minister for Justice, the President of the High Administrative Court (all of them *ex officio*) and a person appointed by the President of the Republic, 15 members elected from among the judges of the Supreme Court, common courts, administrative courts and military courts, four members elected by the Sejm from among the deputies to the Sejm; and two elected by the Senate from among the senators. The term of office of the National Council of the Judiciary is four years.

IV. Supreme Court

The Supreme Court, having its seat in Warsaw, is the highest court authority in the Republic of Poland. This court exercises judicial supervision over the operation of all other courts, ensuring the consistency of interpretation of laws and of judicial practice. The Supreme Court is not a common court; it has its own budget.

The judges of the Supreme Court (Justices), like the common court judges, are appointed by the President of the Republic upon the motion of the National Council of the Judiciary. The Chief Justice of the Supreme Court is appointed by the President of the Republic for a six-year term from among candidates put forward by the General Assembly of Justices.

The Supreme Court considers appeals in cassation and other appeals against court judgments; it adopts resolutions aimed at clarifying legal provisions which raise doubts or the application of which cause disparities in judicial decision-making. It adopts resolutions containing settlements of legal questions referred to it in connection with specific cases.

The Supreme Court is divided into the Civil Law Chamber, the Chamber of Administrative Law, the Chamber of Labour and Social Security Law, the Criminal Law Chamber and the Military Chamber. Each Chamber is directed by a President of the Supreme Court Chamber appointed by the President of the Republic from among the justices.

The authorities of the Supreme Court include the General Assembly of Justices, the Assemblies of Justices of individual Chambers, and the Board of Representatives of Justices.

Within the Supreme Court the Judicature Reports Office prepares and publishes collections of supreme court judgments containing settlements of major legal questions and resolutions entered into the register of interpretation rules.

V. Common courts of justice

The common courts are the appellate, provincial and district courts. These courts decide, *inter alia,* cases concerning criminal, civil, family and juvenile law, commercial law, labour and social security laws, except for cases vested in other courts (for example the Military Courts). Common courts also keep land and mortgage registers and other registers.

As a rule, common courts consider cases as panels of career and lay judges or as single career judge – in open proceedings. Exceptions are set out in laws. Proceedings before courts are conducted following the principle of equality of the parties, with the parties having the right to defence and to appeal to a higher instance unless the law provides otherwise.

A. District courts

District courts acting as courts of the first instance adjudicate all criminal, civil, family and juvenile, labour and commercial law cases, except for those which in the first instance are within the jurisdiction of provincial courts and those reserved to the competence of special courts. District courts also have jurisdiction in cases concerning land and property registers.

As a rule, district courts adjudge as a bench composed of three persons: a career judge as the presiding judge and two lay judges (criminal cases). Cases specified in the law are adjudged by one professional judge (for example, in summary proceedings). In civil proceedings district courts adjudge – as a rule – by a single (career) judge.

District courts are divided into criminal and civil divisions, and, if required, family and juvenile division (family courts), land and property register divisions and separate units for commercial cases (commercial courts) and for labour law and social security cases (labour courts). A division is directed by its chairman, who is the President of the court, Vice-President or a judge.

The district court authority is the President of the court.

Misdemeanour boards are affiliated with the district courts. District courts consider appeals of decisions of the misdemeanour boards and enforce decisions of the boards.

B. Provincial courts

Provincial courts are common courts which either adjudge as the first instance or review the district court judgments.

Provincial courts act in the first instance as a bench composed of three persons (a career judge and two lay judges) or of one person, and exceptionally – in the most serious criminal cases (such as homicide) – five persons (two career and three lay judges) or three career judges (if the case is particularly complex). In the second instance the bench is composed of three career judges (in juvenile cases one career judge).

Provincial courts are divided into divisions, including criminal, civil, family and juvenile divisions (family and juvenile courts), labour and social security divisions (labour and social security courts), commercial divisions (commercial courts) and supervision divisions. Within the provincial court in Warsaw there is an additional unit for antitrust cases (antitrust court). In the provinces where prisons and pretrial detention centres are situated there are also divisions for the enforcement of sanctions.

The authorities of the provincial court are the President of the court, the General Assembly of Judges, and the provincial court Board of Representatives of Judges.

C. Appellate courts

Appellate courts were established in 1990. They constitute the third tier of the common court system. Appellate courts consider appeals of provincial court judgments. Appellate courts adjudge in a bench composed of three judges, and exceptionally, in the most serious criminal cases, five judges.

The authorities of the appellate courts are the President of the court, the General Assembly of Judges and the Board of Representatives of Judges.

D. Specialised divisions of the courts

1. Family courts

Within the district courts are family and juvenile divisions (family courts). These courts have jurisdiction over family custodianship and juvenile cases, proceedings in regard to alcohol addicts and also over cases under the Law on Protection of Mental Health. Hence the family and juvenile courts deal with a whole array of different cases. They have to resolve all problems – except divorces which have been moved to the jurisdiction of provincial courts – connected with family, for example both those associated with normal family matters such as ascertainment of paternity, and those of quasi-criminal character, such as concerning juvenile delinquency. Moreover, the family courts apply provisions of other laws not connected with the family law such as those on coercive placement in a mental health facility, or on the issues of transplantation of human organs. It is also expected that the jurisdiction of family courts will be expanded to cover some new spheres of regulation. Thus it may be said that the family courts are the most interdisciplinary ones.

2. Labour and social security courts

Within the courts there are separate divisions for labour law cases (labour courts), and within the provincial courts and courts of appeal there are separate units for labour and social security law cases (labour and social security courts). In these courts, judgments are rendered by career and lay judges with particular expertise in labour and social security matters. Proceedings in labour and social security cases are conducted under the provisions of the Code of Civil Procedure, in the part regulating special proceedings. Labour law proceedings include matters concerning employment and employment-related claims, claims under other legal relationships to which labour law provisions apply under separate regulations and cases concerning damages claimed from employers under regulations on compensation for accidents at work and occupational diseases.

An employee may also request – before filing the case in court – that the proceedings be instituted before a panel of arbiters.

3. Commercial courts

Within the provincial courts and some district courts (which generally have their seats in capitals of provincials) there are separate organisational units for commercial cases (commercial courts). Judgments in commercial courts are rendered by career and lay judges who are particularly well acquainted with issues connected with commercial law and commercial matters. Disputes are considered under the provisions of the Code of Civil Procedure that provide for the special rules of such. Commercial cases include those arising from civil law relationships between commercial entities within the scope of their business operations – including bankruptcy and composition cases – and the ones concerning relations between partners or shareholders of a company, ones against commercial entities on desisting from activities harmful to the environment and the like and cases which are within the jurisdiction of the courts under the antitrust provisions.

4. Enforcement of sanctions courts

In the provincial courts there are also divisions (courts) for the enforcement of sanctions. The authorities acting in such proceedings are, *inter alia,* courts as such and specialised judges exercising their own powers. Such a judge exercises supervision over the legality and conditions of imprisonment and pretrial detention. The principal responsibilities of enforcement of sanctions courts include deciding cases of conditional release, granting breaks in serving a term of imprisonment (these take the form of meeting with one's relative or another person off the institution for up to 30 hours or on a 14-day furlough on adjournment of the penalty due to illness or other important reasons), issuing decisions concerning the serving of the sentence and considering complaints of prisoners against such court decisions (the Court for the Enforcement of Sanctions considers a complaint as a special, larger bench). In the enforcement proceedings for court orders, the court as a rule adjudicates as a bench composed of one judge.

5. Courts of registration

Registers of legal persons are kept by courts of registration, which are divisions of district courts having their seats in capitals of provinces, and by provincial courts.

The Register Division of the Warsaw provincial court registers trade unions, political parties and periodicals.[1]

VI. Military courts

Military courts are special courts operating in the Armed Forces but they also certain cases in regard to persons who are not members of the Armed Forces. Supervision over military courts in respect of their organisation and the military service is exercised by the Minister for National Defence.

Military courts include garrison and district military courts. Judicial supervision over these courts is exercised by the Military Chamber of the Supreme Court. The first instance military court – the Garrison Court – adjudges in all cases which are not included in the jurisdiction of district court. The District Military Court adjudges in cases of offences committed by soldiers with the rank of major and higher, offences which in common courts are within the jurisdiction of provincial courts, those specified in Article 311, paragraph 3 (armed assault on a superior) and Article 313 (collective insubordination) of the Criminal Code. The District Military Court also adjudicates appeals against judgments and rulings issued in the first instance by the Garrison Court and, in certain cases, rulings issued in preparatory proceedings regarding soldiers with the rank of major and higher. The Military Chamber of the Supreme Court considers in particular appeals against judgments and rulings issued in the first instance by the District Military Court and appeals in cassation.

Only career soldiers may be judges of military courts. A military attorney at law must have the rank of a military officer. A lay judge and "a representative of a body of soldiers" are required to have a military rank at least equal to the rank of a defendant on active duty.

VII. Misdemeanour boards

Misdemeanour boards adjudge cases on petty offences (not considered criminal offences). Members of misdemeanour boards are elected for a four-year term by councils of municipalities within the appropriate court's jurisdiction. Members of the misdemeanour board are independent in making judgments. Legal remedies to a decision of the misdemeanour board are as follows: appeals, demands to refer the case to a court and complaints. Appeals are decided upon by district courts.

A misdemeanour board may impose a penalty of limitation of liberty, a fine or a reprimand. It may also impose additional obligations and additional penalties, including the ban on engaging in a specific activity and the ban on driving motor vehicles. (Relatively short term) imprisonment for misde-

1. The development of an overall, nationwide system of court registers is now under way. The system will integrate information of all the registers, such as land and mortgage register, commercial register and so on.

meanours is to be adjudged by the court. Decisions of misdemeanour boards are enforced by the District Courts of proper jurisdiction.[1]

VIII. Judges, lay judges, court employees and persons working for the courts

A. Judges

Judges are appointed by the President of the Republic upon the motion of the National Council of the Judiciary. The Council receives the prior proposal of the court authority via the Minister for Justice, who may express opinions about the candidates.[2]

Judges are independent. Guarantees of their independence include judicial immunity and disciplinary accountability, immovability, and irremovability (judges are irremovable except for cases enumerated in the law, such as illness, disability or age over 65 or 70).[3] A major guarantee of independence consists in the powers of the National Council of the Judiciary, which under the law "safeguards judicial independence and the independence of the courts."

A judge may not be a member of a political party or engage in any political activity; this restriction does not apply to judges who are deputies to the Sejm or senators.

The basic salaries of judges of courts of the same rank are equal and are a multiple of the average projected yearly salary in the public sector.[4] The

1. The 1997 Constitution does not provide for misdemeanour boards and therefore they are to be abolished (within four years of the day the Constitution comes into force); cases considered by them will be transferred to the jurisdiction of courts.
2. The post of judge may be filled by a person who, *inter alia,* has completed university studies in law, has completed a judicial or prosecutorial training, has passed the examination for judges or prosecutors, has worked as an assistant judge or prosecutor for at least a year, and is at least 26 years of age. The additional requirement for the post of appellate court judge is at least five years of professional experience as a judge; for the post of a supreme court judge the requirement is ten years of such experience, or as a public prosecutor, or counsellor at law, or performance of the profession of attorney at law, or work in state administration at an independent position connected with legal practice. A professor or an associate professor of law may also be appointed to the post of a judge.
3. A judge retires at the age of 70, unless he requests to be retired at the age of 65, or – alternatively – at the age of 55 (a female judge) or at the age of 60 (a male judge) having served 25 or 30 years respectively in the judge's post. Also the National Judiciary Council may take a decision on the retirement of a judge due to illness, etc. A retired judge receives a pension equal to 75% of his most recent remuneration while in service.
4. In 1997 these indexes were as follows:
   appellate court judge - 4.0
   provincial court judge - 3.2
   district court judge - 2.7
   associate judge - 2.0
   trainee - 0.9 to 1.0 (first and second year of the training period respectively).

salary levels of judges of equally ranking courts differ only according to the length of employment and the functions performed[1].

Judges are disciplinarily accountable before their professional bodies.

B. Lay judges

Lay judges for provincial and district courts are chosen by the councils of municipalities covered by the jurisdiction of those courts.[2] The term of office of a lay judge is four years. In adjudicating, lay judges are independent. provincial court lay judges are designated by the Presidents of courts of appeal to consider labour and social security law cases in courts of that instance.

A lay judge – as a rule – may not preside over a trial or session nor perform the functions of a career judge outside a trial.

C. The clerks of the court (*Rechtpfleger*)

The clerks of the court were introduced in 1997 with the aim of relieving judges of responsibilities that are not adjudication in the strict sense of the word.[3] The responsibilities of the clerks of the court are limited to proceedings concerning land and property registers and registration proceedings. The courts have a say in matters that are within the competence of the clerks of the court, since – first – judges are to deal with such matters until there are a sufficient number of the clerks of the court (transitory solution), and – second – a decision issued by a clerk of the court can be challenged by a complaint to the district court (lasting solution).

D. Probation and supervision officers

Probation and supervision officers (family probation and supervision officers and probation and supervision officers for adults) are attached to the courts.

Probation and supervision officers perform their duties on the basis of employment contracts (professional probation and supervision officers) or as volunteers (voluntary probation and supervision officers).[4]

There are some 1 500 employed probation and supervision officers for adults, over 10000 voluntary probation and supervision officers for adults,

1. The indexes of function benefits (versus the average projected salary in the state sector are from 0.3 to 1.1).
2. The function of lay judge may be performed by a person who, *inter alia,* is at least 26 years of age and has been employed or has resided in the place of nomination for at least a year.
3. The conditions for taking the position of the clerk of the court are completion of university studies in law or administration and, in the case of lack of completion of a judicial or prosecutorial training, the completion of a six-month training course.
4. Appointment to the post of a probation and supervision officer is conditional upon the completion of a trial period at the court and on passing an examination (exceptionally the candidate may be exempted from such a requirement).

about 1500 employed juvenile probation and supervision officers, and about 8000 voluntary juvenile probation and supervision officers.

E. Court enforcement officers (sheriff officers)

The officers are public officials attached to district courts. They are appointed by the Minister for Justice.[1] They perform the enforcement functions in civil law cases and have certain other responsibilities, among others the following: enforcing court decisions as to financial and non-financial claims, making seizures to secure claims, enforcing other executory titles and making an inventory before institution of court proceedings or before passing judgment by the court. These officers may also serve processes and other documents, and oversee public auctions.

Court enforcement officers operate under the supervision of the Minister for Justice. They run court enforcement offices. They receive regular remuneration, as well as a commission based on successfully collected enforcement fees (the fees are percentages of enforced pecuniary claims, or lump sums in the case of non-pecuniary claims).

Court enforcement officers have their own professional organisation. The authorities of the organisation are: the National Assembly of Court Enforcement Officers, the National Board of Court Enforcement Officers, Assemblies of officers of individual court enforcement officers chambers and the chambers.

There are around 550 court enforcement officers.

F. Court-appointed experts

Court-appointed experts are persons having expertise in a specific field of knowledge or skill; they are appointed by the court or the public prosecutor in order to provide their opinion in cases which require specialised knowledge. Their opinions regard only factual matters. As a rule, the law itself may not be the subject of a court-appointed expert's opinion.

Court-appointed experts are on lists run by provincial courts; their appointment is for five years. Persons not listed as court-appointed experts can also be summoned as experts.

The court is not bound by the expert's opinion; it assesses it like other evidence, that is, following the principle of free assessment of proof. In court proceedings (or in preparatory proceedings in criminal cases), proof may also be adduced from the opinion of the relevant scientific unit.

G. Sworn translators

In preparatory proceedings and court proceedings a person who has the appropriate professional qualifications and is called by the court or public prosecutor may serve as a translator. Translators and interpreters are usually summoned from a list of sworn translators kept at the provincial court. Their responsibility is to translate testimony, statements and explanations to

1. Some of the requirements of appointment are: completion of higher studies in law or administration, and of sheriff officers' training, and passing the examination.

assist persons who do not know the Polish language and to translate documents being submitted to the court in the course of the proceedings. Sworn translators also translate for the parties and other participants of the proceedings before investigative and judicial authorities. They are also employed in cases where special provisions require the submission of a translation made and certified by a sworn translator (for example in foreign legal transactions).

IX. Statistics (1997)

A. Number of courts

Supreme court 1
Appellate courts 10
Provincial courts 44
District courts 292

B. Number of cases brought and decided

Year 1997	cases brought	decisions
1. *Criminal matters*		
District courts	521276	507799
Provincial courts	227307	228790
Appellate courts	9884	9932
Supreme court	3933	2413
2. *Civil matters*		
District courts	2569519	2647763
Provincial courts	195761	194650
Appellate courts	15823	15038
Supreme court	3899	2501

C. Number of judges

Judges of the Supreme Court 84
Judges of appellate courts 288
Judges of provincial courts 1837
Judges of district courts 4562
Associate judges 926

ROMANIA

I. Political organisation of the state

Article 1 of the Constitution, which entered into force after being approved in the national referendum of 8 December 1991, states that Romania is a sovereign, independent, unitary and indivisible nation state. The form of government in Romania is that of a republic. Romania is a democratic welfare state based on the rule of law, in which human dignity, the rights and freedoms of its citizens, the free development of the personality, justice and political pluralism represent supreme values and shall be guaranteed.

Sovereignty belongs to the Romanian people, who exercise it through their representative bodies and by referendum.

Legislative power is exercised by the Parliament, which is the supreme representative body of the Romanian people and the country's sole legislative authority. It comprises the Chamber of Deputies and the Senate.

The two chambers of parliament are elected by universal suffrage in equal, direct, secret and free elections in accordance with the electoral law.

The number of deputies and senators is laid down in the electoral law in proportion to the country's population.

The Chamber of Deputies and the Senate pass laws, resolutions and motions by a majority of their members.

The Parliament passes constitutional, institutional and ordinary laws.

Constitutional laws are those amending the Constitution. Institutional laws regulate the electoral system, the organisation and functioning of the political parties, the organisation of referenda, the organisation of the government and the Supreme Defence Council, the rules governing a state of emergency and martial law, offences, penalties and the system for executing them, the grant of an amnesty or collective pardon, the organisation and functioning of the Legal Service Commission, the courts, the Public Prosecutor's Office and the Court of Audit, the status of civil servants, administrative proceedings, the general legal system relating to property and inheritance, the general rules governing employment relationships, trade unions and social security, the general organisation of the education system, the general organisation of religious worship, the organisation of local and regional administration and the general rules relating to local self-government, determination of the exclusive economic zone, and other areas in respect of which the Constitution provides for the adoption of institutional laws.

The President of Romania represents the state and guarantees the country's unity and territorial integrity. He or she is elected by universal suffrage in an equal, direct, secret and free election. No one may serve more than two terms as President of Romania. A term is four years.

The principal functions of the President include the promulgation of laws passed by Parliament and the dissolution of the two legislative chambers, following consultations with their Presidents and the leaders of the parliamentary groups, when Parliament has not passed a vote of confidence for the formation of the government.

The Government of Romania comprises the Prime Minister, ministers and other members specified in an institutional law. In conformity with its programme, which is approved by Parliament, it ensures the implementation of the country's domestic and foreign policy and exercises overall control over public administration.

The President of Romania nominates a candidate for the office of Prime Minister following consultations with the party with an absolute majority in Parliament or, if there is no such majority, the parties represented in Parliament. The candidate for the office of Prime Minister asks Parliament for a vote of confidence on the government's programme and list of members.

The government's programme and list of members are debated by the Chamber of Deputies and the Senate at a joint sitting. The Parliament passes a vote of confidence in the government by a majority of deputies and senators.

From the administrative point of view, the country is divided into communes, towns and counties (*judete*). The law provides for certain towns to be declared cities (*municipii*). Public administration in the administrative and territorial units is based on the principles of local self-government and the decentralisation of public services.

At the level of central government, public administration is organised by ministers answerable only to the government, in conformity with the law. At the local level, the public administrative authorities comprise local councils and mayors elected in the manner specified by law in the communes and towns and in the administrative/territorial chambers of the cities. They also include the county councils, whose task is to co-ordinate the work of the councils of the communes and towns in order to provide the public services in which the counties have an interest, and the prefects, who are the government's local representatives and are in charge of the decentralised public services of the ministries and other central government bodies located in the administrative and territorial units.

II. The various types of court

A. The position of the judiciary in relation to the other branches of government

Title III of the Constitution of 8 December 1991 recognises the separation of powers. It lays down that the Parliament "is the supreme representative body of the Romanian people and the country's sole legislative authority" (Article 58) and states that the government "shall implement the domestic policy of the country and exercise overall control over public administration" (Article 101), that "justice shall be administered in the name of the law" and that the "judges shall be independent and subject only to the law" (Article 123).

The separation of powers is expressly mentioned in section 1 of Law No. 92/1992 on the organisation of the courts: "The judiciary shall be separate from the other branches of state government. It shall have its own responsibilities, which shall be carried out by the courts and the Public Prosecutor's Office, in accordance with the principles and provisions of the Constitution and the other laws of the state."

B. Composition and functioning of the courts

The judicial bodies comprise:

- the District Courts, or courts of first instance;
- the County Courts;

– the Courts of Appeal; and
– the Supreme Court of Justice.

There are also military tribunals, which are subject to the limits specified by law. The jurisdiction of the individual courts is laid down by law. The organisation and functioning of the Supreme Court of Justice and the military tribunals are regulated by special laws.

Overall control over each court is exercised by a President, who also has administrative responsibilities. The Presidents of the lower courts and the Courts of Appeal are assisted by Vice-Presidents. They appoint judges to perform duties other than their judicial function, in conformity with the law.

The County Courts and the Courts of Appeal may be divided into one or more sections according to the type of case. If a court is not divided into sections it has mixed jurisdiction. It is the responsibility of the Minister for Justice to determine the number of sections these courts shall have. The Minister determines which courts shall have maritime and inland waterway sections to deal with cases specified by law. The sections of these courts are managed by a President. The Presidents of the courts, or sections as the case may be, form benches to try cases. Where necessary, specialised benches can be set up to deal with specific matters.

Criminal cases involving minors are heard by judges appointed to each court for this purpose by the Minister for Justice.

Cases which, according to the law, come under the original jurisdiction of the District Courts, the County Courts and the Courts of Appeal are heard by a single judge.

Ordinary appeals (*apel*) are heard at the County Courts and the Courts of Appeal by benches of two judges.

Limited appeals (*recurs*) are heard at the County Courts and the Courts of Appeal by benches of three judges.

If the judges hearing an appeal cannot agree on a decision, the case is reconsidered by another bench that includes the members of the original bench and the President or Vice-President of the court or another judge nominated by the President.

1. District Courts

There are District Courts in each county (*judeţ*) and in the City of Bucharest. The area covered by each of these courts within the county is determined by government decree on the recommendation of the Minister for Justice.

The District Courts deal with all cases and applications not assigned by law to the jurisdiction of other courts. The Minister for Justice may decide that certain categories of case in the City of Bucharest shall be heard only by specific district courts, subject to the substantive jurisdiction provided for by law.

2. County Courts

There is a County Court in the main town of each county and one in Bucharest.

All District Courts, both in the counties and in Bucharest, fall within the area of a county court.

The County Courts deal at first instance with cases and applications that come under their jurisdiction by law. They also hear ordinary appeals against judgments delivered by the District Courts, and limited appeals against decisions of the Lower Courts which are not subject to ordinary appeal.

3. Courts of Appeal

Each Court Of Appeal exercises its jurisdiction in a district comprising several county courts. The Courts of Appeal deal at first instance with cases that come under their jurisdiction by law.

As appellate courts, they hear appeals against original judgments by the County Courts and limited appeals against appeal judgments of the County Courts, as well as certain other cases provided for by law.

The County Courts and Courts Of Appeal are divided into civil, commercial, criminal, administrative and, in some cases, maritime sections.

4. The Supreme Court of Justice

The role of this court is to administer justice in accordance with the principles and provisions of the Constitution and the laws of the state and to ensure the correct and uniform application of the laws by all the courts by considering decisions made on appeal and other decisions specified by law. It may also rule on the merits of cases specified by law. In addition, it may ask the Constitutional Court to rule on the constitutionality of laws before their promulgation. Through its Directorate of Research and Documentation, it ensures the clarity of legislation, case law and legal theory. It also selects and summarises decisions for publication in its *Official Report*.

The Supreme Court of Justice consists of a President, a Vice-President, five Presidents of chambers and not more than eight judges.

The court comprises five chambers: civil, criminal, commercial, administrative and military, each with its own responsibilities. Its staff also includes legal assistants.

C. The Public Prosecutor's Office

According to the Organisation of the Courts Act, as amended by Law No. 259 of 30 September 1997, the Public Prosecutor's Office exercises its functions through prosecutors at each court under the control of the Minister for Justice.

The work of the Public Prosecutor's Office is organised according to the principles of strict conformity with the law, impartiality and supervision by superior authorities.

The Public Prosecutor's Office is independent of the other public authorities and carries out its responsibilities solely on the basis of the law and in order to ensure it is observed.

The responsibilities of the Public Prosecutor's Office are as follows:

– It conducts prosecutions in the cases and under the conditions specified by law.

– It supervises the investigations carried out by the police and other bodies. In carrying out this responsibility, its prosecutors direct and supervise the investigators, and their decisions are binding.

– It brings criminal cases before the courts for trial.
– It brings civil actions in the cases provided for by law.
– It participates in criminal proceedings before the courts, under the conditions specified by law.
– It appeals (*recurs*) against judicial decisions, under the conditions specified by law.
– It monitors compliance with the law in the enforcement of judgments and writs of execution.
– It verifies the observance of the law in places of pre-trial detention, prisons, corrective training centres and places of preventive detention.
– It protects the rights and interests of minors and persons deprived of legal capacity.
– It examines circumstances that cause or encourage crime and makes proposals on how to eliminate them and how to improve the criminal law.

The public prosecutors are independent of the courts.

The functions of the Public Prosecutor's Office are exercised by prosecutors attached to the District Courts, the County Courts and the Courts of Appeal. The prosecution service at the District Courts and the County Courts is run by state prosecutors, assisted by deputies, and at the Courts of Appeal by senior state prosecutors, also assisted by deputies.

The state prosecutors attached to the County Courts supervise the prosecution service in their particular area.

The senior state prosecutors attached to the Courts of Appeal supervise the prosecution service in their area either directly or through inspectors.

The prosecution service attached to the Supreme Court of Justice is run by a senior state prosecutor, who is assisted by two deputies.

The senior state prosecutor at the Supreme Court of Justice is promoted or removed from office by the President of Romania on the recommendation of the Minister for Justice.

The senior state prosecutor at the Supreme Court of Justice supervises the entire prosecution service either directly or through inspectors.

The instructions of the Minister for Justice to ensure the observance and application of the law, whether issued directly or through the senior state prosecutor, are mandatory.

The Minister for Justice supervises all the prosecutors through inspectors working for the prosecution services attached to the Supreme Court of Justice or the Courts of Appeal or through other prosecutors delegated for the purpose.

Whenever necessary, the Ministry of Justice, either on its own initiative or at the request of the Judicial Service Commission, may have checks carried out by the general inspectors or by prosecutors attached to the Directorate for Relations with the Public Prosecutor's Office and co-ordinate the policies of the Ministry of Justice to combat crime.

D. Judicial supervision of administrative decisions

The Constitution provides for and guarantees the right of anyone who has suffered damage as a result of the action of a public authority to assert the rights that have been violated and to obtain compensation as appropriate.

The conditions attached to the exercise of this right are laid down in an institutional law (the Administrative Proceedings Act).

Administrative cases are heard by the administrative sections of the County Courts, the Courts of Appeal and the Supreme Court of Justice.

E. Judicial review of the constitutionality of laws

Created with the aim of guaranteeing the supremacy of the Constitution, the Constitutional Court is defined by the institutional law as "the only authority to rule on constitutional matters in Romania".

The court is independent of all public authorities and is subject only to the Constitution and the institutional law by which it was set up.

The responsibilities of the Constitutional Court laid down by the Constitution include review of the constitutionality of the laws, which is exercised both "before the event", in which case it is preventive in nature, and "after the event", by means of an action alleging unconstitutionality.

F. The Court of Audit

G. Judges and persons involved in the administration of justice (registrars, bailiffs, experts, receivers, administrative officers)

Judges and prosecutors are, with the exception of trainees, appointed by a decree issued by the President of the Republic on the recommendation of the Legal Service Commission. Trainee judges and prosecutors are appointed by order of the Minister for Justice. The period of training is two years and begins after the judge has passed the qualifying examination.

Persons involved in the administration of justice are appointed by the Presidents of each court, except for bailiffs, who are appointed by the Minister for Justice.

The conditions for admission to the legal service, the promotion of its members and their rights and duties are laid down in the Organisation of the Courts Act 1992.

H. Rights of supervision

The Legal Service Commission and the Minister for Justice ensure the independence of the courts.

The Minister for Justice is responsible for the proper organisation and functioning of the courts as a public service. Through the judicial inspectors at the Courts of Appeal, he is informed on the operation of the courts and on any situation likely to have an adverse effect on the quality of their work or on the application of the laws and regulations in the Court of Appeal districts.

The Presidents and Vice-Presidents of the courts supervise the organisation and quality of the service, the observance of the laws and regulations within the institution of which they are in charge and the courts in their district. The Presidents of the Courts of Appeal also carry out this function through judicial inspectors attached to the courts.

On no account may the checks carried out lead to interference with the judicial process or to a review of a case that has already been heard. The exercise of the responsibilities assigned to the Minister for Justice by law in connection with the lodging of appeals is not considered to be interference.

I. Other personnel of the law
– lawyers
– notaries

1. The Legislative Council[1]

The Legislative Council is a specialised consultative body of the Romanian Parliament. It gives its opinion on draft legislation with a view to systemising, unifying and co-ordinating all legislation and officially keeps all Romanian legislation up to date. Its individual responsibilities are as follows:

– it analyses and gives its opinion on government bills, private member's bills, draft orders and government decisions of a legislative nature, with a view to subjecting them to the adoption procedure as appropriate;

– it analyses and gives its opinion, when so requested by the chairman of the responsible parliamentary committee, on amendments submitted to it for debate and on government or private member's bills referred to it after being passed by one of the houses of Parliament;

– following a decision of the Chamber of Deputies or the Senate, it draws up itself or co-ordinates the drawing up of codes or other particularly complex laws;

– following a decision of the Chamber of Deputies or the Senate or on its own initiative, it produces studies aimed at systemising, unifying and co-ordinating legislation and makes proposals to the Parliament and, as the case may be, the government;

– it examines the conformity of legislation with the provisions and principles of the Constitution and refers confirmed cases of non-constitutionality to the permanent bureaux of the houses of Parliament and, as the case may be, the government. Within a maximum of twelve months, as laid down in its constitution, it presents proposals to bring the previous legislation into line with the provisions and principles of the Constitution;

– it officially keeps legislation up to date and is in charge of computerisation of the up-dating system;

– it co-ordinates the drawing up and publication of registers of legislation enacted and of collections of legislative instruments in Romanian and other languages and gives its opinion, with regard to co-ordination with the official updating of legislation and on collections compiled by other authorities or by natural or legal persons; and

– it keeps a copy of the original of all laws enacted and the corresponding promulgation orders. The Legislative Council presents an annual report on its work to Parliament.

1. Law No. 73 of 3 November 1993 on the work, organisation and functioning of the Legislative Council was published in the *Official Bulletin,* Part I, No. 260, of 5 November 1993.

2. The Ombudsperson[1]

The aim of the institution of the Ombudsperson is to protect citizens' rights and freedoms in their relations with the public authorities.

The Ombudsperson:

– receives complaints from persons who consider their rights and freedoms have been violated by the public authorities and rules on their complaints;

– ensures that the applications received are dealt with in accordance with the law and requires the public authorities in question or their officials to cease their violation of the petitioner's rights and freedoms, restore those rights and make reparation for the damage suffered.

If the Ombudsperson finds that the Public Prosecutor's Office is competent to settle a complaint referred to him or her or if the complaint is on a court's list or is directed against judicial errors, he or she will bring the case to the attention of the Senior Public Prosecutor attached to the Supreme Court of Justice or the Judicial Service Commission, which are obliged to communicate the conclusions they have reached and the measures taken.

The Ombudsperson, who is appointed by the Senate for four years, is independent of any other public authority. He or she may not perform any other public or private office.

In the exercise of his or her responsibilities, the Ombudsperson makes recommendations that may not be subjected to a review by Parliament or a court.

The Ombudsperson presents a report to Parliament either annually or at the request of the two houses.

1. Law No. 35/1997, published in the 1997 *Official Bulletin*.

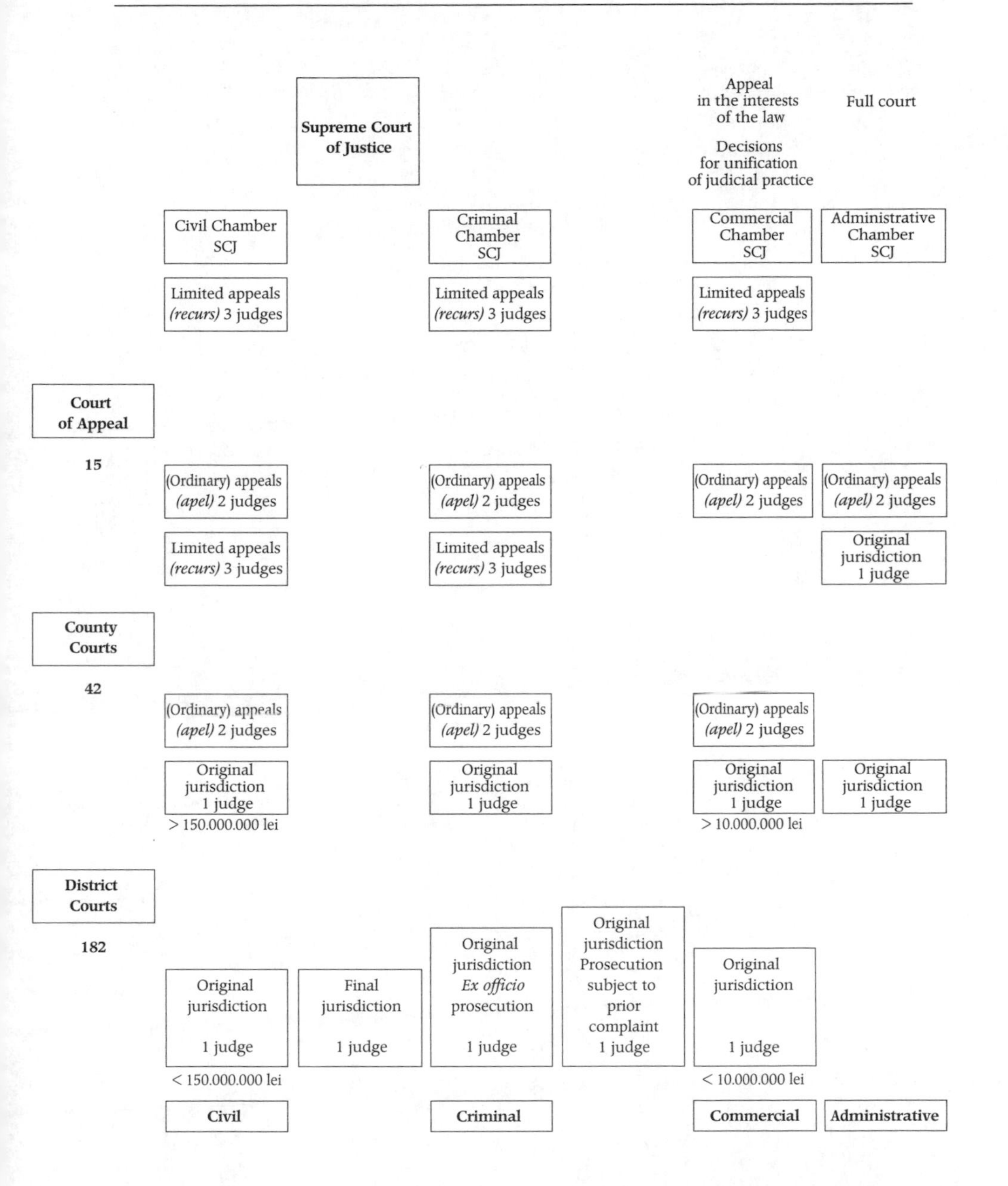
Supreme Court of Justice
Appeal in the interests of the law
Full court
Decisions for unification of judicial practice
Civil Chamber SCJ
Criminal Chamber SCJ
Commercial Chamber SCJ
Administrative Chamber SCJ
Limited appeals (recurs) 3 judges
Limited appeals (recurs) 3 judges
Limited appeals (recurs) 3 judges
Court of Appeal
15
(Ordinary) appeals (apel) 2 judges
(Ordinary) appeals (apel) 2 judges
(Ordinary) appeals (apel) 2 judges
(Ordinary) appeals (apel) 2 judges
Limited appeals (recurs) 3 judges
Limited appeals (recurs) 3 judges
Original jurisdiction 1 judge
County Courts
42
(Ordinary) appeals (apel) 2 judges
(Ordinary) appeals (apel) 2 judges
(Ordinary) appeals (apel) 2 judges
Original jurisdiction 1 judge
Original jurisdiction 1 judge
Original jurisdiction 1 judge
Original jurisdiction 1 judge
> 150.000.000 lei
> 10.000.000 lei
District Courts
182
Original jurisdiction 1 judge
Final jurisdiction 1 judge
Original jurisdiction Ex officio prosecution 1 judge
Original jurisdiction Prosecution subject to prior complaint 1 judge
Original jurisdiction 1 judge
< 150.000.000 lei
< 10.000.000 lei
Civil
Criminal
Commercial
Administrative

Slovak Republic

THE principle of the separation of the executive, the legislature and the judiciary is observed in the legal order of the Slovak Republic. This principle in enshrined in the Constitution, which was adopted on 1 September 1992 and entered into force on 1 January 1993, the day the Slovak Republic came into being.

I. The judiciary

The judiciary is governed by Title VII of the Constitution. Chapter 1 of Title VII deals with the Constitutional Court, and Chapter 2 with the judicial authorities. However, the fact that this title is divided into two chapters does not mean the Constitutional Court is superior to other courts.

II. The Constitutional Court

The Constitutional Court of the Slovak Republic is a special court that is independent both of the legislature and the executive and exercises its jurisdiction over the entire territory of the Republic in order to ensure, in the absence of subordinate institutions, the constitutionality of the laws. In particular, its jurisdiction covers:

– decisions on the conformity of laws with the provisions of the Constitution;

– decisions on the conformity of subordinate legislation with the provisions of the Constitution and other provisions and on the conformity of generally binding local authority regulations with those adopted by the higher executive organs; and

– decisions on the conformity of generally binding legal rules (including laws) with international agreements ratified in accordance with the required procedures.

In addition to the responsibilities set out above, the Constitutional Court fulfils the function of a court with jurisdiction over electoral matters and of a court empowered to hear a charge brought by the National Council of the Slovak Republic (the Slovak Parliament) for an act of high treason of which the President of the Republic has been accused (Article 129 of the Constitution).

The Constitutional Court is a single court. It is composed of six judges appointed by the President of the Republic for seven years from a list of candidates proposed by the National Council.

III. The Courts of First Instance and the Regional Courts

The judicial system in the Slovak Republic consists of three tiers:

– the District Courts, the Courts of First Instance, comprise the lowest tier;
– the Regional Courts comprise the second tier, above which is
– the Supreme Court.

The structure of the various levels of courts with general jurisdiction is laid down in the Administration of Justice Act.

The District Courts sit either as benches (civil, criminal or commercial) of three or five judges or with a single judge, as provided for by law. The benches always include one lay assessor.

The Regional Courts function both as courts of appeal and, in certain cases, as courts of first instance. In their appellate role they rule on appeals against the judgments of the lower courts. They sit as benches made up of the President, judges and one lay assessor.

The Regional Courts also have an administrative section that exercises judicial review over decisions taken by the administrative authorities. The Slovak Republic has no independent system of administrative tribunals.

Judicial review of administrative decisions takes the following two forms:

– rulings on appeals against decisions of the administrative authorities, as provided for by law; and

– review of the legality of decisions taken by an administrative body, which may be either confirmed or set aside.

The judicial system also includes military tribunals, which hear all criminal cases involving the armed forces, prisoners of war and other persons specified by law. There are district military tribunals and a high military court.

At present, there are 55 district courts and 8 regional courts. In their application of the law the Lower Courts are bound by the legal opinion of a higher court in its decision to quash a judgment only when retrying the case after the original decision has been set aside. Otherwise, a legal opinion expressed by one court is not binding on any other court. Nevertheless, judicial decisions and the legal opinions formulated in them play a significant role in the interpretation of the law and thus constitute an important means of standardising interpretation of the laws by the courts. The Supreme Court accordingly publishes the principal decisions of the Slovak courts in an Official Collection, which forms an important source of case law.

IV. The Supreme Court

The Supreme Court of the Slovak Republic is the highest judicial authority in the country. It functions as a court of cassation. It is permitted only in exceptional cases to vary decisions by the Courts of Appeal in criminal proceedings. However, it functions as a court of appeal in cases dealt with at first instance by a regional court.

The responsibilities of the Supreme Court are laid down in the rules of procedure applicable in a given case. In criminal cases heard at first instance by the District Courts, appeals lie to the Regional Courts. If the Chief Public Prosecutor or the Minister for Justice makes an application to set aside a decision of a regional court, it is heard by a chamber of the Supreme Court. In cases heard at first instance by a regional court, appeals lie to the relevant chamber of the Supreme Court. If an application is made to set aside a decision of a chamber of the Supreme Court exercising appellate jurisdiction, it is dealt with by a bench of the Supreme Court consisting of five members. If the Supreme Court finds that the law has not been broken, it will refuse the application. If the law has been broken, it will act accordingly. If the law has been broken to the detriment of the accused, it will simultaneously set aside all or part of the decision that has been challenged. If a new decision has to be taken once the challenged decision has been quashed, the Supreme Court will order the court that reached it to retry the case. In exceptional cases, the Supreme Court may rule on the matter itself by virtue of the specific powers conferred on it, provided that it bases its ruling on the facts of the case as already established. However, under the Code of Criminal Procedure, the Supreme Court does not have the power:

– to find the accused guilty of the offence in respect of which he or she has been discharged or acquitted in the decision appealed against or in respect of which the criminal proceedings have been concluded;

– to find the accused guilty of a more serious criminal offence than that for which he or she has been found guilty in the decision appealed against;

– to sentence the accused to a term of imprisonment exceeding fifteen years or to life imprisonment.

The jurisdiction of the Supreme Court in civil, commercial and administrative matters is governed by the Code of Civil Procedure. In civil or commercial cases heard at first instance by the District Courts, appeals lie to the Regional Courts. If an extraordinary appeal is lodged against a decision of the District Court, the case is heard by a chamber of the Supreme Court. If the Regional Court deals with a case at first instance, an appeal lies to the Supreme Court. When a chamber of the Supreme Court deals with an extraordinary appeal it will dismiss the case if it considers the decision of the Appellate Court was well-founded. If not, it will set it aside. In administrative cases, the Supreme Court is empowered to review as to the merits the decisions of:

– the central administrative authorities;

– state administrative authorities responsible for the entire territory of the Slovak Republic;

– authorities responsible throughout the entire territory of the Slovak Republic for carrying out the administration of the state, to the extent laid down in a special law; and

– self-governing bodies and other legal entities authorised by the law to take decisions in the area of public administration, unless the Supreme Court is competent to do so by virtue of a special law. If the chamber of the Supreme Court considers that the decision challenged is in conformity with the law, it will dismiss the application. If it finds that the administrative decision was legally flawed or that the facts on which it was based are not established, it will reach a judgment setting aside the administrative authority's decision at first instance and remit the case to that authority for re-examination.

The Supreme Court ensures the uniform interpretation and application of generally binding laws and regulations by:

– hearing ordinary and extraordinary appeals against the decisions of the Lower Courts in the cases provided for by law;

– expressing its opinion on matters relating to the uniform interpretation of generally binding laws and regulations;

– examining the conformity with the law of decisions taken by the central administrative authorities of the Slovak Republic;

– ruling on the recognition and enforceability in the Slovak Republic of decisions made by foreign courts, if this is provided for by law or by an international instrument; and

– ruling on other cases provided for by law.

The Supreme Court consists of a President, a Vice-President and other judges. It sits in benches consisting of a President and two other supreme court judges. In the case of extraordinary appeals the bench is made up of its President and four other supreme court judges. The court is divided into criminal, civil, commercial and administrative chambers, each of which is headed by a President appointed by the President of the Supreme Court. They organise and direct the work of the chambers. The latter also express their opinion on matters relating to the uniform interpretation of generally binding laws and regulations. The full court also issues its opinions on such matters, especially with regard to cases that come under the jurisdiction of more than one chamber and those that give rise to disagreement. In addition, it examines reports on the effectiveness of generally binding laws and regulations and, on this basis, presents draft proposals for new legislation. The Supreme Court has no lay assessors.

The courts may not refuse to apply rules enacted by the executive (subordinate legislation). However, they are entitled under the Constitution to ask the Constitutional Court to determine the conformity of these rules with the law and to suspend judgment in a specific case until such time as the Constitutional Court has given its ruling. The Constitutional Court's judgment on the legality (constitutionality) of the rule in question is binding on all the courts.

According to the Constitution, the judicial authorities shall carry out their work independently of any other state bodies, including those responsible for the administration of the courts at all levels of jurisdiction. The Ministry of Justice is responsible for the administration of the Higher Courts, while this responsibility is shared in the case of the Supreme Court by its President and the Minister for Justice. The Presidents of the Lower Courts are in charge of their own administration and are assisted by the relevant staff. In the exercise of his or her administrative duties, the only action taken by the Minister with respect to a court decision is to raise an objection asserting a breach of the criminal law. The Supreme Court rules on the Minister's objection. In the interests of ensuring the uniform interpretation of the laws, the Minister can also ask for a matter to be brought before the Supreme Court when there is a disagreement between the Lower Courts on a point of law, whatever its nature may be. This does not constitute a legal remedy since the Supreme Court does not annul or amend the judicial decision in question but only serves to ensure the uniformity of future judgments.

V. Judges

The sole purpose of the judicial administration is to guarantee the existence of the conditions for the normal and proper functioning of the courts. It therefore provides sufficient human resources – judges and specialised staff – in the majority of cases as well as sufficient funds to acquire the premises and equipment necessary to achieve this end. Since the review of judicial decisions is the responsibility of the Higher Courts, the supervisory bodies only oversee the judges from the point of view of whether they are carrying out their tasks properly and order any statutory disciplinary measures required to rectify the situation. The public authorities are not empowered to order disciplinary measures against judges but they may apply to the disciplinary tribunals, which are composed of judges, to institute specific proceedings in this regard.

Under the Constitution, judges are elected by the National Council (Parliament) of the Slovak Republic on the government's recommendation. They are initially elected for a term of four years (a kind of probationary period), after which they are elected for life by the National Council on the government's recommendation.

The President and Vice-President of the Supreme Court are elected by the National Council on the government's recommendation from among the Supreme Court judges for a term of five years, which may be renewed once. The Presidents and Vice-Presidents of the Regional Courts are appointed and dismissed by the Minister for Justice. The Presidents of the District Courts are nominated by the Presidents of the Regional Courts.

A judge's term of office ends:

- after four years beginning with the date of the first appointment unless the appointment has been renewed for life;
- upon his or her resignation; or
- upon his or her dismissal by the National Council (after it has requested the opinion of the relevant disciplinary tribunal) for the reasons set out in Article 147, paragraphs 1 and 2 of the Constitution.

There are currently 1 200 professional judges at all the courts (for 5.5 million inhabitants).

Republic of Slovenia

I. Introduction

The Constitution of the Republic of Slovenia lays down the right to freedom of work and choice of profession. The same applies to the field of professions relating to practising lawyers, judges, prosecutors, naturally on the assumption that certain legal conditions are fulfilled.

There are district, regional, higher courts and the Supreme Court in the Republic of Slovenia. There are 44 district courts, 11 regional courts, four higher courts and there is just one court of the highest instance, that is, the Supreme Court of the Republic of Slovenia.

On 31 March 1997 there were 221 judicial posts filled at the District Courts, 196 at the Regional Courts, and there were 82 judicial posts filled according to the data as of 31 December 1996, while there were 31 judicial posts filled at the Supreme Court of the Republic of Slovenia.

II. Characteristics of judicial organisation

A. Constitutional/institutional guarantees

The independence of the judiciary is already guaranteed by the separation of legislative, executive and judicial powers (Article 3 of the Constitution of the Republic of Slovenia, the *Official Gazette of the Republic of Slovenia,* No. 33/91). Each branch of the authority is independent from the other, however all three branches of authority are mutually interconnected and interwoven (a system of checks and balances). Judges are independent in exercising their judicial function in accordance with the Constitution and with the law (Article 125 of the Constitution of the Republic of Slovenia). All of this is in effect guaranteed at the constitutional level and is directly implemented, the more precise manner of implementation being determined by individual laws.

B. Appointments, promotion, security of tenure, disciplinary measures

The judges are elected according to the legal order of the Republic of Slovenia. This is laid down by the Constitution of the Republic of Slovenia, which stipulates by Article 130: "The National Assembly shall elect judges upon the recommendation of the Judicial Council." It is understood that by being elected to the office of judge, the judge is appointed to the vacant judicial post. When the Judicial Council adopts the act on electing the judge, it determines the salary class of the judge appropriate for the advertised judicial post. A judge enters his judicial service on the day when he takes the following oath before the President of the National Assembly: "I hereby swear to perform the function of judge in accordance with the Constitution and the law and to pass judgments in good conscience and impartially."

The judge fulfils the conditions for promotion to a higher judicial post if he fulfils the conditions, stipulated by this law for appointment to such a judicial post, as well as conditions stipulated by this law for the promotion of judges. The conditions and the manner of promotion are more specifically determined by the Law on the Judicial Service in Articles 24, 25 and 26. By entering judicial service a judge obtains the right to promotion. Promotion includes promotion in salary classes, promotion to a higher judicial post and promotion to the post of councillor. Promotion is decided upon by the Judicial Council after completion of the procedure for establishing professionalism and success in judicial work, however the decision to promote a judge to the post of supreme court judge is taken by the National Assembly at the proposal of the Judicial Council. A judge is promoted to a higher salary class every three years and he can be promoted to the next higher judicial post. Appointment on the basis of promotion is published in the *Official Gazette of the Republic of Slovenia.*

A judge elected to a judicial function acquires a position, guaranteed by the Constitution, the law on courts and the present law. The judge is in an employment relationship with the Republic of Slovenia, elected as judge with a permanent mandate, which implies a high degree of protection and firmness of judicial function. No one participating in a lawsuit can be called responsible for the opinion he has given when passing judgment in the court. A judge cannot be held in detention, nor can criminal proceedings be initiated against him without the consent of the National Assembly if he is suspected of having committed a criminal offence while performing his judicial function.

The Constitution of the Republic of Slovenia stipulates the participation of the citizens in the implementation of judicial authority (lay judges); the law further more precisely determines the cases and forms of direct participation of the citizens in exercising judicial authority. The citizens participate in implementing judicial authority as lay judges at the regional courts. The chairman of the Higher Court appoints and dismisses lay judges at regional courts from the area of jurisdiction of the Higher Court.

A disciplinary court decides on disciplinary procedures brought against judges. A judge cannot be accused before the Disciplinary Court for an opinion given while ruling in the court. The chairman of the court can initiate disciplinary procedures against the judge, which is the basis on which the disciplinary prosecutor is obliged to initiate disciplinary procedures. Disciplinary action is taken against a judge accused of breaching his judicial obligations or of irregularity in the performance of judicial service. Disciplinary sanctions as determined by the Law on the Judicial Service are the following:

- transfer to a different court;
- suspension of promotion;
- salary reduction.

If a judge has violated the Constitution or severely infringed the law, and the National Assembly at the proposal of the Judicial Council does not dismiss the judge, the Disciplinary Court takes one of the above-mentioned disciplinary measures.

Disciplinary procedures against a judge may not be initiated more than two years after the infringement occurred. The implementation of a disciplinary sanction expires after one year.

Decisions in first level disciplinary procedures are made by the Disciplinary Court, composed of a supreme court judge as chairman of the court, two high court judges, a district court judge and a regional court judge. Appeals against the decision of a first level disciplinary court are decided upon by a second level disciplinary court, composed of seven supreme court judges.

C. Legal education and training

The judge is guaranteed the right to education and other rights deriving from the judicial service. A judge is entitled to participate in forms of education, consultations and other meetings of legal experts. The participation of a judge is decided on the basis of an application by the chairman of the court, who must ensure that judges from various legal fields receive equal access to participation in the above-mentioned educational and consultative forms.

D. Working conditions (funding, salaries, personnel/logistics, physical security)

Funds for the functioning of the courts are provided from the budget of the Republic of Slovenia. The salaries of the judges are laid down by the law. A judge is entitled to receive a salary corresponding to the judicial post or position to which he is appointed. Judges are divided into three pay groups, within which salary classes are defined and expressed as coefficients. The first pay group covers district and regional court judges and councillors of district courts. The second pay group encompasses councillors at regional courts, high court judges and councillors of high courts. The third pay group encompasses supreme court judges and councillors of the Supreme Court. The base for calculating a judge's salary is the same as for parliamentary deputies. The allowance for judges from the first pay group is 25%, for judges from the second pay group 35%, and for judges from the third pay group 50%.

A court has the required number of higher professional personnel and professional personnel for performance of legal work, who receive petitions by parties for entry into the records and, under the guidance of and by order of the judge, hear the clients, witnesses and experts in individual matters outside the main trial, make preparations for the trial, report at the sessions of the senates and draft court decisions. For the purpose of the conduct of proceedings and for first decisions concerning the land registers, court registers and payments under the Court Order, the courts of first instance have the necessary number of court clerks. Each court has an adequate number of administrative, technical and other court personnel. Their tasks, the manner of their functioning and their particular responsibilities are laid down by the law and by the Court Procedural Code. The number of professional personnel, court clerks, administrative, technical and other court personnel for each court is determined by the Minister for Justice after receiving the prior opinion of the Judicial Council.

All court buildings and buildings of state prosecutors are guarded by security officers, equipped with metal detectors, as well as a the security service in charge of security. With regard to the physical protection of judges, they are not protected outside their offices; the judge would however be provided with immediate protection in case of danger.

E. Education and training of personnel involved in the administration of justice

No special provisions concerning the education of administrative-technical and other personnel performing certain tasks in the courts are stipulated by law. However, individual provisions are included in the Court Procedural Code, which determine the internal organisation of courts, the operation of courts and the assignment of individual matters. Article 199 of the Court Procedural Code stipulates that judicial personnel have the right and duty to acquire further vocational education within the educational forms organised by the ministry competent for justice, or by the ministry responsible for state administration. All judicial personnel must pass the examination on the provisions of the Court Procedural Code within the framework of educational programmes; the examination is taken before a commission of the ministry competent for justice within one year of employment of the candidate. Judicial personnel must take the examination every five years until they have been employed at the court for 20 years. Those who do not register for the examination, or do not pass it even at their second attempt within the further two months, are considered not to fulfil the conditions for their posts.

F. Protection against inappropriate influence (relationship with executive authority, reassignment of cases)

The Constitution of the Republic of Slovenia stipulates the separation of legislative, executive and judicial powers. Each branch of authority is independent within the framework of competence determined by individual statutes. However, individual branches of authority incorporate certain fields in which one branch of authority intervenes with or supervises another branch of authority. In the case of judicial and executive branches of authority, the intervention occurs in the field of judiciary administration as determined by Article 74 of the Law on Courts. The judiciary administration is responsible for providing general conditions for the successful exercising of judicial authority, in particular the preparation of laws and other regulations in the field of organisation and operation of courts, for care of education and vocational training of personnel, for provision of professional, material, work space and technical conditions, further for the provision of international legal aid, for the enforcement of penal sanctions, for statistical and other research into the operation of the courts, and for other administrative tasks provided by law. In matters of judiciary administration, the ministry competent for justice communicates with the courts through the Presidents or the heads of courts.

A certain amount of intervening, although not substantive, takes place also in the field of petitions for review, as determined by Article 72 of the Law on Courts. A party who considers that the court is unduly protracting his/her case may address a complaint about procrastination (petition for review) to the President of the court, or lodge such a complaint with the ministry competent for justice. If the petition for review is not obviously groundless, the President of the court asks the judge immediately to file on allegations of the petition and the progress of the case. If the petition for review has been lodged with the ministry competent for justice, the ministry may ask the President of the court to act according to the above provision and to inform the ministry of his/her findings. The ministry competent for justice may send the petition for review to the President of a higher court, and if the party complains about the work of a higher court to the President of the Supreme

Court with the suggestion that the work of the court regarding the subject of the complaint be inspected the findings of the inspection are reported to the ministry.

Nobody may interfere with the contents of a judge's decision except a higher court within its competence.

G. Relations with the press

Courts follow the reports of mass media in their region and inform the public about their work and problems. Following press reports and informing the public is the responsibility of the President of the court or, upon his/her authorisation, of a person responsible for public relations. Information about matters being settled at courts is given in written form, or exceptionally – in the event of matters of great interest – at press conferences, only to reporters holding press cards. The written information of a court is as a rule transmitted to the mass media through the Slovenian Press Agency, or directly to the mass media covering the region for which the information is intended.

H. Impartiality

1. Conflict of interest

In Article 23, the Constitution of the Republic of Slovenia stipulates that each person is entitled to have all issues relating to his/her rights and obligations and to have any criminal charges laid against him/her decided without undue delay by an independent, impartial court constituted according to statute. The basic principle of justice is the principle of independence and impartiality. This principle is linked to the principle of legality according to which a judge is bound only by the Constitution and law in his/her decision-making. A judge can impartially judge only if he/she is in his/her work completely independent of other state bodies and political parties. Therefore, no state body may interfere with judicial decisions or instruct a judge in any way. Independence of the courts is a necessary condition for establishing the principle of the state governed by the rule of law. The principle of independence is linked with certain other principles, particularly with the principles of the permanence of the judicial function, intransferability of judges, judicial immunity and incompatibility of functions.

2. Membership and participation in professional associations and political parties

The Constitution of the Republic of Slovenia stipulates that the office of a judge is incompatible with office in any other state body, local government body or any organ of any political party, and with such other offices and activities as are specified by statute (Article 133 of the Constitution of the Republic of Slovenia). The Law on Judicial Service in Article 3 also stipulates that a judge may not perform functions or activities deemed incompatible with the office of judge under provisions of the Constitution or of the Law. A judge may not perform the work of a lawyer or notary or any commercial or other profit-making activity. A judge may not hold a management position or be a member of an administrative or supervisory board in a commercial company or any other legal person engaged in profit-making activity. A judge may not accept any employment or work that would obstruct his/her performance as a judge, harm the reputation of the judicial service or create the impression that he/she is not impartial in his/her performance as a judge. However, a judge may be engaged in teaching, publishing, scientific, research or other similar work within the legal profession, provided that such activity does not interfere with his performance of judicial service. For the performance of such work a judge may not enter into employment relations. If a judge is elected as President of the Republic, parliamentary deputy, judge in the Constitutional Court, Prime Minister, or human rights ombudsman, or their deputy, or if a judge is appointed a minister, the office of judge and all rights and obligations deriving from judicial service are suspended. A judge may not accept any position or work which would obstruct him/her in the performance of his tasks or harm the reputation of his/her position or create the impression that he/she is not impartial in his/her performance as a judge.

I. Availability of (judicial) remedies

In the legal system of the Republic of Slovenia, each person is guaranteed the right of legal remedy. Each person is guaranteed the right of appeal and the right to any other legal remedy in relation to decisions of any court, government body, local government body and statutory authority which determines the rights, obligations or legal entitlements of such a person. The appeal is an ordinary legal remedy. With reference to legally effective and final decisions of judicial and other above-mentioned bodies, extraordinary legal remedies can also be pursued in all civil, criminal and administrative procedures.

Statutes, provisions for implementation and other general acts have to conform with the Constitution. If a court believes that the statute to be used in a proceeding is unconstitutional, the proceedings must be suspended and proceedings must be in the Constitutional Court. The resumed Constitutional Court is the court which, within the legal order of the Republic of Slovenia, decides on conformity with the Constitution, thus performing the function of supervision of constitutionality and legality. The procedure for the judicial review of constitutionality and legality of regulations and general acts issued for the exercise of public powers begins with the submission of a written request by a petitioner or with a resolution of the Constitutional Court on the acceptance of an initiative for initiating proceedings. The review of constitutionality and legality of regulations and general acts issued for the exercise of public powers includes an evaluation of the conformity of statutes and other general acts with ratified international treaties and with the general principles of international law. Any person may lodge a written initiative to begin the procedure provided that he/she shows standing to sue. The Constitutional Court may wholly or partially abrogate any law that is in conflict with the Constitution. The abrogation takes effect on the day after the publication of the decision on the abrogation, or after the lapse of the time limit determined by the Constitutional Court. A statute or a part of a statute abrogated by the Constitutional Court does not apply to relationships that had arisen before the day such abrogation came into effect if by that day such relationships had not been finally adjudicated.

On the basis of the provision of Article 133 of the Law on Courts, the decision of the European Court of Human Rights is enforced directly by the competent court of the Republic of Slovenia if so provided by a ratified treaty.

If a decision of the European Court of Human Rights establishes that a final court decision to the prejudice of the convicted person has violated any human right or fundamental freedom, the time limit for the lodging of a request for the protection of legality begins on the day of serving on the convicted person the decision of the European Court of Human Rights. This is the provision of Article 421 of the Penal Code.

J. Fair trial (fairness of proceedings, publicity of trial, equality of arms, possibility of appeal)

Each person in the Republic of Slovenia shall be guaranteed equality in the protection of his/her rights in any proceeding before a court and any other government body. The court must endeavour to carry through the proceedings without undue delay and to render impossible any abuse of rights of the parties involved in these proceedings. A proceeding, carried through before a court, is of course based on the principle of justice. The principle of publicity (this being a constitutional category) means that the work of courts is public, the proceedings are conducted in public and all judgments are delivered in open court; the exceptions, however, are defined by law. In assuring publicity, it is however necessary to respect to the highest possible degree the principle of independence of the court and of the protection of personal rights and liberties.

The equality of arms of the parties shall be guaranteed in every proceeding before a court. In criminal proceedings this is expressed in the principle of contradictoriness and in the principle of formal defence according to which every defendant has the right to defend himself by assistance of a counsel, in civil proceedings; however, a party does have the possibility to assert his/her rights by hiring a barrister to represent him/her.

Everybody has the right to appeal or to any other legal remedy in relation to the decisions of any court and other statutory authorities, local government body and bearers of public mandates which determine upon his/her rights, obligations or legal entitlements.

K. Length of proceedings

The court must endeavour to ensure that the proceedings are carried out without undue delay, and prevent any abuse of the rights of the parties in the proceeding. The duration of a proceeding can, however, be affected, by different factors which do not depend on the functioning of a court (for example: the complexity of the case; evasion by the parties, procrastination of the proceedings by the parties and so on).

Based on the courts' statistics for the year 1996, the duration of 46% of the criminal proceedings before regional courts was longer than one year and 23.4% of the proceedings lasted between six months and one year. In civil proceedings 26.5% of cases before regional courts lasted between six months and one year, 25.8% of the cases between one and three years, and 5.5% lasted over three years.

L. Execution of judicial decisions (civil, criminal and administrative)

The general provision on execution of judicial decisions is given in Article 3 of the Law on Courts, stipulating that the enforcement of a court decision may not be prejudiced by the decision of another state body.

The execution of judicial decisions in criminal cases is regulated by the Law on Criminal Procedure. A judgment becomes final if the same cannot any longer be disputed by appeal or if there is no appeal against it. A final judgment will be executed when the same has been served and when no legal obstructions exist for its execution. If no appeal is filed or if the parties renounce or withdraw the appeal, the judgment is enforceable when the term for appeal has expired and/or from the day when the parties renounced or withdrew the appeal. If the court which delivered the judgment in the first instance is not competent for its execution, it shall send a certified copy of the judgment with an attestation of enforceability to the body competent for execution. If the fine, as stipulated by this law, cannot be recovered even by force, the court will proceed so as to adjudge one day of prison for each initiated tenth part of the net average month salary achieved in the economic sector in the Republic of Slovenia. The decisions of courts shall be executed when they become final; the decrees however, shall be executed immediately, save when the body that issued the decree has not disposed otherwise. Should there arise doubt about the permissibility of the execution of judicial decision or about the correct calculation of the fine, or, if the final judgment does not contain the stipulation on inclusion of the arrest or time previously served, or if the court has not included them correctly, then a chairman of the first instance court will decide upon it in a separate decision.

In civil procedure (civil action) the court shall issue an authoritative decree on contentious relationship and/or disputable right. If the decision does not produce an effect by itself, when, for example, the decision does not constitute, modify or cancel the legal relationship (such is the effect of constitutive judgments or judgments changing a legal right or status) or, when the purpose of the judicial decision is not just to establish the existing right and legal relationships (declaratory judicial decision); therefore, when the question concerns the judicial decisions which impose on the defendant a certain fee, service, omission or permission (tributive or condemnatory decisions), it is not possible to guarantee legal protection only in civil actions. In a civil action a court imposes on the defendant the fulfilment of a certain obligation (debtor from the creditor-debtor relationship) by means of a judicial decision. If the defendant does not comply with this executive order, compulsory enforcement is required. For the final fulfilment of creditor-debtor rights in enforcement proceedings it is, therefore, necessary to make use of direct force. The court concedes the execution on the basis of executory title, the executory titles are: executory judicial decision and settlement in court/compromise in court, enforceable decision in administrative procedure, and others.

A decision issued in administrative procedure is enforceable if the same has become final and if the time limit set for the voluntary fulfilment of the obligation has expired.

The time limit for the voluntary fulfilment of the obligation begins as of the day on which the decision has been served on the debtor. If only a part of the decision has become enforceable, the execution may only be conceded for that part. The executory title is suitable for execution if it contains both the creditor and the debtor as well as the subject, kind, extent and time of the fulfilment of obligation. If a final judgment or any other court decision has been changed by a decision of the Constitutional Court of the Republic of Slovenia issued on the basis of the constitutional complaint, the same will be executed in accordance with the decision of the Constitutional Court.

III. Role and status of public prosecutors

A. Appointment, promotion, security of tenure, disciplinary measures

State prosecutors are appointed by the Government of the Republic of Slovenia at the proposal of the Minister for Justice, while the State Prosecutor General of the Republic of Slovenia is appointed by the National Assembly at the proposal of the government for a period of six years with the possibility of reappointment. The Appointment Act is published in the *Official Gazette of the Republic of Slovenia.*

With appointment to office, a state prosecutor acquires the right to promotion. Promotion covers promotion in salary categories, promotion to a higher post and the promotion to the position of councillor. Unless otherwise stipulated by the Law on the Office of the State Prosecutor, the provisions of the Law on the Judicial Service apply accordingly to the promotion of state prosecutors, to the determining of the criteria for selection and promotion, and in assessing the work of state prosecutors. The personnel commission decides on promotion and salary categories and on promotion to the position of councillor, while the body competent to appoint state prosecutors in accordance with the provisions of the Law of the Office of the State Prosecutor decides on promotion to a higher post.

The office of state prosecutor is a permanent office. In respect of the entitlements deriving from his employment by the Republic of Slovenia, a state prosecutor is equal to a judge, save where otherwise stipulated by the Law on the Office of the State Prosecutor.

A state prosecutor is liable to disciplinary measures if he violates the duties of a state prosecutor or the reputation or dignity of the office of state prosecutor. A state prosecutor is not liable to disciplinary measures for opinions he expresses in his work or any other matter with which he is dealing. The State Prosecutor General and the Minister for Justice have the right to demand the initiation of disciplinary proceedings against a state prosecutor. Disciplinary sanctions include: dismissal from the office of state prosecutor, the suspension of promotion and salary reduction. In disciplinary proceedings, decisions are taken in the first instance by a disciplinary tribunal and the provisions applying to disciplinary proceedings against a judge shall apply accordingly.

B. Legal education and training

The provisions of the Law on the Judicial Service apply accordingly to the training of state prosecutors.

C. Working conditions (funding, salaries, personnel/logistics, physical security)

The salary of a state prosecutor is determined according to the same bases, with the same bonuses and in the same manner as the salary of a judge in a corresponding position. The personnel commission decides on classification in salary categories.

The office of state prosecutor is a permanent office. In respect of the entitlements deriving from his employment by the Republic of Slovenia, a state prosecutor is equal to a judge, save where otherwise stipulated by the Law on the Office of the State Prosecutor.

D. Scope of powers (review of legality of administrative decisions, special tasks)

The basic role and task of a state prosecutor is to lodge and present criminal charges and carry out other procedural activities of a prosecutor in criminal proceedings, unless otherwise stipulated by law. A state prosecutor lodges initiatives for prosecution and legal remedy in matters pertaining to misdemeanours, lodges procedural acts in civil and other judicial proceedings and in administrative proceedings where stipulated by law.

A state prosecutor of the Republic of Slovenia has the right to lodge an important extraordinary legal remedy both in criminal and in civil procedures, that is, a request for the protection of legality.

There is a special group of state prosecutors in the Republic of Slovenia formed for special purposes and dealing with specific areas of criminal activity such as organised crime and money laundering.

E. Relationship between the prosecuting authority and the judiciary

State prosecutor's offices are independent state bodies the position and competencies of which are regulated by the Law on the State Prosecutor's Office.

A state prosecutor's office is a state body within which criminal prosecution in the name of the state is carried out. Within the division of power it may be conditionally classified under the executive branch, both from functional and organisational aspect and does therefore not belong to the judicial branch. However it has a somewhat different position within the executive branch from other executive bodies. Within the executive branch, a state prosecutor's office is an independent body. The division between the function of adjudication and the function of prosecution was one of the basic conditions for the separation of the judiciary from the executive branch and for the independence of the judiciary. The organisation of a state prosecutor's office according to the division of competence (subject matter, territorial, functional) is parallel to the judiciary, however it differs essentially from it by its internal structure. None of the constitutional principles for the regulation and functioning of the judiciary apply to the state prosecutor's office. This body is organised in such a manner that the functioning of the body is performed by one person; a higher body may not influence a subordinate body, the public nature of work is not emphasised, and the like. In comparison with courts, the state prosecutor's offices are organised on a hierarchic basis, since the superior state prosecutor may give to state prosecutors and state prosecutor's offices general instructions for their work in individual kinds of matters or even in an individual matter.

Sweden

I. Introduction[1]

Sweden is divided into 21 counties (*län*). The counties are primarily administrative units but are also of importance for the competence of some administrative and other special courts. Each county is divided into a number of municipalities, governed by elected councils and exercising important local self-government. Some of the municipalities (those qualified formerly as cities) were, according to older rules, also responsible for the ordinary jurisdiction of first instance, but nowadays all courts are state courts.

In the following section the question of jurisdiction in constitutional matters is outlined. Section III presents the General Courts for civil and criminal matters. In addition, comment is made about the so-called real estate courts and the Environment Courts. The Labour Court is also dealt with as well as comments on the Market Court. Finally, the administrative courts are dealt with as well as some remarks on special institutions of control.

The independence of the courts is guaranteed in the Constitution. Neither the Parliament (*Riksdagen*) nor any public authority may determine how a court shall adjudicate a particular case or how a court shall in other respects apply a rule of law in a particular case.

The judges are appointed by the government. With the exception of a number of the justices in the Supreme Administrative Court (*Regerings-rätten*) judges must have a university law degree. Judges can be removed from office only under specific circumstances mentioned in the Instrument of Government, one of the Swedish fundamental laws. Besides these permanent judges, associate judges (*assessor*) and assistant judges (*fiskal*) may sit in court. The Courts of First Instance and the Courts of Appeal also have lay assessors (*nämndemän*). They are elected by the municipal councils or the county councils.

A special authority, the National Courts Administration (*Domstolsverket*) assists the general courts and the administrative courts in different matters, for example administration, education and budget.

II. Jurisdiction in constitutional matters

The Swedish Constitution consists of four fundamental laws: the Instrument of Government (*Regeringsformen*), which came into force in 1975 replacing the 1809 instrument, the Act of Succession (*Successionsordningen*), the Freedom of the Press Act (*Tryckfrihetsförordningen*) and the Fundamental Law on Freedom of Expression (*Yttrandefrihetsgrundlagen*).

Sweden has no special constitutional court. As regards judicial review, ordinary courts are competent to decide not to apply a statutory instrument if it is evident that it is not compatible with the Constitution.

1. For further information please contact: Justitiedepartementet /The Ministry of Justice, Enheten för processrätt och domstolsfrågor, 103 33 Stockholm, Sweden. Tel.: +46 8 405 10 00; Fax: + 46 8 791 76 95; E-mail: registrator@justice.ministry.se; Web site: www.regeringen.se. Domstolsverket /The National Courts Administration; 551 81 Jönköping, Sweden. Tel.: +46 36 15 53 00; Fax: +46 36 16 57 21; E-mail: registrator@dv.dom.se; Web site: Not yet available.

III. THE GENERAL COURTS

The basic rules concerning the organisation of the general courts are given in the Code of Judicial Procedure (*Rättegångsbalken*) of 1942, effective since 1948 (as amended later).

The country is divided into a number of circuits, each with a District Court (*tingsrätt*). The actual number of districts is 95. A District Court is organised with a chief judge (*lagman*) and a number of other judges (*rådmän*). In ordinary civil cases the court consists of three judges, and in some minor civil cases, one. In criminal cases, and in some civil cases concerning family law, the court is composed of one presiding judge and three lay assessors. Larger district courts are usually organised in divisions. These divisions can be specialised.

The second instance in an ordinary case is the Court of Appeal (*hovrätt*). Sweden has six courts of appeal; the oldest is Svea Court of Appeal in Stockholm, founded in 1614. The Courts of Appeal are divided into divisions. Each case is heard by at least three judges. In criminal cases the Courts of Appeal consist also of at least two lay assessors. These courts hear civil and criminal appeals without restriction as to the importance of the case, although leave to appeal is required in some minor cases.

The last instance is the Supreme Court (*Högsta domstolen*), which has its seat in Stockholm. The Supreme Court is composed of 16 justices (*justitieråd*), or such higher number which may be required, working in two divisions. The divisions are not specialised but hear all types of cases. The Supreme Court hears civil and criminal appeals, but cases are admitted only under certain conditions. The leading idea is that a case shall be admitted only if there is a need for creating a precedent, but a case can also be admitted if a serious mistake has been made in the Lower Court. As the word appeal indicates, the Supreme Court may, if a case is admitted, deal not only with questions of law but also with questions of fact. The bench in the Supreme Court consists of five justices.

The Supreme Court is also the Court of First and Last Instance concerning punishable acts committed in office by ministers. Prosecution in such cases must be decided on by the Parliamentary Standing Committee on the Constitution (*Konstitutionsutskottet*). Moreover, the Supreme Court also has original jurisdiction in proceedings brought against justices, the Parliamentary Ombudsmen (*Riksdagens ombudsmän* or *Justitieombudsmannen*), the Chancellor of Justice (*Justitiekanslern*), the Prosecutor-General (*Riksåklagaren*), judges or advocates-general of the European Court of Justice, judges of the European Court of First Instance, appeal court judges and judge referees (*revisionssekreterare*) in the Supreme Court for alleged punishable acts committed in office or in claims for damages arising from such acts.

Twenty-two of the District Courts function (with a special composition) as so-called real estate courts (*fastighetsdomstolar*). These courts deals with cases concerning formation of real estate, expropriation, land leases, certain rent questions, etc. Certain matters concerning the relations between landlord and tenant are, in the first instance, dealt with by special boards, called Regional Rent Tribunals (*hyresnämnder*) and Regional Tenancies Tribunals (*arrendenämnder*).

For cases concerning certain aspects of the environment, five of the District Courts function, with a special constitution, as environment courts (*miljödomstolar*). Appeals are heard by the Environment Court of Appeal (*miljööverdomstolen,* the Svea Court of Appeal with a special constitution). These environment courts were established on 1 January 1999. At the same time the National Licensing Board for Environment Protection and the Water Rights Court where dissolved.

The only time juries are employed in Sweden are in cases concerning the Freedom of the Press Act and the Fundamental Law on Freedom of Expression. Such cases are tried before certain district courts. Unless both parties renounce the option, the court proceedings proper are preceded by a hearing before a jury of nine persons.

Questions in the fields of administrative law may, in general, not be brought before the General Courts. It should be remarked, however, that contracts between public authorities and private persons or companies, as well as actions in tort against the state, are regarded as regular matters of civil law, for which the General Courts are competent.

IV. The Labour Court

Matters concerning collective bargaining agreements and some other questions of labour law fall within the exclusive competence of the Labour Court (*Arbetsdomstolen*), which is a single instance for the whole country with its seat in Stockholm. The Labour Court passes first and final decisions on these matters, without any possibility of appeal. The Labour Court is also competent to hear appeals in cases concerning other labour disputes between parties who do not belong to any organisation of employers or employees. Such cases are heard by the District Courts in the first instance.

The Labour Court, which was founded in 1928, is composed of a maximum of four chairmen, four vice-chairmen and 17 other members (three of whom should have special knowledge of the labour market and 14 who represent employers, employers' organisations and organisations of employees). The chairman and the vice-chairman should have experience as judges. The normal quorum is one chairman and four to six other members including two to four members representing in equal numbers employers and employees. The functions of the Labour Court are strictly judicial; it interprets and enforces existing agreements in the same way as an ordinary court and does not interfere with mediation or with the finding of compromises in labour disputes. Special officers exist for that purpose.

V. The Market Court

Cases concerning a number of questions belonging to the field of market law (rules against restraint of trade, the rules about improper marketing practices and so on) is handled by the District Court of Stockholm. Appeals against judgments in this field may be carried to the Market Court (*Marknadsdomstolen*). The Market Court is composed of one chairman, one vice-chairman and five other members. The chairman, the vice-chairman and one of the other members should have experience as judges. The rest of the members should be experts in economics. The bench in the Market Court consists of four members, among them the chairman or the vice-chairman.

VI. The administrative courts

The task of the administrative courts may be described as one of maintaining due observance of the law within the public administration – at central, regional and local level. In these, the proceedings take a form corresponding quite closely to the proceedings at the Courts of General Jurisdiction. However, in contrast to general courts, proceedings in writing are predominant, although oral hearings are becoming increasingly common.

The principal rule in administrative laws is that appeals against administrative decisions can be carried to the Administrative Courts. The first instance is the County Administrative Court (*länsrätt*). Sweden has 23 county administrative courts (due to reorganisation one county has three courts). Appeals against judgments of these courts may be carried to the Administrative Court of Appeal (*kammarrätt*); there are four in number. In most cases a special leave to appeal is required to have a case tried by an administrative court of appeal. The highest administrative court is the Supreme Administrative Court (*Regeringsrätten*) which – like the Supreme Court – in principle only try cases which are of interest from the point of view of possible precedents. The Supreme Administrative Court is composed of 14 justices (*regeringsråd*), or a higher number if required.

The County Administrative Courts are organised with a chief judge (*lagman*) and a number of other judges (*rådmän*). Most cases are adjudicated by one judge with three lay assessors. Cases before the Administrative Courts of Appeal are generally adjudicated by three judges, but in certain cases, for example those related to custody of children, lay assessors are also included in the court. In the Supreme Administrative Court, the bench usually consists of five justices.

In certain matters appeals against decisions made by administrative authorities are carried not to the courts but to a higher authority, for example the national board within the field of action, and sometimes ultimately to the government.

In this type of matter there is a possibility for the individual litigant, if the decision was made by an authority, to apply to the Administrative Court of Appeal or, if the decision was made by the government, to apply to the Supreme Administrative Court for a judgment whether the actual decision is in accordance with the law or not (*rättsprövning*).

The Court of Patent Appeals (*Patentbesvärsrätten*) is a special administrative court which deals with appeals against decisions made by the Swedish Patent and Registration Office regarding patent and trade mark rights for instance.

VII. Special institutions of control

The best known of these institutions is probably the Office of the Parliamentary Ombudsmen, the first of whom was appointed in 1809. At present there is one office with general authority. It is divided between four ombudsmen, one of whom has certain leading functions.

Since the end of the second world war, several countries have set up similar offices based on the Swedish model. The ombudsmen, who are almost always prominent judges, are appointed by the parliament for a term of four years. In many instances the same person has been re-appointed for several terms. Their chief duty is to see that the courts and civil service observe and enforce the nation's laws, especially those which safeguard the freedom, security and property of its citizens. The ombudsmen are assisted by a legally-trained staff. They may make inquiries and obtain whatever information they consider necessary. Furthermore, they supervise actions of the local government authorities and of any person who in any way exercises public executive powers.

The Instrument of Government also provides for the office of the Chancellor of Justice, who undertakes approximately the same supervision of the courts and administrative organs as the Parliamentary Ombudsmen. The Chancellor of Justice, who is a government appointee and usually someone with a distinguished record of service in the judiciary, follows the same procedures as the ombudsmen. The office also supervise the limits of the freedom of the press in accordance with the Freedom of the Press Act and the limits of the freedom of expression in accordance with the Fundamental Law on Freedom of Expression. He also has authority to represent the state in civil litigation and serves the government as its chief legal adviser.

See overleaf for diagram showing General Courts and Administrative Courts in Sweden.

VIII. The General Courts and the Administrative Courts in Sweden

The Supreme Court
Högsta domstolen
Stockholm

The Appeal Court
Hovrätten
Stockholm
Jönköping
Malmö
Göteborg
Sundsvall
Umeå

The District Court
Tingsrätten
95 courts

The Administrative Supreme Court
Regeringsrätten
Stockholm

The Administrative Appeal Court
Kammarrätten
Stockholm
Göteborg
Sundsvall
Jönköping

The Administrative County Court
Länsrätten
23 courts

SWITZERLAND

INTRODUCTION

Under Articles 64 and 64*bis* of the Federal Constitution, the organisation of the courts, judicial procedure and the administration of justice are the responsibility of the cantons. This applies both to civil and criminal law.

There are marked differences of court organisation and judicial procedure between the cantons. For the purposes of this survey the cantons of Berne and Geneva have been taken as examples. Cantonal judges are elected by the people or by the cantonal parliament, and have to be re-elected periodically. As a rule, the presiding judges of the District Courts (*tribunaux de district*) and judges at higher cantonal courts are lawyers, while assessors at district courts and special tribunals (commercial, labour, tenancies, etc.) are lay judges. Article 106 of the Constitution provides for a federal court to administer justice in federal matters. It consists of 30 judges and 15 substitutes elected by the Federal Assembly, that is the Swiss Parliament (section 1 of the Federal Judicature Act) (*loi fédérale d'organisation judiciaire*). Any Swiss citizen with the right to vote is eligible. However, in practice all federal judges are lawyers who have followed a wide range of careers (cantonal judges, barristers, professors). The seat of the Federal Court is Lausanne. Since it was set up its functions have grown significantly as a result of the development of federal law. The first Federal Judicature Act dates from 5 June 1849, while the act in force at present (which has been revised many times) dates from 16 December 1943. It defines the jurisdiction of the different chambers, or "courts" comprising the Federal Court. In all the cases submitted to it, the various chambers may sit as reduced benches of three judges and rule (unanimously) on actions and appeals they consider inadmissible, manifestly ill-founded or well-founded (p. 36 (a) of the Federal Judicature Act).

The appended chart distinguishes between the following main branches of jurisdiction:

- civil;
- debt recovery and bankruptcy;
- criminal;
- constitutional;
- administrative.

II. CIVIL JURISDICTION

A. Cantonal Courts

Cantonal law provides for one or (usually) two levels of jurisdiction in civil cases. Only one level is provided for in the case of minor disputes and commercial disputes in those cantons that have commercial courts. When it is possible to appeal to the Federal Court, some cantons provide for only one level of jurisdiction. There are great differences between the cantons with regard to the possibility of having the facts and evidence reviewed on appeal.

At first instance, the proceedings are often oral and the presence of a lawyer is optionally.

B. Federal Court

1. Appeals in civil cases[1]

A uniform system of civil law has been in force in Switzerland since 1 January 1912. The Federal Court's task is to ensure the uniform application of this law throughout the Confederation. This is, in fact, its only task, since the establishment of the facts and the assessment of the evidence are left exclusively to the Cantonal Courts (see below).

In civil disputes of a financial nature, appeals are only admissible if the claim before the last Cantonal Court amounts to at least 8000 Swiss Francs (page 46 of the Federal Judicature Act). The Federal Court deals with disputes concerning industrial property and other financial cases, fully listed on page 45 of the Federal Judicature Act, irrespective of the value of the claim.

The parties may themselves lodge appeals and plead their own cases. They may be represented only by lawyers and professors of law at Swiss universities. As a general rule, oral hearings are held in financial cases only if the value of the claim exceeds 15000 Swiss Francs. The appeal must be lodged with the authority that gave the decision within thirty days of its written notification.[2]

2. Pleas of nullity in civil matters[3]

In cases where no appeal is available, the parties may lodge a plea of nullity with the Federal Court when the cantonal authority has applied cantonal or foreign law instead of overriding federal law or when that authority has infringed the provisions or federal law concerning the power of authorities.

3. Sole jurisdiction[4]

The Federal Court has sole jurisdiction to hear:

– civil law disputes between the Confederation and a canton or between cantons (Article 110, paragraph 1 (1) and (3) of the Constitution, page 41 (1) (a) of the Federal Judicature Act);

– civil actions against the Confederation where the amount of the claim is at least 8000 Swiss Francs (with some exceptions) (Article 110, paragraph 1 (2)) of the Constitution, page 41 (1) (b) of the Federal Judicature Act);

– cases referred to it by agreement between the parties, instead of to the Cantonal Courts, if the amount of the claim is at least 20000 Swiss Francs (Article 111 of the Constitution, page 41 (c) of the Federal Judicature Act);

– financial disputes between a canton and an individual citizen (where they do not fall within the jurisdiction of the Administrative Courts), if requested by one of the parties, provided the amount of the claim is at least 8000 Swiss Francs (Article 110, paragraph 1 (4) of the Constitution, page 42 of the Federal Judicature Act).

1. Pages 43 ff. of the Federal Judicature Act.
2. Page 54 of the Federal Judicature Act.
3. Pages 68 ff. of the Federal Judicature Act.
4. Pages 41 ff. of the Federal Judicature Act.

Proceedings are governed by the Federal Law on Federal Civil Procedure, of 4 December 1947.

III. Jurisdiction in matters of debt recovery and bankruptcy

In these cases a clear distinction must be drawn between the decisions of the Debt Recovery and Bankruptcy Offices (*offices des poursuites et des faillites*) on the one hand and those taken by the courts on the other (lifting of attachment, actions for recovery of property, declarations of bankruptcy, objections to the order of priority of creditors in bankruptcy, actions to dispute sequestration, actions in revocation, and confirmation of a composition with creditors).

The Debt Recovery and Bankruptcy Offices are subject to supervision by the Higher Cantonal Courts. The Federal Court exercises supreme supervision.

Any decision taken by a Debt Recovery and Bankruptcy Office may be referred to the cantonal supervisory authority. An appeal may be lodged against the latter's decisions within ten days to the Debt Recovery and Bankruptcy Chamber (*Chambre des poursuites et des faillites*) of the Federal Court, regardless of the amount of the claim. An appeal may be lodged at any time for a denial of justice or an unjustified delay.

IV. Criminal jurisdiction

The Criminal Courts are organised differently in the various cantons. Fewer and fewer now have assize courts. Criminal procedure is a matter for the cantons, but the criminal law has been uniform throughout the Confederation since 1942. The Criminal Cassation Chamber (*Cour de cassation pénale*) of the Federal Court ensures the uniform application of federal law. With few exceptions, a plea of nullity for an infringement of federal law may be lodged against any cantonal judgment in a criminal case.[1] This remedy may be exercised by both the accused and the Public Prosecutor. Since the entry into force on 1 January 1993 of the Federal Criminal Injuries Compensation Act (*Loi fédérale sur l'aide aux victimes d'infractions*), the victim of crime has also been able to file a plea of nullity, provided that he or she has been a party to the cantonal proceedings and the judgment has affected his or her civil claims.

With some exceptions (see below), the Cassation Chamber is bound by the facts established by the Cantonal Courts.

The Federal Constitution (Article 112) and the Criminal Code[2] make certain offences subject to federal jurisdiction (for example offences linked to the use of explosives or committed against the federal authorities). These cases are investigated by federal examining judges under the supervision of the Indictment Chamber (*Chambre d'accusation*) of the Federal Court and

1. Pages 268 ff. of the Federal Criminal Procedure Act.
2. Page 340.

heard by the Federal Criminal Court (five judges) or (in extremely rare cases, the last being in 1933) by the three judges of the Criminal Bench (*Chambre criminelle*) assisted by a jury of twelve (Federal Assizes – *assises fédérales*).

V. Constitutional jurisdiction

Some cantons have set up constitutional courts.

A public law appeal (*recours de droit public*) to the Federal Court may be lodged against all cantonal orders (*arrêts*) or decisions that violate the Federal Constitution, the Constitution of a canton or an international treaty and against which there is no other legal remedy.

There are two different public law courts that deal with the public law appeal, unless it is linked to another appeal pending before the Federal Court, in which case the court hearing the main appeal also hears the public law appeal.

The constitutional freedoms most often invoked are the right to property (Article 22*ter* of the Constitution), freedom of trade and industry (Article 31 of the Constitution), personal freedom (unwritten constitutional law, Article 5 of the European Convention on Human Rights), protection against arbitrary decisions, denial of justice and equality before the law (Article 4 of the Constitution).

The Federal Court is, however, bound by the federal laws and international treaties to which Switzerland is a party (Article 113, paragraph 3 of the constitution).

Every citizen and foreign national has the right of appeal without necessarily being represented by counsel. Complaints are automatically examined. Appeals are decided by three, five or seven judges, depending on whether they are directed against a decision in an individual case, raise a question of principle or challenge a cantonal legislative measure.

Proceedings normally take the form of an exchange of written submissions, but the court can order evidence to be taken.

VI. Administrative jurisdiction

A. Cantonal law

Administrative courts with fairly wide powers or independent boards are given the task of supervising the correct application of cantonal administrative law. The cantons are obliged to set up a judicial authority to deal with administrative disputes.[1]

The Federal Court may not consider whether cantonal administrative law has been fairly applied except from the standpoint of whether the decision was arbitrary (Article 4 of the Constitution). However, it may quash a decision that breaches a citizen's constitutional right or conflicts with federal law or an international treaty.

1. Page 98 (a) of the Federal Judicature Act.

B. Federal law

The administrative proceedings of federal authorities are governed by the Federal Administrative Procedure Act (*Loi fédérale sur la procédure administrative*) of 20 December 1968 and the Federal Judicature Act.

The Federal Court (public law chambers) decides as the Court of Last Instance on administrative law appeals against decisions of the federal government departments, the Federal Council, the Federal Chancellery and independent federal enterprises or establishments, unless the Federal Administrative Procedure Act provides for an appeal to the Federal Council.

Appeals against decisions of cantonal or federal bodies on social insurance matters (which come under federal law) lie with the Federal Insurance Tribunal (*Tribunal fédéral des assurances*) at Lucerne, which functions as a social insurance chamber of the Federal Court.[1]

Administrative law appeals may be lodged on the grounds of an infringement of federal law, including excessive or wrongful use of discretionary power, and of the inaccurate or incomplete establishment of the relevant facts (with some restrictions). On the other hand, the Federal Court cannot (with certain exceptions) review the expediency of a decision.

There is no special tribunal for tax matters or for social matters other than social insurance. Nor is there a court of audit. However, there are numerous independent appeal boards which resemble tribunals.

The decisions of the Federal Council are not subject to review by the Federal Court, but the court does examine Federal Council orders before they are passed to determine whether they are covered by the law.

The first public law chamber consists of seven judges and the second of five. Both normally sit with three judges but may sit with five.

1. Page 122 of the Federal Judicature Act.

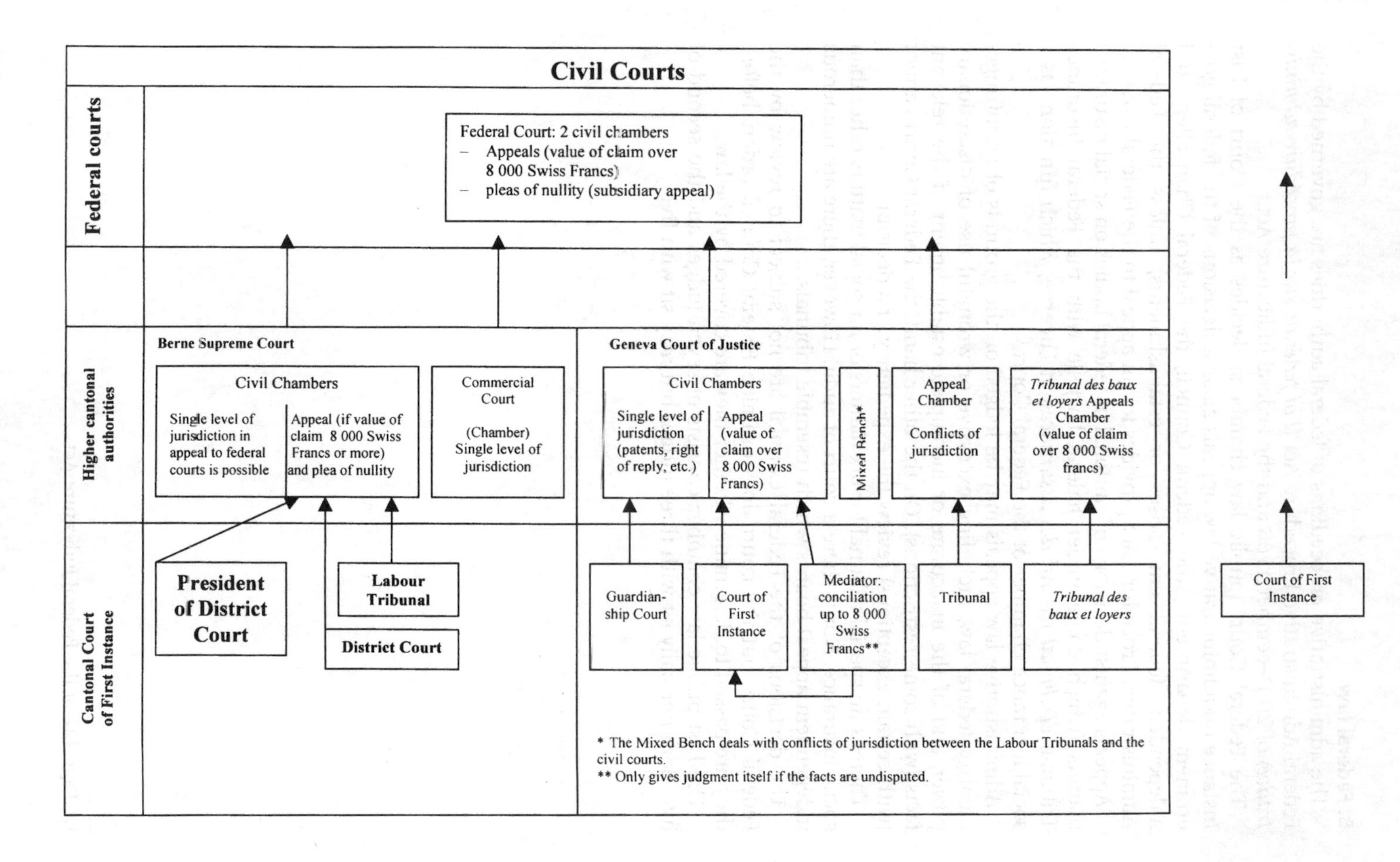
Civil Courts
Federal courts
Higher cantonal authorities
Cantonal Court of First Instance
Federal Court: 2 civil chambers
– Appeals (value of claim over 8 000 Swiss Francs)
– pleas of nullity (subsidiary appeal)
Berne Supreme Court
Civil Chambers
Single level of jurisdiction in appeal to federal courts is possible
Appeal (if value of claim 8 000 Swiss Francs or more) and plea of nullity
Commercial Court
(Chamber) Single level of jurisdiction
Geneva Court of Justice
Civil Chambers
Single level of jurisdiction (patents, right of reply, etc.)
Appeal (value of claim over 8 000 Swiss Francs)
Mixed Bench*
Appeal Chamber
Conflicts of jurisdiction
Tribunal des baux et loyers Appeals Chamber (value of claim over 8 000 Swiss francs)
President of District Court
Labour Tribunal
District Court
Guardianship Court
Court of First Instance
Mediator: conciliation up to 8 000 Swiss Francs**
Tribunal
Tribunal des baux et loyers
Court of First Instance
* The Mixed Bench deals with conflicts of jurisdiction between the Labour Tribunals and the civil courts.
** Only gives judgment itself if the facts are undisputed.

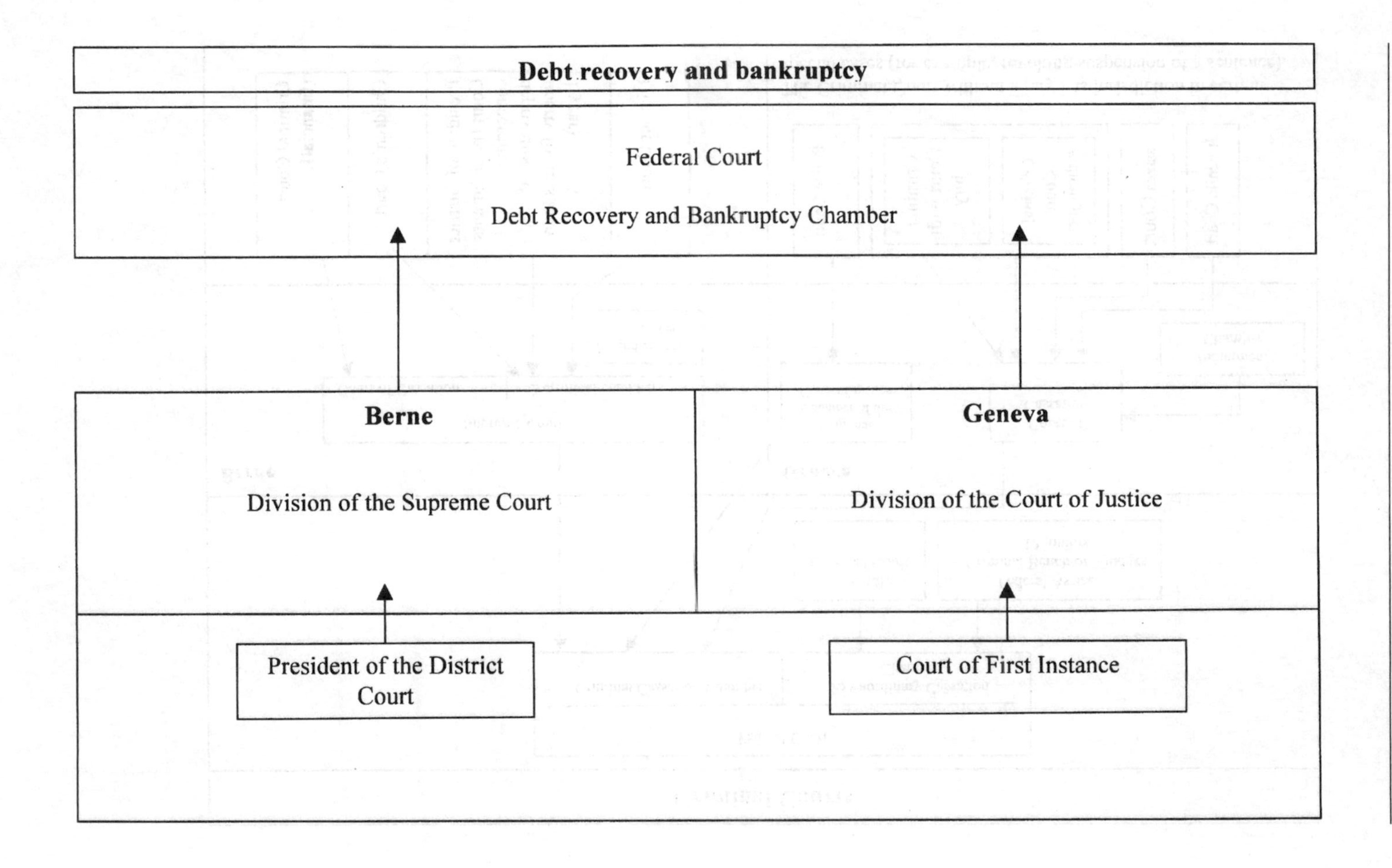

Debt recovery and bankruptcy
Federal Court
Debt Recovery and Bankruptcy Chamber
Berne
Division of the Supreme Court
Geneva
Division of the Court of Justice
President of the District Court
Court of First Instance

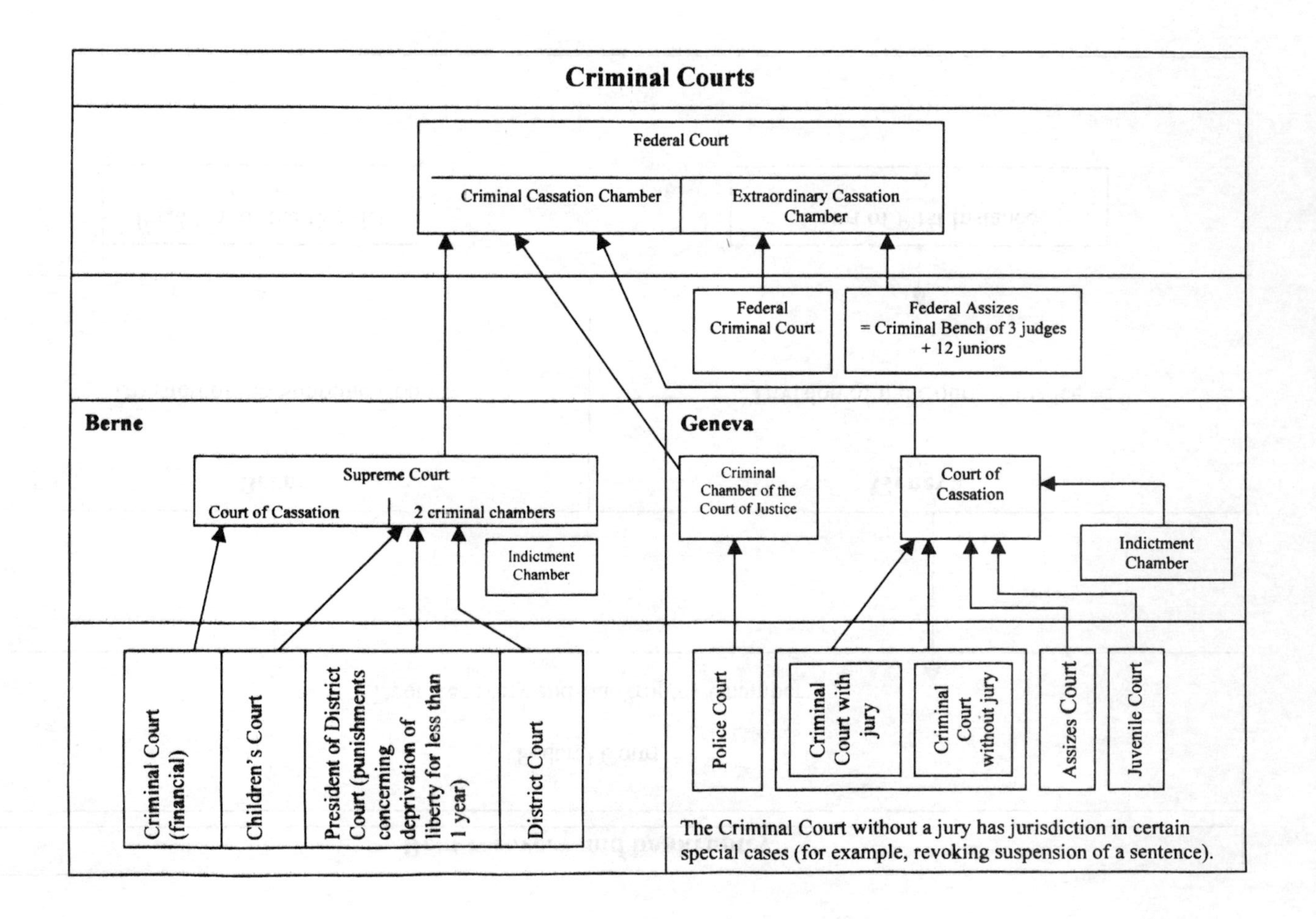

Criminal Courts
Federal Court
Criminal Cassation Chamber
Extraordinary Cassation Chamber
Federal Criminal Court
Federal Assizes = Criminal Bench of 3 judges + 12 juniors
Berne
Supreme Court
Court of Cassation
2 criminal chambers
Indictment Chamber
Criminal Court (financial)
Children's Court
President of District Court (punishments concerning deprivation of liberty for less than 1 year)
District Court
Geneva
Criminal Chamber of the Court of Justice
Court of Cassation
Indictment Chamber
Police Court
Criminal Court with jury
Criminal Court without jury
Assizes Court
Juvenile Court
The Criminal Court without a jury has jurisdiction in certain special cases (for example, revoking suspension of a sentence).

Constitutional jurisdiction

Federal Court: 2 public law divisions ("courts") for constitutional and administrative law (public law)

Public Law Appeal: subsidiary remedy for a violation of citizens' constitutional rights (federal and cantonal constitutions)

- violation of inter-cantonal agreements and international treaties
- appeals concerning federal and cantonal political rights (elections and voting)

↑

Decrees and final decisions of cantonal authorities
(legislative, executive or judicial)

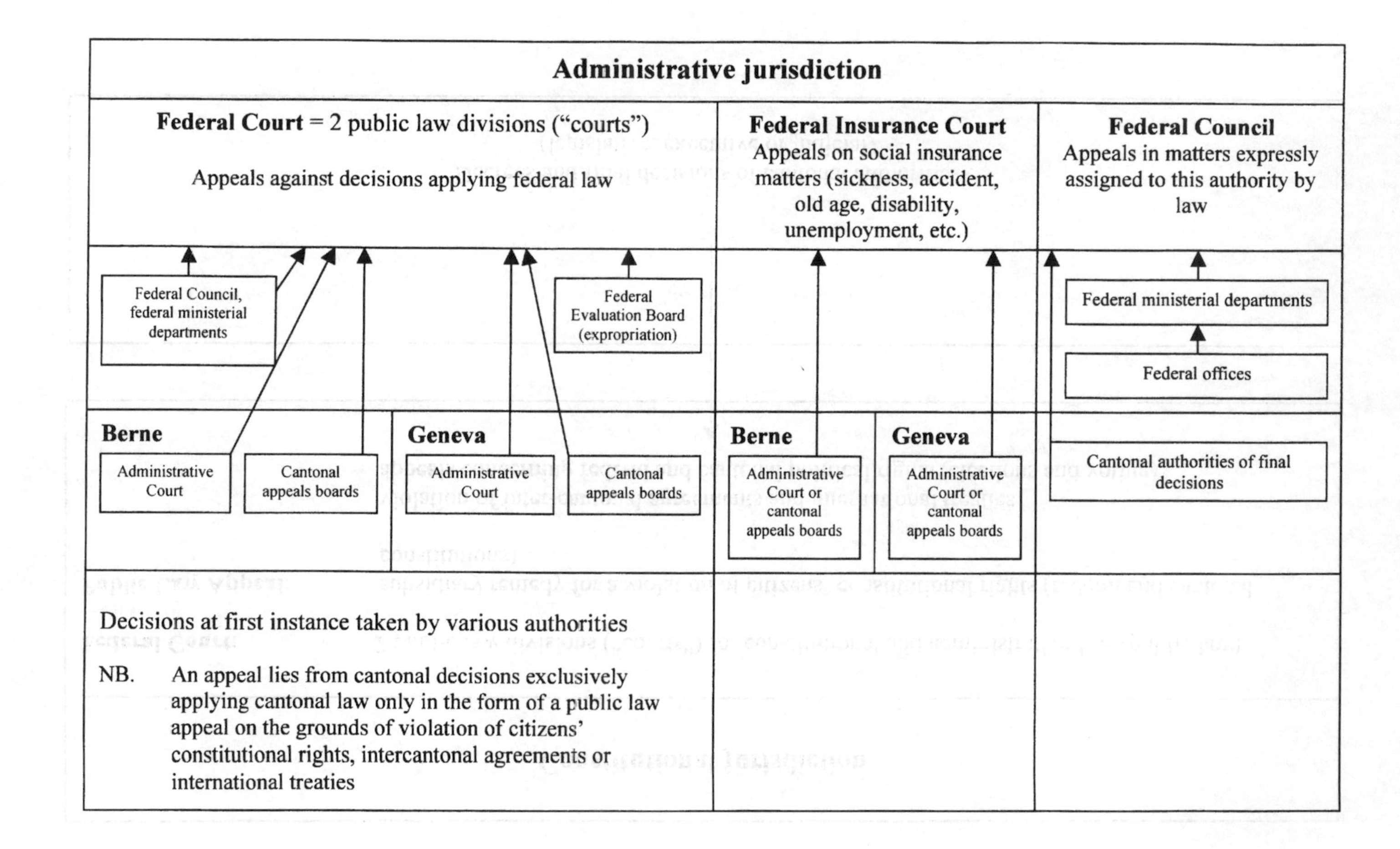
Administrative jurisdiction
Federal Court = 2 public law divisions ("courts")
Appeals against decisions applying federal law
Federal Insurance Court
Appeals on social insurance matters (sickness, accident, old age, disability, unemployment, etc.)
Federal Council
Appeals in matters expressly assigned to this authority by law
Federal Council, federal ministerial departments
Federal Evaluation Board (expropriation)
Federal ministerial departments
Federal offices
Berne
Administrative Court
Cantonal appeals boards
Geneva
Administrative Court
Cantonal appeals boards
Berne
Administrative Court or cantonal appeals boards
Geneva
Administrative Court or cantonal appeals boards
Cantonal authorities of final decisions
Decisions at first instance taken by various authorities
NB. An appeal lies from cantonal decisions exclusively applying cantonal law only in the form of a public law appeal on the grounds of violation of citizens' constitutional rights, intercantonal agreements or international treaties

"The former Yugoslav Republic of Macedonia"

ACCORDING to the Constitution promulgated in 1991, "the former Yugoslav Republic of Macedonia" is an independent, sovereign, civil and democratic state in which the system of government is based on the rule of law.

The Constitution establishes the separation of powers between the legislature, the executive and the judiciary.

Under the Constitution, judicial authority is exercised by autonomous and independent courts that give judgment on the basis of the Constitution and ordinary laws and of international treaties ratified in conformity with the Constitution.

The courts are organised as a single system and extraordinary courts are prohibited.

According to the Courts Act of 1995, the unity of judicial authority is provided by the establishment of

– 27 courts of first instance,
– 3 courts of appeal, and
– the Supreme Court.

– The courts of first instance have original jurisdiction for all civil and criminal cases, including those involving petty offences.

– The courts of appeal hear appeals against the judgments given by the courts of first instance and carry out other functions conferred on them by law.

– The Supreme Court is the highest judicial authority in "the former Yugoslav Republic of Macedonia".

- it ensures the uniform application of the laws by the courts.
- it hears appeals against the decisions of its benches in the cases provided for by law.
- as a third tier of jurisdiction, it hears final appeals against judgments given by the courts of appeal and the decisions of its benches in the cases provided for by law.
- it has jurisdiction over administrative cases in the cases provided for by law;
- it hears extraordinary appeals against final judgments of the Lower Courts; and
- it carries out other tasks assigned to it by law.

The Constitution and the Courts Act provide that the Supreme Court shall sit as a bench.

The law specifies the cases heard by a single judge.

ACCORDING to the Constitution, promulgated in 1991, "the former Yugoslav Republic of Macedonia" is an independent, sovereign, civil and democratic state in which the system of government is based on the rule of law.

The Constitution establishes the separation of powers between the legislature, the executive and the judiciary.

Under the Constitution, judicial authority is exercised by autonomous and independent courts that give judgment on the basis of the Constitution and ordinary laws and of international treaties ratified in conformity with the Constitution.

The courts are organised in a single system and extraordinary courts are prohibited.

According to the Courts Act of 1995, the unity of judicial authority is protected by the establishment of:

– 27 courts of first instance;

– 3 courts of appeal; and

– the Supreme Court.

The courts of first instance have original jurisdiction for all civil and criminal cases, including those involving petty offences.

The courts of appeal hear appeals against the judgments given by the courts of first instance and carry out other functions conferred on them by law.

The Supreme Court is the highest judicial authority in "the former Yugoslav Republic of Macedonia".

[illegible] ensures the uniform application of the laws by the courts;

[illegible] hears appeals against the decisions of its benches in the cases provided for by law;

[illegible] as a third tier of jurisdiction, it hears appeals against judgments given by the courts of appeal and the decisions of its benches in the cases provided for by law;

[illegible] it has jurisdiction over administrative cases in the cases provided for by law;

[illegible] it hears extraordinary appeals against final judgments of the lower Courts; and

[illegible] carries out other tasks assigned to it by law.

The Constitution and the Courts Act provide that the Supreme Court shall [illegible].

[illegible] laws specify the cases heard by a single judge.

Turkey

I. Introduction

Turkey is a republic. Its capital city is Ankara. Legislative authority is vested in the Grand National Assembly. Executive authority is exercised by the President of the Republic and the Cabinet. Judicial authority is exercised in the name of the Turkish nation by independent courts. The judges are guided in their decisions by the Constitution, the law and legal principles and their conscience.

The Turkish judicial system may be divided into six main areas of jurisdiction, which will be examined in turn. These are the types of court: the Constitutional Court, the Jurisdictional Conflict Court (*Uyusmazlik Mahkemesi*), the Courts of Ordinary Jurisdiction, the Administrative Courts, courts martial and tribunals dealing with fiscal matters.

II. Constitutional jurisdiction

The Constitutional Court

The Constitutional Court (*Anayasa Mahkemesi*), set up by the Constitution of 1982, sits in Ankara. Its functions and jurisdiction may be summarised as follows:

It examines the constitutionality, with regard to both formal requirements and content, of laws and legislative decrees and the Rules of Procedure of the Grand National Assembly. As far as constitutional amendments are concerned, it examines only formal requirements. However, legislative decrees issued during a state of emergency, a period of martial law or in wartime may not be the subject of an appeal to the Constitutional Court with regard to either formal requirements or the merits.

Examination of whether laws meet the formal conditions laid down in the Constitution is limited to verifying the existence of the required majority when the final vote was taken. In the case of constitutional amendments, the court merely ensures that the majorities necessary for their proposal and adoption have been observed and that the condition that they may not be debated under the urgent procedure rules has been complied with. An examination of the formal criteria may be requested by the President of the Republic or by one-fifth of the members of the Grand National Assembly. An application to annul a law on the grounds of a procedural defect may not be made in the form of a constitutional objection.

The Constitutional Court, in its capacity as the Supreme Court, tries the following for breaches of the law committed in their official capacity: the President of the Republic; the members of the Cabinet; the President, members of, and Chief Public Prosecutors attached to, the Court of Cassation, the Council of State, the Military Court of Cassation and High Military Administrative Court; the Chief Public Prosecutors and Deputy Public Prosecutors of the Republic and the President and members of the "Supreme Council of Judges and Public Prosecutors" (the Legal Service Commission) and of the Court of Audit.

The functions of public prosecutor at the Supreme Court are carried out by the Chief Public Prosecutor or Deputy Chief Public Prosecutor of the Republic.

The judgments of the Supreme Court are final.

The Constitutional Court also exercises other functions assigned to it by the Constitution.

The Constitutional Court consists of eleven regular members and five substitutes.

The President of the Republic appoints two members and two substitutes from the Court of Cassation, two members and one substitute from the Council of State, one member from the Military Court of Cassation, one member from the High Military Administrative Court and one member from the Court of Audit, chosen from among the three candidates nominated for each vacant seat by a majority vote by the plenary session of each court from among their respective Presidents and members. One member must be nominated by the Council of Higher Education from among higher education lecturers in law, economics or political science who are not members of the Council itself. Three members and one substitute are appointed directly within the categories mentioned.

Sessions of the Constitutional Court are attended by its President and ten members. The President replaces excused members by substitutes.

The Constitutional Court examines the files of cases other than those it has dealt with as supreme court. However, where it considers it necessary it summons the parties to make oral pleadings.

The Constitutional Court's decisions are taken by an absolute majority.

III. Conflicts of jurisdiction

The Jurisdictional Conflict Court (*Uyusmazlik Mahkemesi*), which sits in Ankara, is empowered to make a final decision on conflicts of jurisdiction and judgment between ordinary, administrative and military courts.

The court consists of a President and six members. The President is elected by the Constitutional Court from among its members and substitutes. Three of the six members are elected by the Court of Cassation from among the Presidents and members of its civil divisions and three by the Council of State from among the Presidents and members of its divisions.

In conflicts relating to military matters, the composition of the Jurisdictional Conflict Court is different: two of the six members are elected by the Court of Cassation, two by the Council of State and two by the Military Court of Cassation.

Decisions of the court can be taken only in the presence of all its members and by an absolute majority.

IV. Ordinary jurisdiction

Ordinary jurisdiction is organised at two levels. There are no courts of appeal. As a rule, judgments delivered by local courts (courts of first instance) may be challenged in the Court of Cassation in Ankara. However, there are certain exceptions, of which the following are the most important.

In civil law:

– judgments delivered by the Civil Magistrates' Courts in disputes involving sums not exceeding a certain amount of money; and

– decisions by the supervisory authorities in debt claims not exceeding a certain amount of money,

are not subject to challenge in the Court of Cassation.

In criminal law:

– sentences to fines not exceeding a certain amount of money; and

– acquittals in cases of offences punishable by a maximum fine of a certain amount of money,

are not subject to challenge in the Court of Cassation.

The system of ordinary jurisdiction must therefore be examined firstly at local level and then at national level. At local level, ordinary jurisdiction is exercised by the Trial Courts. At national level only the Court of Cassation functions as a higher supervisory authority.

A. Trial courts

Here a distinction must be made between civil and criminal jurisdiction. However, in many places both criminal and civil cases are tried by the same court acting in separate capacities, that is as a civil or criminal magistrate's court or as a civil or criminal court for more serious offences, as the case may be.

1. Civil jurisdiction

General courts

Civil jurisdiction is generally exercised by the Civil Courts or magistrates. The former have general jurisdiction, that is, they are always competent in the absence of a legal provision to the contrary. Consequently, the civil magistrates and the courts specialising in certain areas, such as land registration, are responsible for trying the cases specified in the relevant statutory provisions.

– *Civil magistrates*

In each administrative district there is at least one Civil Magistrate's Court (*Sulh Hukuk Mahkemesi*).

The Civil Magistrates' Courts generally have jurisdiction in civil cases involving claims not exceeding a certain amount of money. They also deal with maintenance proceedings between parents in direct line and between brothers and sisters, as well as with eviction proceedings.

The Civil Magistrates' Courts consist of a single magistrate.

– *Civil Courts*

In each administrative district (sub-prefecture) there is at least one Civil Court (*Asliye Hukuk Mahkemesi*).

As explained above, the Civil Courts deal with all civil cases that do not fall within the jurisdiction of civil magistrates' courts or special courts.

The functions of the Civil Courts, which should, according to the law, consist of a President and two members, are at present exercised by single judges because of the lack of a sufficient number of judges.

– *Commercial Courts*

At present, there are Commercial Courts (*Ticaret Mahkemeleri*) in only a few large cities (such as Istanbul, Ankara, Izmir, Adana, etc).

The Commercial Courts are divisions of the Civil Courts. There is no commercial court as such, and commercial cases are dealt with by civil courts acting in this capacity.

Commercial disputes in which the amount of the claim does not exceed a certain amount of money are dealt with by the Civil Magistrates' Courts.

The Commercial Courts consist of a President and two members.

Special tribunals

– *Labour tribunals*

Jurisdiction in labour and social cases is exercised by the labour tribunals (*Is Mahkemeleri*). Their function is to settle disputes arising from breaches of contracts of employment and from the application of the Labour Code and the Social Insurance Act.

However, labour tribunals are set up only in towns where this is justified by the number of cases. Elsewhere, such cases are referred to other courts by the Legal Service Commission.

– *Land registration tribunals*

These tribunals (*Kadastro Mahkemeleri*) deal with cases arising from the application of the Land Registration Act, which should normally come under the jurisdiction of the Civil Courts and Civil Magistrates' Courts.

Each of these tribunals consists of a single judge.

Supervisory authorities in actions for debt recovery: these authorities (*Icra Tetkik Mercileri*) are responsible for supervising the debt recovery offices and for examining complaints and objections against the acts of these offices. They may also pass criminal judgments for breaches of the law in the area of debt recovery.

Each such supervisory authority consists of one judge. At present, many places do not have separate judges to carry out these functions and they are exercised by the Civil Court judges instead.

2. Criminal jurisdiction

General courts

Criminal jurisdiction is generally exercised by the Criminal Courts (*Asliye Ceza Mahkemeleri*), the Assize Courts (*Agir Ceza Mahkemeleri*) and the Criminal Magistrates' Courts. The Criminal Courts have general jurisdiction, that is, they are always competent in the absence of any provision of law to the contrary.

– *Criminal Magistrates' Courts*

The Criminal Magistrates' Courts (*Sulh Ceza Mahkemeleri*) generally have jurisdiction for minor criminal offences.

As a rule, each administrative district has one such court, which consists of a single magistrate. In places where there is no magistrate this function is exercised by the judges of the Criminal Courts.

– *Criminal Courts*

As explained above, the Criminal Courts deal with all offences that do not fall within the jurisdiction of the Criminal Magistrates or the Assize Courts.

There is one criminal court in each administrative district. It must by law consist of a President and two members, but owing to the lack of sufficient judges most of them sit with a single judge.

– *Assize Courts*

The Assize Courts (*Agir Ceza Mahkemeleri*) have jurisdiction for crimes carrying the death penalty, penal servitude or a prison sentence of more than five years.

They consist of a President and two members.

Special tribunals

– *Press tribunals*

Certain offences falling within the jurisdiction of both the Criminal Magistrates and the Criminal Courts are tried exclusively by the latter if they are mentioned in the Press Code or have been committed in the form of publication in the press. However, in places with more than three judges these courts have a special bench made up of three judges of the highest rank, that is to say they consist of a President and two members. In these cases they are called "press tribunals" (*Toplu Basin Mahkemeleri*).

– *State Security Courts*

The State Security Courts have been set up to deal with offences against the indivisible unity of the state, both from the point of view of the territory and the Turkish nation, against the free democratic order or against the Republic, the characteristics of which are defined in the Constitution of 1982, as well as offences directly affecting the internal or external security of the state.

The State Security Courts consist of a President, two members and two substitutes, a prosecutor and a sufficient number of deputy prosecutors.

The President, one member, one substitute and the prosecutor are appointed from among senior judges and state prosecutors; one member and one substitute are appointed from among senior military judges, and the deputy prosecutors from among state prosecutors and military judges. All appointments are made in accordance with the procedures laid down in the relevant laws.

Appeals against the decisions of the State Security Courts lie to the Court of Cassation.

The functioning, powers and responsibilities and other provisions relating to proceedings before the State Security Courts are laid down by law.

B. Court of Cassation

The Court of Cassation (*Yargitay*) is the Court of Last Resort in relation to judgments and sentences passed by the Ordinary Courts. It also deals as a court of first and last instance with certain actions for compensation brought against senior judges and public prosecutors.

The members of the Court of Cassation are elected by the Legal Service Commission, in a secret ballot by an absolute majority of votes cast by all its members, from among senior judges and state prosecutors and persons considered to be members of this profession.

1. Divisions

There are 32 divisions (*Daire*), 21 civil (*Kukuk Daireleri*) and 11 criminal (*Ceza Daireleri*). The civil divisions include a sufficient number of commercial divisions (*Ticaret Daireleri*) and debt and bankruptcy divisions (*Icra-Iflas Daireleri*).

Each division consists of a President and four members. Its decisions are taken by a majority.

2. Plenary Civil Bench

The plenary Civil Bench (*Hukuk Genel Kurulu*) functions are to examine decisions by the Court of First Instance and to ensure uniformity of court judgments.

When a civil division of the Court of Cassation quashes a decision of a local court but the latter disagrees and upholds its original decision, this decision, if made the object of a further appeal, is considered by the plenary Civil Bench. If the Bench also quashes the decision of the Local Court, the latter must comply with its ruling.

One of the most important functions of the Court of Cassation is to safeguard the uniformity of court decisions throughout the country. When a civil division of the Court of Cassation intends to depart from previous rulings on a particular subject or when it has given different rulings in similar cases or when there is a discrepancy between the decisions of two civil divisions, the matter is considered and decided by the plenary Civil Bench.

The plenary Civil Bench consists of the first President of the Court of Cassation and the Presidents and members of the civil divisions, including the commercial division and the debt and bankruptcy divisions.

The quorum is two-thirds of the total membership of the civil divisions. Decisions are taken by an absolute majority of the total number of members.

3. Plenary Criminal Bench

The plenary Criminal Bench (*Ceza Genel Kurulu*) has the same functions as its civil counterpart, that is, the examination of rulings made by courts of first instance and the uniformity of court decisions.

It consists of the first President of the Court of Cassation and the Presidents and members of the criminal divisions.

What has been said of the plenary Civil Bench with regard to the quorum for hearings and decisions also applies to the plenary Criminal Bench, except that the Chief Public Prosecutor takes part in the hearing and the decision where the uniformity of court judgments is concerned.

4. Grand General Assembly

The Grand General Assembly (*Büyük Genel Kurul*): if there is a difference between the rulings of the two plenary benches (civil and criminal) or between a division and one of the plenary benches, or between a civil division and a criminal a division, the conflicting rulings are examined and a decision is taken by the Grand General Assembly.

The Chief Public Prosecutor also takes part in the hearing and the decision where the uniformity of court judgments in criminal cases is concerned.

C. Public prosecutors

Each criminal court has a chief prosecutor and a sufficient number of deputy prosecutors. In places where there is an assize court, there is no separate Public Prosecutor's Office for the Criminal Court. This is because the Assize Courts are, as has been said above, divisions of the Criminal Courts.

The Court of Cassation has a sufficient number of prosecutors in addition to the Chief Public Prosecutor.

V. Administrative jurisdiction

According to the Constitution, all administrative acts are subject to scrutiny by the judicial authorities. Public administrative bodies are required to provide compensation for damage caused by their actions.

Administrative jurisdiction is exercised by local administrative courts and by the Council of State, which sits in Ankara and is the Court of Last Resort regarding decisions and judgments of the Administrative Courts. The Council of State also rules as a court of first and last instance in certain proceedings specified by law. However, certain administrative authorities also have semi-judicial functions, namely the District Councils, the Provincial Councils, the Disciplinary Boards, the Minimum Wage Arbitration Boards and the Tax Assessment Appeals Boards. However, the decisions of these administrative authorities are subject to final scrutiny by the Administrative Courts and the Council of State.

In addition, as will be indicated below, the Council of State is the Court of Second and Last Instance for tax disputes.

VI. Military jurisdiction

Military jurisdiction is exercised by military courts and disciplinary tribunals (which are always military). The Military Courts may judge non-military personnel only for military offences specified by the relevant law.

The persons and offences falling within the jurisdiction of military courts in wartime or during a state of emergency are also defined by law.

The majority of the members of the Military Courts must be judges.

The hierarchy of the Military Courts and tribunals is as follows:

A. Trial courts

- Disciplinary tribunals
- Military courts
- Martial law tribunals, which are extraordinary tribunals and deal with certain offences defined by law.

B. Military Courts of Cassation

VII. Fiscal jurisdiction

Fiscal jurisdiction is divided into three categories: taxes, customs and excise, and budgetary.

A. Tax jurisdiction

Tax jurisdiction is exercised at first instance by the Tax Tribunals (*Vergi Mahkemeleri*), at which cases are dealt with by specialist judges. The only avenue of appeal is to the Council of State.

Disputes concerning customs and excise duties are also dealt with by the Tax Tribunals.

B. Budgetary jurisdiction

Budgetary jurisdiction is exercised at national level by the Court of Audit (*Sayistay*), which sits in Ankara.

The Court of Audit is responsible, in accordance with the functions assigned to it by law, for scrutinising on behalf of the Grand National Assembly all receipts and expenditure and the assets of departments covered by the general and subsidiary budgets, for giving final rulings on the management of the accounts, for advising the Grand National Assembly on draft laws relating to the final accounts, for carrying out monitoring and verification procedures and for taking the relevant decisions.

UKRAINE

IT is important to note that nowadays the drafts of the new Law of Ukraine concerning the judicial system and its structure is under the consideration of the *Verkhovna Rada* of Ukraine.

The reform of the judicial system in Ukraine is an integral part of legal reform as a whole. Thus, great attention was paid by those drafting the law to the elaboration of the new legal instruments aimed at regulating the problems connected with improvement of the judicial system.

Six drafts of the new Law of Ukraine concerning the judicial system and its structure were recently presented to the *Verkhovna Rada* of Ukraine.

One of the drafts was presented by the Cabinet of Ministers of Ukraine (the government). The others were presented by the Commissions of the *Verkhovna Rada* of Ukraine.

The drafts were elaborated in close collaboration with practising lawyers, judges, scientists, officials of the Supreme Court of Ukraine and the Highest Arbitration Court of Ukraine.

The attached information in table form concerns the current Law of Ukraine from the year 1981, "on Legal Proceedings in Ukraine".

For the structure of courts of general jurisdiction see overleaf.

The structure of courts of general jurisdiction[1]

The Plenum of the Supreme Court of Ukraine	**The Supreme Court of Ukraine**	**The Court Collegium** on civil cases
The Military Collegium		**The Court Collegium** on criminal cases
	The Presidium of the Supreme Court of Ukraine	

It considers cases in the framework of its competences as the Court of First Instance, in order of cassation, in the order of supervision and in connection with revelation of new evidence

The Presidium of the Court	**The Supreme Court of the Republic of Crimea**	The Court Collegium on civil cases The Court Collegium on criminal cases

It considers cases in the framework of its competences **as the Court of First Instance, in order of cassation, in the order of supervision and in connection with revelation of new evidence**

Regional (*Oblast*) Court	**Kyiv and Sevastopol city courts**	**Military regional courts, the Navy Court**	**The inter-regional courts**
The Court Presidium The Court Collegiums on civil and criminal matters	**The Court Presidium** The Court Collegiums on civil and criminal matters	It considers cases in the framework of its competences **as the Court of First Instance, in order of cassation, in the order of supervision and in connection with revelation of new evidence**	The Court of **First Instance, considers cases in establishments with restricted access**

They consider cases **as courts of first instance, in order of cassation, in the order of supervision and in connection with revelation of new evidence**

1. The Law on Legal Proceedings in Ukraine.

Sales agents for publications of the Council of Europe
Agents de vente des publications du Conseil de l'Europe

AUSTRALIA/AUSTRALIE
Hunter Publications, 58A, Gipps Street
AUS-3066 COLLINGWOOD, Victoria
Tel.: (61) 3 9417 5361
Fax: (61) 3 9419 7154
E-mail: Sales@hunter-pubs.com.au
http://www.hunter-pubs.com.au

AUSTRIA/AUTRICHE
Gerold und Co., Graben 31
A-1011 WIEN 1
Tel.: (43) 1 533 5014
Fax: (43) 1 533 5014 18
E-mail: buch@gerold.telecom.at
http://www.gerold.at

BELGIUM/BELGIQUE
La Librairie européenne SA
50, avenue A. Jonnart
B-1200 BRUXELLES 20
Tel.: (32) 2 734 0281
Fax: (32) 2 735 0860
E-mail: info@libeurop.be
http://www.libeurop.be

Jean de Lannoy
202, avenue du Roi
B-1190 BRUXELLES
Tel.: (32) 2 538 4308
Fax: (32) 2 538 0841
E-mail: jean.de.lannoy@euronet.be
http://www.jean-de-lannoy.be

CANADA
Renouf Publishing Company Limited
5369 Chemin Canotek Road
CDN-OTTAWA, Ontario, K1J 9J3
Tel.: (1) 613 745 2665
Fax: (1) 613 745 7660
E-mail: order.dept@renoufbooks.com
http://www.renoufbooks.com

CZECH REPUBLIC/ RÉPUBLIQUE TCHÈQUE
USIS, Publication Service
Havelkova 22
CZ-130 00 PRAHA 3
Tel./Fax: (420) 2 2423 1114

DENMARK/DANEMARK
Munksgaard
35 Norre Sogade, PO Box 173
DK-1005 KØBENHAVN K
Tel.: (45) 7 733 3333
Fax: (45) 7 733 3377
E-mail: direct@munksgaarddirect.dk
http://www.munksgaarddirect.dk

FINLAND/FINLANDE
Akateeminen Kirjakauppa
Keskuskatu 1, PO Box 218
FIN-00381 HELSINKI
Tel.: (358) 9 121 41
Fax: (358) 9 121 4450
E-mail: akatilaus@stockmann.fi
http://www.akatilaus.akateeminen.com

FRANCE
C.I.D.
131 boulevard Saint-Michel
F-75005 PARIS
Tel.: (33) 01 43 54 47 15
Fax: (33) 01 43 54 80 73
E-mail: cid@msh-paris.fr

GERMANY/ALLEMAGNE
UNO Verlag
Proppelsdorfer Allee 55
D-53115 BONN
Tel.: (49) 2 28 94 90 231
Fax: (49) 2 28 21 74 92
E-mail: unoverlag@aol.com
http://www.uno-verlag.de

GREECE/GRÈCE
Librairie Kauffmann
Mavrokordatou 9
GR-ATHINAI 106 78
Tel.: (30) 1 38 29 283
Fax: (30) 1 38 33 967

HUNGARY/HONGRIE
Euro Info Service
Hungexpo Europa Kozpont ter 1
H-1101 BUDAPEST
Tel.: (361) 264 8270
Fax: (361) 264 8271
E-mail: euroinfo@euroinfo.hu
http://www.euroinfo.hu

ITALY/ITALIE
Libreria Commissionaria Sansoni
Via Duca di Calabria 1/1, CP 552
I-50125 FIRENZE
Tel.: (39) 556 4831
Fax: (39) 556 41257
E-mail: licosa@licosa.com
http://www.licosa.com

NETHERLANDS/PAYS-BAS
De Lindeboom Internationale Publikaties
PO Box 202, MA de Ruyterstraat 20 A
NL-7480 AE HAAKSBERGEN
Tel.: (31) 53 574 0004
Fax: (31) 53 572 9296
E-mail: lindeboo@worldonline.nl
http://home-1-worldonline.nl/~lindeboo/

NORWAY/NORVÈGE
Akademika, A/S Universitetsbokhandel
PO Box 84, Blindern
N-0314 OSLO
Tel.: (47) 22 85 30 30
Fax: (47) 23 12 24 20

POLAND/POLOGNE
Głowna Księgarnia Naukowa
im. B. Prusa
Krakowskie Przedmiescie 7
PL-00-068 WARSZAWA
Tel.: (48) 29 22 66
Fax: (48) 22 26 64 49
E-mail: inter@internews.com.pl
http://www.internews.com.pl

PORTUGAL
Livraria Portugal
Rua do Carmo, 70
P-1200 LISBOA
Tel.: (351) 13 47 49 82
Fax: (351) 13 47 02 64
E-mail: liv.portugal@mail.telepac.pt

SPAIN/ESPAGNE
Mundi-Prensa Libros SA
Castelló 37
E-28001 MADRID
Tel.: (34) 914 36 37 00
Fax: (34) 915 75 39 98
E-mail: libreria@mundiprensa.es
http://www.mundiprensa.com

SWITZERLAND/SUISSE
BERSY
Route d'Uvrier 15
CH-1958 LIVRIER/SION
Tel.: (41) 27 203 73 30
Fax: (41) 27 203 73 32
E-mail: bersy@freesurf.ch

UNITED KINGDOM/ROYAUME-UNI
TSO (formerly HMSO)
51 Nine Elms Lane
GB-LONDON SW8 5DR
Tel.: (44) 171 873 8372
Fax: (44) 171 873 8200
E-mail: customer.services@theso.co.uk
http://www.the-stationery-office.co.uk
http://www.itsofficial.net

UNITED STATES and CANADA/ ÉTATS-UNIS et CANADA
Manhattan Publishing Company
468 Albany Post Road, PO Box 850
CROTON-ON-HUDSON,
NY 10520, USA
Tel.: (1) 914 271 5194
Fax: (1) 914 271 5856
E-mail: Info@manhattanpublishing.com
http://www.manhattanpublishing.com

STRASBOURG
Librairie Kléber
Palais de l'Europe
F-67075 STRASBOURG Cedex
Fax: (33) 03 88 52 91 21

Council of Europe Publishing/Editions du Conseil de l'Europe
F-67075 Strasbourg Cedex
Tel.: (33) 03 88 41 25 81 – Fax: (33) 03 88 41 39 10
E-mail: publishing@coe.int – Web site: http://book.coe.fr